W9-DIY-080

1 TIMOTHY
2 TIMOTHY
TITUS

ABINGDON NEW TESTAMENT COMMENTARIES

Victor Paul Furnish, General Editor
Perkins School of Theology,
Southern Methodist University

EDITORIAL BOARD

Jouette M. Bassler
Perkins School of Theology,
Southern Methodist University

John H. Elliott
University of San Francisco

Pheme Perkins
Boston College

Vernon K. Robbins
Emory University

D. Moody Smith
The Divinity School, Duke University

Rex D. Matthews, *ex officio*
Abingdon Press

ABINGDON NEW TESTAMENT COMMENTARIES

1 TIMOTHY
2 TIMOTHY
TITUS

JOUETTE M. BASSLER

Regis College Library
1 MARY STREET
TORONTO, ONTARIO, CANADA
M4Y 2R5

WITHDRAWN

BS
2735.2
B 34
1996

Abingdon Press
Nashville

ABINGDON NEW TESTAMENT COMMENTARIES:
1 TIMOTHY, 2 TIMOTHY, TITUS

Copyright © 1996 by Abingdon Press

All rights reserved.
No part of this work may be reproduced or transmitted in any form or by any means, electronic or mechanical, including photocopying and recording, or by means of any information storage or retrieval system, except as may be expressly permitted by the 1976 Copyright Act or in writing from the publisher. Requests for permission should be addressed in writing to Abingdon Press, 201 Eighth Avenue South, Nashville, TN 37203.

This book is printed on acid-free, recycled elemental chlorine–free paper.

Library of Congress Cataloging-in-Publication Data

Bassler, Jouette M.
    1 Timothy, 2 Timothy, Titus / Jouette M. Bassler.
        p. cm.—(Abingdon New Testament commentaries)
    Includes bibliographical references and index.
    ISBN 0-687-00157-9 (pbk. : alk. paper)
    1. Bible. N.T. Pastoral Epistles—Criticism, interpretation, etc.
I. Title. II. Series.
BS2735.2.B34 1996
227'.8307—dc20   96-3018
                                                                    CIP

Scripture quotations, unless otherwise indicated, are from the New Revised Standard Version Bible, copyright © 1989, by the Division of Christian Education of the National Council of the Churches of Christ in the United States of America.

Scripture quotations noted REB are from The Revised English Bible. Copyright © 1989 by The Delegates of the Oxford University Press and The Syndics of the Cambridge University Press. Reprinted by permission.

Scripture quotations noted NJB are from The New Jerusalem Bible, copyright © 1985 by Darton, Longman & Todd, and Doubleday & Company, Inc. Reprinted by permission of the publishers.

Scripture quotations noted RSV are from the Revised Standard Version of the Bible, copyright 1946, 1952, 1971 by the Division of Christian Education of the National Council of Churches of Christ in the USA. Used by permission.

Scripture quotations noted NAB are from The New American Bible—Revised New Testament. © 1986 Confraternity of Christian Doctrine, Washington, D.C.

Scripture quotations noted NEB are from The New English Bible. © The Delegates of the Oxford University Press and The Syndics of the Cambridge University Press 1961, 1970. Reprinted by permission.

96 97 98 99 00 01 02 03 04 05—10 9 8 7 6 5 4 3 2 1

MANUFACTURED IN THE UNITED STATES OF AMERICA

For John

CONTENTS

FOREWORD

The *Abingdon New Testament Commentaries* series provides compact, critical commentaries on the writings of the New Testament. These commentaries are written with special attention to the needs and interests of theological students, but they will also be useful for students in upper-level college or university settings, as well as for pastors and other church leaders. In addition to providing basic information about the New Testament texts and insights into their meanings, these commentaries are intended to exemplify the tasks and procedures of careful, critical biblical exegesis.

The authors who have contributed to this series come from a wide range of ecclesiastical affiliations and confessional stances. All are seasoned, respected scholars and experienced classroom teachers. They take full account of the most important current scholarship and secondary literature, but do not attempt to summarize that literature or to engage in technical academic debate. Their fundamental concern is to analyze the literary, socio-historical, theological, and ethical dimensions of the biblical texts themselves. Although all of the commentaries in this series have been written on the basis of the Greek texts, the authors do not presuppose any knowledge of the biblical languages on the part of the reader. When some awareness of a grammatical, syntactical, or philological issue is necessary for an adequate understanding of a particular text, they explain the matter clearly and concisely.

The introduction of each volume ordinarily includes subdivisions dealing with the *key issues* addressed and/or raised by the New Testament writing under consideration; its *literary genre, structure, and character;* its *occasion and situational context,* including its wider social, historical, and religious contexts; and its *theological and ethical significance* within these several contexts.

In each volume, the *commentary* is organized according to literary units rather than verse by verse. Generally, each of these units is the subject of three types of analysis. First, the *literary analysis* attends to the unit's genre, most important stylistic features, and overall structure. Second, the *exegetical analysis* considers the aim and leading ideas of the unit, deals with any especially important textual variants, and discusses the meanings of important words, phrases, and images. It also takes note of the particular historical and social situations of the writer and original readers, and of the wider cultural and religious contexts of the book as a whole. Finally, the *theological and ethical analysis* discusses the theological and ethical matters with which the unit deals or to which it points, focusing on the theological and ethical significance of the text within its original setting.

Each volume also includes a *select bibliography,* thereby providing guidance to other major commentaries and important scholarly works, and a brief *subject index.* The New Revised Standard Version of the Bible is the principal translation of reference for the series, but the authors draw on all of the major modern English versions, and when necessary provide their own original translations of difficult terms or phrases.

The fundamental aim of this series will have been attained if readers are assisted, not only to understand more about the origins, character, and meaning of the New Testament writings, but also to enter into their own informed and critical engagement with the texts themselves.

Victor Paul Furnish
General Editor

PREFACE

My objective in this commentary has been to combine skepticism concerning the Pauline authorship of these letters, respect for the pseudonymous author's literary and rhetorical skills, and sensitivity to the ethical and theological dimensions of his argument. This means, among other things, that my primary focus has not been on a comparison of this author with Paul, either as writer or as theologian. Though some comparison is inevitable, given the attributed authorship, I wanted above all to understand this author in his own social and historical context and within his own theological idiom. The attempt to respect this author as a creative writer and theologian does not, however, imply approval of all his arguments and conclusions. I hope I indicate clearly enough not only where the author's exhortations and theology have merit but also where they are problematical in light of the theological and ethical legacy of the early church. The special orientation of this series, with its concern not only for literary and exegetical issues but for theological and ethical ones as well, has provided an excellent context for exploring all these dimensions of the texts.

The format of the series excludes footnotes and the series guidelines encouraged keeping in-text references to secondary literature to a minimum. Those familiar with research on the Pastoral Letters will, however, recognize my indebtedness to previous scholarship. Special mention should be made of Jürgen Roloff's commentary on 1 Timothy. His incisive literary and theological analyses of this letter are without equal, the result of years of scholarly reflection. I have learned much from his work, and I hope that it shows.

It is with deep gratitude that I acknowledge the assistance of John H. Elliott, whose helpful suggestions, gently proffered, kept me attuned to the social dynamics of the Mediterranean world. Victor Paul Furnish, my colleague and the General Editor of the series, has been encouraging and supportive through every phase of the production of the book. Special thanks go also to Rex Matthews of Abingdon Press for nurturing this series through its long gestation period with such patience and for shepherding this particular volume through the various production stages with such skill. I am indebted to Lucy Cobbe for help with the index, to Donna Yarri for checking the citations, and to Mary Ann Marshall for assistance with word processing. The book could never have been written, though, without John's abiding support. I dedicate it to him, *gnēsios syzygos,* though it may seem an odd choice, for the Pastoral Letters nowhere capture the magic of a good marriage.

Jouette M. Bassler

LIST OF ABBREVIATIONS

AB	Anchor Bible
AnBib	Analecta biblica
Apoc. Bar.	*Apocalypse of Baruch*
Barn.	*Barnabas*
b. Sanh.	Babylonian Talmud, tractate *Sanhedrin*
CBQ	*Catholic Biblical Quarterly*
CD	Cairo text of the *Damascus Document*
Did.	*Didache*
Ebib	Etudes bibliques
EKKNT	Evangelisch-katholischer Kommentar zum Neuen Testament
Eusebius *Hist. Eccl.*	Eusebius, *History of the Church*
1 [2] Clem.	*First [Second] Clement*
FRLANT	Forschungen zur Religion und Literatur des Alten und Neuen Testaments
Gk.	Greek
GNB	*The Bible in Today's English Version (Good News Bible)*
Heb.	Hebrew
Herm. Man.	*Hermas, Mandate*
Ign. *Magn.*	Ignatius, *Letter to the Magnesians*
Ign. *Smyr.*	Ignatius, *Letter to the Smyrnaeans*
Ign. *Trall.*	Ignatius, *Letter to the Trallians*
Irenaeus *Adv. Haer.*	Irenaeus, *Against Heresies*
JBL	*Journal of Biblical Literature*
Josephus *Ag. Ap.*	Josephus, *Against Apion*
Josephus *Ant.*	Josephus, *The Antiquities of the Jews*

Josephus *J. W.*	Josephus, *The Jewish War*
JRelS	*Journal of Religious Studies*
JSNTSup	Journal for the Study of the New Testament—Supplement Series
JTS	*Journal of Theological Studies*
LXX	Septuagint
NAB	*The New American Bible*
NEB	*The New English Bible*
NIGTC	The New International Greek Testament Commentary
NIV	*The Holy Bible, New International Version*
NJB	*The New Jerusalem Bible*
NovTSup	Novum Testamentum, Supplements
NRSV	The New Revised Standard Version Bible
NT	New Testament
NTD	Das Neue Testament Deutsch
NTS	*New Testament Studies*
OT	Old Testament
Pol. *Phil.*	Polycarp, *Letter to the Philippians*
Prot. Jas.	*Protevangelium of James*
REB	*The Revised English Bible*
RNT	Regensburger Neues Testament
RSV	The Revised Standard Version of the Bible
SBLMS	SBL Monograph Series
SBLSBS	SBL Sources for Biblical Study
Tertullian *Adv. Marc.*	Tertullian, *Against Marcion*
T. Dan	*Testament of Dan*
T. Gad	*Testament of Gad*
T. Moses	*Testament of Moses*
THKNT	Theologischer Handkommentar zum Neuen Testament
ZNW	*Zeitschrift für die neutestamentliche Wissenschaft*

INTRODUCTION

The letters to Timothy and Titus occupy a unique position within the body of letters attributed to the apostle Paul. They alone are addressed to single individuals, though their exhortations often concern the entire church, or portions of it. (By way of contrast, the letter to Philemon is also addressed to Apphia, Archippus, and the entire church that met in Philemon's house.) These three letters are united by a distinctive vocabulary and style that seem, at the same time, to distinguish them from the other Pauline letters. The opponents mentioned in the three letters are described—and combated—in similar ways. And all three letters show a pervasive concern for pastoral oversight of the church and, in the case of 1 Timothy and Titus, for specific church leadership roles as well. Because of their many similarities and because of this concern, the three letters have, since the eighteenth century, been referred to collectively as the Pastoral Letters or Epistles.

AUTHORSHIP

Absolutely crucial to the interpretation of these letters is the position taken on the question of their authorship. Though they were written in Paul's name and accepted as Pauline by the early church, a number of scholars in the nineteenth century, and even more in the twentieth, have raised serious questions about the accuracy of this ascription. Several features of the letters contribute to the debate over their authenticity—their language and style; their theology; the historical circumstances, including the level of church structure and organization, that they reflect; and the witness to them in early Christian writings. The arguments are laid out at some length elsewhere; only a brief summary is presented here (see especially Knight 1992; Prior 1989).

The witness of early Christian writings is ambiguous. The letters are mentioned in an early listing of authoritative Christian writings (the Muratorian Canon), but the date of the list is disputed; some scholars assign it to the late second century, others to the fourth. The Pastorals are not found in a manuscript collection of the Pauline letters that dates from about 200 C.E. ($\mathfrak{P}^{46}$) and seem to have been absent from earlier collections as well (Gamble 1985, 40). They appear in all later major manuscripts, however, except the reputable Vaticanus (B). Irenaeus (c. 180 C.E.) explicitly mentions the letters and assumes their Pauline authorship (*Adv. Haer.* 3.3.3). Athenagoras, writing about the same time, clearly quotes 1 Tim 2:2. Polycarp, writing four decades earlier, seems to quote several passages from the letters. It is much less clear whether the author of *1 Clement* (95 C.E.) or Ignatius (113 C.E.) knew and quoted the letters. They do not appear in Marcion's canon of sacred books (c. 140 C.E.), but it is disputed whether this is because he did not know of them or, as Tertullian alleges, because he rejected them (*Adv. Marc.* 5.21).

More telling are the historical circumstances reflected in the letters. The interest in and complexity of church leadership roles—which included bishops, elders, deacons, and perhaps widows—go far beyond that found in the undisputed letters: qualifications are listed; ordination rites are mentioned; disciplinary procedures are established. The historical situations presupposed by the letters—Timothy left behind to minister to the churches in Ephesus, Titus left to complete a mission on Crete—cannot be reconciled with what we know of Paul's travels from the undisputed letters or from Acts. Even supporters of the authenticity of these letters must rely on the hypothesis that Paul was released from the imprisonment described at the conclusion of the book of Acts; that he then engaged in further work in Ephesus and on Crete, after which he wrote 1 Timothy and Titus; and that he was then imprisoned a second time, during which time he wrote 2 Timothy (Fee 1988; Spicq

1969). Though later writings lend some support to this hypothesis (*1 Clem.* 5:7; Eusebius *Hist. Eccl.* 2.22.1-6), it is not strong and is in fact contradicted by Acts, which is not only absolutely silent about Paul's possible release from the Roman prison, but also broadly hints that the imprisonment culminated in Paul's death (20:24-38).

The distinctive language and style of these letters raise further questions about authorship (Harrison 1921, 1964). A substantial portion of the vocabulary consists of words not found in the undisputed letters but common in the philosophical writings of the time. Sentence construction—use of prepositions, conjunctions, and so on—is demonstrably different in these letters. The style is wooden, devoid of the passion and eloquence that characterize the undisputed letters. Attempts have been made to explain these discrepancies by appealing to Paul's use of secretaries to write at least some of his letters (Rom 16:22; see also 1 Cor 16:21; Gal 6:11; Phlm 19). If the contents of a letter were outlined to a secretary, but not dictated, variations in vocabulary and style could arise from the secretary's completion of the letter. Yet unlike some of the undisputed letters, the Pastorals give no hint of the use of a secretary, whereas those undisputed letters that do reveal a secretary's hand retain the distinctive Pauline vocabulary and style. The secretary hypothesis does not provide a satisfactory resolution of the authorship question.

The differences between the theology in the undisputed letters and the theology of the Pastorals probably provide the most significant evidence for pseudonymity (see below, pp. 31-34). Among the problems that have been noted is the absence in these letters of any reference to God's righteousness or to the cross of Christ, arguably the central issues in the main Pauline letters. There is also a noticeable shift in christological language: "Son," prominent in the undisputed letters, is never used in the Pastorals, but "Savior," found only at Phil 3:20 in the undisputed letters, is used frequently in the Pastorals for both God and Christ. Indeed, the author seems to refer to Christ as God in one verse (Titus 2:13), though in another he insists on Christ's humanity (1 Tim 2:5). The Spirit is rarely mentioned in the Pastorals, and never as a down payment on, or the first fruits of, the promised redemption (cf. 2 Cor 1:22; Rom 8:23). There is a new interest in "godliness," in "sound" or "healthy" consciences, in preserving the "deposit" of faith, and a distinctive interpretation of both the incarnation and the parousia as epiphanies of God's saving will.

Such shifts—and there are many others—in theological language and perspective can be attributed to changed circumstances and external influences, even to Paul's increased age. Many, however, find a better explanation of this and the other issues noted above in the hypothesis of pseudonymity. This is the hypothesis that will govern the following explication: the Pastoral Letters were not written by Paul, but by a later churchman writing in Paul's name several decades after Paul's death. Though pseudonymity can mask gender as well as name, the author's comments on the behavior and roles of women identify him beyond question as male (see, e.g., 1 Tim 2:9-15; 2 Tim 3:6; Titus 2:5).

The hypothesis of pseudonymity carries with it several important corollaries. First, precise dating of the letters is difficult. If Polycarp did, in fact, know and quote the Pastorals (see above)—and there is no firm consensus on the point—they must have been written before the middle of the second century. The author of the Pastorals seems to rely to some extent on the book of Acts (though again the point is disputed), which would mean a date of composition some-time after 90 C.E., perhaps in the first decade of the second century. Second, the place of composition is equally uncertain. Many have seen in the letters' relatively large number of references to persons associated with Ephesus a clue to their point of origin (Hultgren 1984), while others argue for a link with Rome. There is inadequate evidence to resolve the issue. Third, if the author is pseudonymous, so are the addressees. It is necessary to separate the interpretation of the letters from the historical figures of Timothy and Titus and to regard the author's references to these men instead as part of his literary fiction.

It is difficult to assess fully the ethical dimensions of the letters' pseudonymity. Writing in the name of another was a relatively common phenomenon in both Jewish apocalyptic and Greco-Roman philosophical circles (Meade 1986; Malherbe 1977a). The claim is often made that this convention was employed out of modesty and as a way to honor a respected figure of the past. It is often further claimed that the author expected the pseudonymity to be recognized by readers and that there was thus no intent on his part to deceive (Donelson 1986, 9-23; cf. Ellis 1992). Yet it is impossible to prove these points, and evidence from later Christian circles shows that vigorous efforts were made at that time to identify documents written pseudonymously in an apostle's name and that such documents, once identified, were invariably rejected. Thus the author of the Muratorian Canon rejected certain letters from Paul to the Alexandrians and Laodiceans as "forged in Paul's name for the sect of Marcion, and several others, which cannot be received in the catholic Church; for it will not do to mix gall with honey."

The case of the Pastoral Letters is particularly perplexing, for there are a number of passages within these letters containing personal details that, if composed by the author, would seem to suggest a calculated attempt to deceive (2 Tim 1:4-5; 4:9-15; Titus 3:12-14). The suggestion is sometimes made that these passages are fragments of genuine letters, or that they derive from oral traditions about Paul. Such an argument, however, even if true, does not answer or eliminate the question of the pseudonymous author's intent in incorporating them into his letters.

Clearly the author of these letters himself revered, and was writing to churches that revered, the apostle Paul. He was confronting a situation that seemed to him to distort the apostle's message and to endanger the apostle's churches. Writing in Paul's name, he attempted to bring the apostle's word—as he understood it—to bear on the situation. It seems clear that he wanted the letters to be read as Paul's, but we cannot recover his thoughts on the ethics of his endeavor. The church, in canonizing the letters, was certainly influenced by the claim of Pauline authorship, but the prevailing criterion for their acceptance was probably that of use. For good or for ill, and regardless of the circumstances of their origin or their author's intent, these letters proved useful to the church in the struggle for self-preservation and self-definition (McDonald 1988, 146-63). From the end of the second century they are cited regularly as part of the church's scripture.

Genre, Character, and Sources

Though a major factor in the composition of these letters was the appearance of teachers within the community of faith whose views the author regarded as wrong and whose techniques he regarded as harmful (see below, pp. 25-31), the letters are nevertheless essentially hortatory documents, not polemical ones. That is, the author's major goal was to exhort the community, various groups within it, and the leaders of it to embrace or continue in certain modes of behavior and to avoid other modes. His major goal was not to attack or refute the opposing teachers directly.

As hortatory documents, the letters are filled with direct and indirect commands, reminders, rationales (both theological and practical), vice and virtue lists, and especially models of behavior— both exemplary (usually using the figure of Paul) and reprehensible (usually using the example of the opposing teachers). A pervasive hortatory device that influenced the composition and structure of these letters is the pairing of these contrasting examples (see 1 Tim 4:1-16; 2 Tim 3:1-13; Titus 1:5-16). The negative example of the opponents thus reinforces the positive example of Paul, and both lend support to the letters' various exhortations.

In spite of their similar goals and character, 1 Timothy and Titus differ significantly from 2 Timothy. The former contain primarily, but not exclusively, exhortations concerning the community, both as a whole and in its constituent parts. These letters are similar in tone, content, and form to administrative letters from authorized officials to subordinates, who were in turn responsible for the administration of particular domains (Wolter 1988, 156-202). Timothy and Titus function in these two documents primarily as mediators of the instructions. Second Timothy, on the other hand, consists primarily of personal exhortation. Because it is presented as a letter from Paul as he awaits his apparently imminent execution, this letter takes on a number of attributes of what is called "testamentary" literature, that is, writings that purport to be the last literary legacy of a dying patriarch. Thus, like Dan, Benjamin, and other pseudonymous figures in the *Testaments of the Twelve Patriarchs,* and even like the farewell speech of Paul in Acts 20:17-35,

Paul predicts his death in this letter (4:6-8), warns of troubles to come (3:1-9), rehearses his own faithfulness (3:10-11), and exhorts his "child" to remain faithful to his teachings (4:1-5). In this letter the community plays essentially no role. The emphasis is on the close personal relationship between Paul and Timothy and on the latter's role as Paul's successor.

Though all three letters are essentially hortatory, they have different but complementary contents and functions. First Timothy and Titus provide the official mandate for the community, while 2 Timothy emphasizes the importance of unbroken continuity and fidelity to the traditions preserved and presented by Paul. Their complementarity can be seen in other ways as well. It is in 1 Timothy, for example, that the contours of concrete problems in the community emerge most clearly: women exercising teaching roles in the church (2:11-15), overuse and apparent misuse of the widow's office (5:3-16), a real—but indistinct—problem with some elders (5:17-25), and disrespectful behavior by slaves (6:1-2). Titus covers much the same material as 1 Timothy, but, except for instructions to slaves (Titus 2:9-10), with no apparent reference to concrete problems. This shorter letter does, however, strongly reinforce the message of subordination that the author presents in 1 Timothy as a solution to the problems mentioned there (Titus 1:6, 10; 2:5, 9; 3:1). In both of these letters, opposing teachers figure prominently as a threat to the community, yet the author does not directly rebut or refute these teachers. Much of 2 Timothy, however, addresses the question of the proper mode and content of Christian teaching (1:13-14; 2:1-2, 14-16, 22-25; 3:14-16; 4:1-2), and thus *this* letter constitutes a substantive response to the tactics of the opponents (Johnson 1978/79). It is likely that the three letters were always intended to circulate together and to function in these complementary ways.

The author employed several sources when he wrote these letters. He was familiar with a number of Pauline letters; certainly Romans and 1 Corinthians and Philippians, and probably 2 Corinthians and Philemon as well. Moreover, he was familiar with them as a collection and composed his own collection in conscious imitation and expansion of it. He was also probably familiar with Acts, for the reference to "things that happened to me in Antioch, Iconium, and Lystra" (2 Tim 3:11) seems to allude to events reported in Acts 13–14. He may have had access to some personal traditions about Paul not found in Acts. There is a striking correspondence between the names of friends and opponents in these letters and names found in a second-century apocryphal document entitled *The Acts of Paul*. The authors of the Pastorals and the *Acts of Paul* may have relied on the same oral legends to compose their quite different documents (MacDonald 1983). Beyond this, the author cites a number of liturgical or credal fragments, though it is often difficult to determine their exact extent and nature (see, e.g., 1 Tim 2:5-6; 3:16; 2 Tim 2:11-13; Titus 2:11-14; 3:4-7). He also borrowed heavily from household management traditions, vice and virtue lists, and documents on church order and organization. Though his style is not elegant and transitions are often clumsy and abrupt, the author created out of this diverse material an effective appeal for order, stability, and faithfulness.

There are few problems with the text of the letters that substantively affect their meaning. These problems are noted and discussed in the following commentary.

OCCASION AND CONTEXT

The "double pseudonymity" of these letters makes it exceedingly difficult to define with real precision their occasion and context. Since they are not only pseudonymous in authorship but also in addressees, they could have arisen in, and been intended for, churches anywhere within the Pauline mission field. Though many have proposed a connection with the church in Ephesus, this remains only a hypothesis, and a disputed one at that. Thus while one can presume that the basic attributes, institutions, and ideals of the Roman Empire—the (extended) household, a stratified society, the values of honor and shame, virtues promoted by Greco-Roman philosophers—form the social context of these letters, the *specific* circumstances in the Roman province of Asia or the city of

Ephesus in about the year 100 C.E. may—or may not—have been a factor in their composition.

The problems that the author addresses, however, are mostly *internal* to the churches. To be sure, he is concerned that the behavior of church members should meet with the approval of outsiders (1 Tim 3:7; 5:14; 6:1; Titus 2:5, 8, 10), and this suggests that these members were marginalized to some degree from the wider culture. There are few verses, however, that suggest fear of actual persecution (2 Tim 3:12). Indeed, the author insists on prayers and courtesy for outsiders, even for high officials (1 Tim 2:1-2; Titus 3:2), presupposes the freedom to worship God openly (1 Tim 4:13-16) and to enjoy God's good creation (1 Tim 4:4), and hopes for the salvation of all (1 Tim 4:10). Though 2 Timothy is presented as Paul's letter from a Roman prison and though suffering is one of its pervasive themes, this suffering is primarily correlated with opposition by other teachers and abandonment by former colleagues, not with a hostile external social environment.

The Pastoral Letters are written as if to two different persons, one in Ephesus and one on Crete, each facing, it would seem, different opponents. Moreover, "Paul" recalls opposition he himself faced in the past (1 Tim 1:19-20; 2 Tim 1:15), describes opposition that Timothy and Titus face (1 Tim 1:3-7; 6:3-5, 20-21; 2 Tim 2:14-26; Titus 1:10-16; 3:9-11), and predicts opposition in the future (1 Tim 4:1-5; 2 Tim 3:1-5). Though the letters thus seem to reflect a temporal and spatial diversity of opposition, the presupposition of pseudonymity permits—indeed encourages—the hypothesis that all references to opponents describe the same historical phenomenon, that experienced by the author's church. Indeed, there is great homogeneity in the portraits of all the opposing teachers, yet the author's style of argumentation does not permit a clear determination of the nature and extent of the threat they posed. Only rarely does he offer even a glimpse of the content of their message. Instead he engages primarily in name-calling and even then relies on stereotypical accusations deriving from the conventional attacks leveled by contemporary philosophers against their rivals, the sophists or rhetoricians. The highly traditional and polemical language of these attacks thus reveals little about the actual nature or behavior of the opposing teachers. In particular, charges of greed (1 Tim 6:5; Titus 1:11), hypocrisy (2 Tim 3:5; Titus 1:16), moral corruption (1 Tim 1:9-10; 2 Tim 3:2-4), and deception (2 Tim 3:13) cannot be taken at face value (Karris 1973).

Because of the paucity of reliable information about the opponents, there is a tendency to "mirror read" the author's emphases. That is, it is tempting to assume that because the author stresses, for example, God's will to save all (1 Tim 2:4), the opponents limited salvation to an elite few. Such a method, though grounded, perhaps, in a reasonable assumption, yields unverifiable results and should be used with great caution.

In spite of the difficulties involved, however, some fairly reliable information about the opponents can be extracted from these letters. This information is not enough to provide a complete picture, but it does suggest the rough contours of the situation that the author was addressing. Some statements that the author makes, for example, stand out from the background of his stock polemics and seem to reflect the actual situation. The author provides one piece of direct information about the message of the opponents: They claim that a (or the) resurrection has already taken place (2 Tim 2:18). Because the author does not comment on this teaching but simply instructs "Timothy" to avoid such "profane chatter," it is difficult to determine the meaning of such a statement. It probably assumes a dissociation of the human spirit from the material body and a resurrection solely of the spirit, which is thus possible apart from the body and prior to physical death (cf. 1 Cor 15:12-19). This presupposes a profoundly negative view of the body and thus of the material world, but this view is confirmed by other passages in these letters.

One such passage is the description of certain people who will, in the future, "forbid marriage and demand abstinence from foods" (1 Tim 4:3). Under the assumption that what is predicted for the future by "Paul" corresponds to the author's present, and under the further assumption that all facets of the opposition described in these letters reflect the same local phenomenon, a reasonably coherent picture of this opposition emerges. Judging from the author's counterargument (1 Tim 4:4, the only direct rebuttal found in these letters), an argument that stresses the goodness of creation, the opponents' asceticism was probably rooted in a rejection or denigration of the created or material world. Such an attitude is also suggested by the reproach, directed against certain "rebellious people," that "to the pure all things are pure, but to the corrupt and unbelieving nothing [i.e., nothing in the material world] is pure" (Titus 1:15).

The theological basis for the opponents' asceticism is thus radically different from Paul's own justification for the celibate life. Though Paul promoted and practiced celibacy, he did not insist on it for all Christians, because he rooted it, not in a negative view of creation (cf. Rom 1:20; 1 Cor 8:6), but in his more practical conviction that it was a way of life better suited to enduring the traumas of the end of the age (1 Cor 7:25-35). Thus, although the opponents' asceticism superficially resembled Paul's celibate stance and may indeed have been inspired by it, the author of the Pastoral Letters vehemently rejects asceticism in Paul's name.

Unlike their views on the resurrection and asceticism, a third component of the opponents' message can only be deduced from the argument of these letters. The author says that the opponents "profess to know God" (Titus 1:16) and warns Timothy against "what is falsely called knowledge" (1 Tim 6:20). He describes correct faith as "knowledge of the truth" (Titus 1:1; see also 1 Tim 4:3) and links that knowledge with salvation (1 Tim 2:4; 2 Tim 2:25). This emphasis on knowledge suggests that it was an important component of the opponents' message; if so, it provides a significant clue to their identity.

The features associated with the opponents—rejection of the material, created world; a spiritualized view of the resurrection; and an emphasis on knowledge—all characterized the movement known as Gnosticism that emerged in the church in the second century (though its roots go back somewhat earlier). In its fully developed forms, this diverse movement espoused a radical dualism that often viewed the material world as the heinous creation of an inferior god, a prison for captured spirits whose true origin was a transcendent sphere of light and knowledge. Elaborate myths were developed to explain the tragic creation of the material world and true salvation was understood as liberation from that world. This salvation was only available to those whose origin was the transcendent sphere and was achieved by obtaining knowledge of that origin, which enabled a return to it. In Christian Gnosticism, Christ was seen as the bearer of this saving knowledge, an emissary from the transcendent world who took on only the appearance of a physical body. As a consequence of this dualistic worldview, Gnostics were either hostile or indifferent to the actions of the body, some groups of them embracing asceticism, others libertinism.

It is not clear how closely we should identify the opponents in the Pastoral Letters with the fully developed forms of Gnosticism. Without further evidence, the disparagement of the material world hinted at in 1 Tim 4:3-4 falls short of the radical dualism of later Gnostic systems. The accusation that opponents dealt in "myths" (1 Tim 1:4; 4:7; 2 Tim 4:4; Titus 1:14) was a stock charge in philosophical polemics and cannot be reliably used to link them with the elaborate descriptions of the origin of the "aeons" that were part of Gnostic lore. Yet the opponents were probably part of a movement, widespread and diverse, that evolved into Gnosticism, for they seem to have possessed, in undeveloped form, attributes and beliefs that became characteristic of it.

It is more difficult to define the nature of the link between the opponents and Judaism. To be sure, the author describes them in various places as "desiring to be teachers of the law" (1 Tim 1:7), as "paying attention to Jewish myths" and "commandments" (Titus 1:14), and even as being "of the circumcision" (Titus 1:10). Some assume on the basis of these phrases that the author faced opponents on two fronts, one Jewish, promoting the law, and one Gnostic, promoting esoteric speculations. Yet these references to Jewish traditions are similar to phrases Paul uses in Romans and Galatians to describe opponents (see, e.g., Rom 2:17-21; Gal 2:12) and their presence in these pseudonymous letters may reflect the author's desire to give the opponents a "Pauline" flavor. Certainly nothing in the content of the letters indicates that the Jewish law or circumcision played a significant role in the conflict or that Judaizing outsiders were threatening the church. If there was a connection between the opponents and Judaism, it may have been in their use of Jewish Scripture as a foundation for their theological speculations (see comments on 1 Tim 1:8-11).

It is clear that the opponents, whatever their current beliefs, originated within the author's church. Moreover, although the author speaks of them as theologically distant—having suffered shipwreck in, or renounced, the faith (1 Tim 1:19; 4:1) or having "swerved from the truth" (2 Tim 2:18)—it does not seem that they were physically distant. They continued to be a factor in the life of the church. They are, for example, to be avoided (1 Tim 6:20; 2 Tim 2:14, 16; Titus 3:9), suggesting the lively possibility of contact. They are to be admonished (Titus 3:10), requiring contact; and their presence breeds useless debates and quarrels within the community (1 Tim 6:4; 2 Tim 2:23; Titus 3:9).

The author vigorously opposes these quarrels and speculations (see, e.g., 1 Tim 1:4; 2 Tim 2:23; Titus 3:2, 9), but, oddly, not so much for their content as for their divisive and unsettling consequences. Though the author disparages opponents as idle talkers (Titus 1:10), they themselves certainly understood their activity more positively. Their "disputes about words" (1 Tim 6:4; see also 2 Tim 2:14) and "controversies" may have appeared to more sympathetic ears as vigorous theological debates and investigations, based perhaps on Jewish Scripture, perhaps even on Paul's own letters (Donelson 1986, 121-27). Against such speculations, which were both theologically unsettling and socially divisive, the author holds up the sound, reliable teaching preserved and transmitted by the ordained leaders of the church (1 Tim 1:10-11; 4:6; 6:20). This concern for sound teaching and reliable teachers is pervasive in these letters and lies behind the author's keen interest in leadership roles in the church (1 Tim 3:1-13; 5:17-25; Titus 1:5-9).

It is not easy to judge the opponents' numbers or strength. In some passages the author dismisses them as a vague and numerically unthreatening "some" (1 Tim 1:6, 19; 4:1; 6:10, 21), but this was a typical rhetorical device and thus an unreliable indicator of their actual numbers. Other passages, especially 2 Tim 4:3-4, suggest that they enjoyed considerable success in the church, and if the portrayal of Paul in that letter as an abandoned, beleaguered leader reflects the reality of the author's church, the opponents may well have had superior strength. Yet conflict is a useful tool to codify values and reinforce group identity and cohesion (Elliott 1981, 113-18). The author may have emphasized—or exaggerated—the urgency of the situation to lend weight to his exhortations. It is unlikely, however, that he "invented" the opposition. Opponents posed a genuine threat, and recognition of this clarifies a number of puzzling aspects of these letters.

Though the author presents the danger posed by the opponents as a doctrinal one (1 Tim 1:3; 6:3; 2 Tim 2:18; 4:3), it is clear from his response that it had a significant, if not dominant, social component as well. The influence of the opposing teachers created instability in the Christian community, both within the families that constituted the community and in the structure of the community itself. The author, for example, charges that the teachers "make their way into households and captivate [or capture] silly women" (2 Tim 3:6). Though the stock polemics that the author drew on included the charge of targeting women (Karris 1973), his pervasive concern with the proper role of women suggests that the charge is here rooted in reality. The opponents were successful in interesting the women of the community in their ascetic message, and this destabilized the traditional family (Titus 1:11). In response, the author repeatedly reinforces traditional family hierarchy and traditional childbearing roles for women.

Interestingly, the second-century *Acts of Paul* describes the apostle as promulgating a message of celibacy, converting a prominent young woman to it, and, in the process, severing her connections with her traditional family. It is impossible to prove, but nevertheless conceivable, that the opponents defended their actions with similar legends about Paul. If so, the author of the Pastoral Letters responds with the device of pseudonymity, countering legends about Paul with letters purportedly from him (MacDonald 1983).

The presence of the opposing teachers also eroded lines of ecclesial authority. There were competing teaching voices within the church, the bishops and/or elders who were officially assigned that role (1 Tim 3:2; 5:17; Titus 1:9) and the opponents who were clearly attempting to usurp it. The erosion of authority may even have penetrated the ranks of the elders themselves (see 1 Tim 5:19-22).

The author responds by denigrating the opposing teachers' doctrines and especially their tactics, while reinforcing "orthodox" teachers by tracing their teachings back to Paul. He also used the metaphor of the household to promote his vision of an orderly social entity.

Though the author refers to the church as the household of God in only one passage (1 Tim 3:15), the image informs in a variety of ways his understanding of the church and thus his exhortations to its members. It promotes, for example, the concept of loyalty and thus undergirds his outrage at the disloyalty of the opposing teachers (2 Tim 1:15; 4:16). It implies clear lines of authority and the subordination of various groups. It highlights the importance of mutual obligations, hospitality, respect for age and experience, and responsible oversight of financial resources. So strong was the identification of the church as a household and so important were households within it that the distinction between the two—real households and metaphorical household—was blurred and relations within the former became definitive for roles within the latter. The actions of the opposing teachers are presented as a fundamental breach of household etiquette (see 1 Tim 6:4; 2 Tim 1:15; 3:2-4; Titus 1:11), and the author responds by excluding them from the household of faith.

THEOLOGY AND ETHICS

The Pastoral Letters have not been noted for their profound theology (cf. Young 1994). Most of the explicitly theological passages are quoted fragments of hymns or creeds or rely heavily on liturgical language for their formulation (see, e.g., 1 Tim 1:17; 2:5-6*a*; 3:16; 4:10; 6:16; 2 Tim 1:9-10; 2:11-13; Titus 2:11-14; 3:4-7). These fragments seem to be tacked onto the argument— sometimes rather awkwardly—instead of woven into it, and they present the impression of a miscellaneous collection of theological affirmations rather than a carefully thought out perspective. Yet there is a theological center in all of this that informs and undergirds in a more sustained way the diverse and often mundane exhortations: God, the one God, the living God, desires the salvation of all (1 Tim 2:4, 6; 4:10; 6:13; Titus 2:11). This serves as the warrant for the exhortations to the quiet and dignified behavior that not only deflects suspicion but also elicits the approval of the non-Christian world. It also motivates the admonitions to good works that appear throughout these letters. It even seems to influence the way the opponents are treated, that is, with an eye to their repentance and salvation (1 Tim 1:20; 2 Tim 2:24-26).

The centrality of this concern is also reflected in the language used to refer to God. In addition to the familiar Christian term, "Father" (1 Tim 1:2; 2 Tim 1:2; Titus 1:4), and the hellenistic Jewish phrases, "King of kings" or "King of the ages" (1 Tim 1:17; 6:15), the term, "Savior," has new prominence. This is new, at least, in the Pauline corpus and rare elsewhere in the New Testament as a reference to God (Luke 1:47; Jude 25), though it is frequently found in Judaism. It is also the most characteristic designation for God in the Pastoral Letters (1 Tim 1:1; 2:3; 4:10; Titus 1:3; 2:10; 3:4), reinforcing the author's emphasis on God's desire to save all.

Christ is also called "Savior," sometimes in a passage that refers to God in the same way (2 Tim 1:10; Titus 1:4; 2:13; 3:6). (Apart from the Pastoral Letters, "Savior" as a christological term is found a dozen times in the New Testament [e.g., John 4:42; Acts 5:31; Phil 3:20], but it is common only in the second letter of Peter [2 Pet 1:1, 11; 2:20; 3:2, 18].) If God is designated "Savior" because of God's will and plan to save, Christ is so designated because he both accomplishes God's saving will and reveals it. His role in the work of salvation is described in traditional language: He gave himself as a ransom for all (1 Tim 2:6; Titus 2:14; cf. Mark 10:45) and he pours out the Holy Spirit on the faithful (Titus 3:6; cf. Acts 2:32-33; John 20:22). More characteristic of these letters is the insistence that Christ also—perhaps even primarily—reveals God's saving will.

The author underscores this revelatory role by using the language of epiphany to describe both Jesus' first appearance on earth and his return at the end of the ages. Though Jesus' coming at the final judgment is described elsewhere in the Greek New Testament as a *parousia* (literally, an arrival or a presence), this event is directly or indirectly associated with a revelation of sorts (Mark 13:26; Rom 2:15-16; 1 Cor 4:5; 2 Thess 1:7-10; 2:8). Nevertheless, the use of the Greek word *epiphaneia* (literally, "manifestation" or "appearance") pure and simple for this event is unparalleled in the New Testament (see 1 Tim 6:14; 2 Tim 4:8; Titus 2:13). Even more striking is the use of the same term to describe Jesus' earthly life. The two events, though designated by the same Greek term, differ significantly in what they make manifest. The second manifests or reveals Jesus' divine glory (Titus 2:13); the first reveals God's saving will (2 Tim 1:8-10; Titus 3:4). Thus in these letters, it is first and foremost God who is Savior, for it is God's saving will and plan that have been executed. Christ is Savior because he both reveals and executes God's saving intent.

This seems at times to subordinate Jesus to God (1 Tim 2:5). Nevertheless, God's saving nature so defines God that Jesus' revelation of God's saving will is a revelation of God's self, and the author can elsewhere identify the two, not only by using the same title ("Savior") for them, but also by (apparently) referring to Jesus as God (Titus 2:13, one of only a handful of New Testament texts to do so; see also John 20:28; Heb 1:8).

The author retains a strong Pauline message of grace. In fact, he goes to some rhetorical lengths to emphasize it (1 Tim 1:12-16; 2 Tim 1:8-10; Titus 3:3-5). At the same time, there is also a strong emphasis on good deeds (see, e.g., Titus 2:14; 3:1, 8, 14) and frequent reminders of a pending judgment (1 Tim 5:24; 2 Tim 1:18; 4:1, 8). Final salvation clearly rests on the obedient life (1 Tim 2:15; 4:7-10, 16; 6:11-16, 19), but "grace" trains the believer in that life (Titus 2:11-12).

The author does not explore at length, as Paul does, the role of the Holy Spirit in that divine training. Indeed, he speaks rarely of the activity of the Spirit: once of its role in prophecy (1 Tim 4:1), once of its role in preserving the tradition (2 Tim 1:14), and once in a liturgical passage that hints at Paul's concept of the Spirit as both the seal of justification and the enabler of the life of righteousness (Titus 3:5-7, cf. Rom 8:1-17; 2 Cor 5:5; Gal 5:16-26). Without Paul's theological depth, but in Paul's spirit, the author clearly conceives the Christian life as one that is lived out "in between"—in between the two epiphanies, in between the experience of grace and the experience of judgment. As for Paul, so for this author, salvation is future and preceded by judgment. But trained by grace, taught by good "orthodox" teachers (1 Tim 4:16; Titus 1:9), and guided by the letters' "Paul," the elect have a strong hope of eternal life (Titus 1:2).

A fundamental presupposition throughout these letters is that there is an indissoluble connection between beliefs and behavior, between doctrine and ethics. Stated simply—and repeatedly—sound teaching and sound behavior go hand in hand. This is the basis for the author's exhortations and the stick he wields against the opposing teachers. Though there is every indication that these teachers led lives characterized by ascetic withdrawal and not debauchery, the author repeatedly links them and their teachings to moral chaos (1 Tim 6:3-5; 2 Tim 2:16; 3:1-9; Titus 1:16). The author's understanding of "sound behavior" was, of course, strongly influenced by the social conventions of the Greco-Roman culture, conventions that prized moderation, modesty, and the maintenance of order and traditional lines of authority. Certain consequences of the opponents' message (e.g., nontraditional roles for women) and the very fact that in assuming the role of teachers they were undermining the hierarchy of the church were to this author the first signs of moral collapse. His denunciation of them is thus couched more in terms of where their teaching will lead than in terms of their demonstrably immoral behavior. Likewise, the socially acceptable behavior he promotes is not only prudent for a marginalized group but also functions as testimony to the truth of the gospel (1 Tim 1:8-11; Titus 2:1).

COMMENTARY: 1 TIMOTHY

SALUTATION (1:1-2)

The letter's salutation conforms to Paul's established formula (itself derived from hellenistic and Jewish letter-writing conventions): the name of the sender, followed by the name of the addressee, with a concluding blessing on the addressee (see, e.g., 1 Cor 1:1-3; also Acts 15:23; Rev 1:4-5).

◊ ◊ ◊ ◊

Unlike most of the letters in the Pauline corpus, the Pastoral Letters have no cosenders (cf. 1 Cor 1:1) and are addressed strictly to individuals. Timothy's church is not included in the address (cf. Phlm 1-2), even though, as we shall see, most of the instructions in this letter concern the church. Instead the salutation is narrowly focused on the relationship between God (and Christ Jesus), Paul, and Timothy.

Paul is introduced here, as in most of the Pauline letters, as "apostle of Christ Jesus." The similar but somewhat fuller salutation in Titus reveals how this author construed the role of the apostle. His task was to preserve the faith of the elect and increase the knowledge of truth, so at its very heart it involved being entrusted with the gospel (Titus 1:1-3; see also 1 Tim 1:11). There is no concept of an office here—that is, no ongoing institution—for the letters mention no other apostles besides Paul and none are expected to assume the role when Paul departs. Others can fill his roles of herald and teacher (2:7; cf. 2 Tim 2:2; 4:2), but Paul is the single apostolic link between God and these churches.

He fills that role, the author says, "by the command of God . . . and of Christ Jesus." The usual salutation terminology involves the *will* of God (1 Cor 1:1; 2 Tim 1:1), which indicates God's control of this event as of all others. "Command," however, suggests a more personal connection between God and the apostle. It suggests, in fact, a direct commission (see 1:11; Titus 1:3). The author does not differentiate the roles of God and Christ Jesus in this commissioning: both, it seems, stand behind the command. God, however, is designated Savior (Gk. *sōtēr*), echoing Old Testament language and concepts (Isa 12:2; Wis 16:7; Sir 51:1; see also Luke 1:47; Jude 25). Here it suggests that God's saving will and plan lie behind the manifestation of Jesus Christ and the proclamation of the gospel (2:3-4; Titus 3:4-7). Christ Jesus is also called "Savior" in these letters (see comments on 2 Tim 1:10; Titus 1:3-4; 2:13; 3:6) because he is the vehicle for manifesting and executing God's saving will. Thus Christ is also, as here, "our hope." This phrase, shorthand for "our hope of eternal life" (Titus 1:2; 3:7), functions almost as a christological title here (see also 2:13; Col 1:27).

Two other, more common, designations are found in the blessing formula: "God the Father and Christ Jesus our Lord." The absence of the pronoun "our" with the word "Father" seems odd, and the text has been "corrected" in later manuscripts. Yet God is presented in this letter as giving life to (i.e., "fathering") *all* things (6:13), while Christ is only acknowledged as Lord by some. Thus the absence of the pronoun with "Father" and its presence with "Lord" could indicate the author's awareness of the difference between God's relationship to the world and Christ's relationship to the community of believers.

Timothy is described, not in terms of his relationship to God or to God's will, but only in terms of his relationship to Paul. According to the undisputed Pauline letters, that relationship was one of younger coworker to older mentor, but it obviously included bonds of affection that led Paul to use the intimate kinship term "child" when referring to him (1 Cor 4:17; Phil 2:19-22). This author continues that practice, but here adds the adjective "loyal" (Gk. *gnēsios*), which also means "legitimate" or "real." As the letters unfold the treachery of the opposing teachers (see 1:6-7; 4:1; 2 Tim 1:15; 4:14-15), the significance of that adjective becomes clear.

◊ ◊ ◊ ◊

The brief salutation not only contains terms and concepts significant for the theology and Christology of this letter, it also presents information about Paul and Timothy that provides important support for the letter's exhortations. Paul is apostle by command—for example, by direct commission—of both God and Christ, who thus stand behind his teachings and exhortations. The one who receives these teachings is Paul's loyal "child" and therefore his legitimate "heir." It will be through Timothy, then—for example, through these letters addressed to Timothy—that Paul's genuine legacy comes. Readers are thus assured that if they are obedient to these teachings, they will experience the saving will of God and the hope of eternal life.

PREFACE (1:3-20)

The letter opens, not with the usual Pauline expression of thanks (cf. Rom 1:8-15; 1 Cor 1:4-9) or praise to God (2 Cor 1:3-7; Eph 1:3-14), but with a reminder of certain teachers who have endangered the church at Ephesus with their deviant doctrines and meaningless talk. An apparent digression on the proper function of the law (vv. 8-11) interrupts the description of the false teachers, and a second digression on Paul's conversion (vv. 12-16), presented in the form of a delayed thanksgiving, seems to lead even farther afield. After a formal doxology (v. 17), however, the author returns to his charge to Timothy and to the subject of opponents in the church (vv. 18-20), providing some structural unity to the chapter.

The entire chapter functions as a prologue or preface to the body of the letter (chaps. 2–6), which consists of instructions to Timothy concerning various activities, church leaders, and groups within the church (see 1:18). It describes a contentious situation that is the setting, if not the occasion, for these instructions, thereby imparting to them a note of urgency and import (see also 6:20-21). It also grounds Paul's apostolate firmly in Christ's actions and judgment, confirming the legitimacy of Paul's office (see 1:1) and thus the authority of his instructions. Likewise, Timothy is confirmed as

Paul's legitimate heir (see 1:2) and thus as a reliable mediator of the Pauline traditions (see also 6:20).

The Problem of Opposing Teachers (1:3-7)

The author does not begin with a formal expression of thanksgiving or a pious beatitude (cf. 2 Tim 1:3; Eph 1:3), but refers immediately to the problem of "certain people" who teach a different doctrine. In this the letter resembles most closely Galatians, which opens with a statement of astonishment over how the Galatians have turned to a "different gospel," following "some" who pervert the gospel of Christ.

The Greek text of verse 3 begins abruptly with a comparative clause: "Just as I urged you while I was going to Macedonia to remain in Ephesus. . . . " The sentence does not, however, contain the "so also" clause necessary to finish the thought (cf., e.g., 2 Cor 1:5). The translators of the NRSV have rendered the sentence as a direct exhortation ("I urge you . . . "), the first of many within this letter. Others think that 1:18, though distant, picks up the thought of the opening clause. Indeed, the incomplete sentence in verse 3 could serve as an open-ended introduction to the remaining contents of the letter, thus presenting all the letter's exhortations as an extension of the earlier instruction to correct certain people in Ephesus.

These people are not identified by name (cf. 1:20), a frequent tactic in this letter and in other polemical writings of the period (see 1:3, 6, 19; 4:1; 5:15, 24; 6:10, 21; see also Rom 3:8; 2 Cor 3:1). The effect is to portray the troublemakers as shadowy figures with an indistinct past and to obscure their actual numbers and influence. They are apparently, however, members or former members of the church and not outsiders, for they are subject to instruction by a church leader (v. 3; see also Titus 1:13) and have "deviated from" the sincere faith they apparently once had (v. 6; see also 4:1).

The author focuses on the activities of these people. Of primary importance is the fact that they are teaching different doctrine. (In Greek this is expressed by a single compound verb [heterodidaskalein], found here for the first time and possibly coined by the author.) The theological content of their teaching is not clearly specified here or anywhere else in 1 Timothy (cf. 2 Tim 2:18), but throughout the letter there is a concern for sound teaching and correct teachers (1:10; 2:7, 12; 3:2; 4:1, 6, 11, 13, 16; 5:17; 6:1-3). These issues are pervasive in 2 Timothy and Titus as well (2 Tim 1:11, 13-14; 2:2, 15, 24; 3:10, 16; 4:2-3; Titus 1:9, 11; 2:1, 3, 7), indicating that competing teachers and doctrines probably provided the immediate occasion for these letters (see Introduction).

The significance of the reference to myths and endless genealogies (v. 4) is harder to assess. The content of the myths, like that of the false doctrines, is nowhere given, though myths are mentioned again in 4:7 and 2 Tim 4:4 and identified more closely as Jewish myths in Titus 1:14. Genealogies are also mentioned again in Titus 3:9, where they are associated with "stupid controversies, . . . dissensions, and quarrels about the law," but, as with the myths, no indication is given of their content or source. The terms have been taken to refer to gnosticizing speculations on cosmological secrets or to speculative interpretations of Jewish Scripture. It was, however, a standard feature of the attacks leveled by philosophers against their rivals, the sophists, to discredit their ideas as "mere myths" (see, e.g., Lucian *Lover of Lies* 9). The author of these letters uses the same techniques to discredit his opponents, so the reference to "myths" or "meaningless talk" (v. 6) may be more rhetorical convention than reliable description. The emphasis, at any rate, is not on the empty content of the opponents' teachings, but on their unnecessary complexity, for the author's main objection to them is the way they have enouraged "speculations" rather than the *oikonomia theou* (v. 4).

This Greek phrase, which appears only here in the Pastoral Letters, is translated in the NRSV as "divine training," though it is found nowhere else with this meaning until the end of the second century in the writings of Clement of Alexandria. The phrase usually refers to God's administration of the universe, including the divine plan for the universe and the divine execution of that plan (see Eph 1:10; 3:9). This more general sense is probably intended here, for there are hints throughout these letters of a divine plan operating in the universe and coming now to fruition (2:6*b*; 6:15; 2 Tim 1:8-10; Titus 1:2). This plan is not hidden in "myths," to be extracted by elaborate theological or theosophical investigations; it is recognized by (or grounded in) simple faith (so NJB, REB).

The goal of instructing the opponents is given in verse 5: to promote the "love that comes from a pure heart, a good conscience, and sincere faith." The author's primary thought is probably not that instruction of the opponents will produce these qualities in them (see, however, 2 Tim 2:24-25), but that by silencing these opponents, these qualities, which come only from God (1:14, 19), can flourish in the church. Love, faith, and conscience are not clearly defined in these letters, though love and faith often appear together and in combination with other virtues as characteristic of the Christian life (see, e.g., 2:15; 4:12; 6:11). The adjectives "pure" and "sincere" (literally, "unhypocritical") have a polemical edge, hinting at the opponents' impure hearts and insincere faith (see also 1:19; 2 Tim 1:5). Likewise the conscience can be either good and pure (as here and in 1:19; 3:9; 2 Tim 1:3) or seared and corrupt (as in 4:2; Titus 1:15), and the word serves in these letters primarily to highlight the moral contrast between the opponents and true Christians. The actual role of the conscience in directing the moral life is not developed (cf. Rom 2:12-16; 1 Cor 8:7-13; 10:23-30).

The final charge against these opponents is that they desire to be "teachers of the law, without understanding either what they are saying or the things about which they make assertions" (v. 7). The author seems to have teachers of the *Jewish* law in mind (see also Titus 1:10, 14), for the Greek word found here *(nomodidaskaloi)* is used elsewhere in the New Testament only to describe teachers of the Mosaic law (Luke 5:17; Acts 5:34). This connection with Judaism is not, however, given any emphasis. What is stressed is that the teachers do not understand what they are saying; that is, they are incompetent (see also 6:4; Job 35:16).

Correct Use of the Law (1:8-11)

Having charged the would-be teachers of the law with total ignorance of their subject, the author reveals the superior knowledge he and Timothy possess ("we know . . . ") by giving the correct understanding of the law. It is difficult to determine from this retort, however, what the opposing teachers were saying about the law. It is unlikely that the words, "the law is good" (clearly an allusion to Rom 7:16; see also Rom 7:12), are directed against an antinomian stance, for while the opponents are charged with factiousness (6:4), meaningless talk (1:6), and asceticism (4:3), they are not explicitly accused of lawless behavior, though they are implicitly linked with it (see below). It is also unlikely that the author is correcting a rigorous legalism that bases salvation on strict obedience to an external code. Even though the numerous references to conscience and faith (1:5, 14, 19) could be construed as a counteremphasis on inner moral discernment, nowhere in this letter, nor in 2 Timothy or Titus, does legalism *per se* clearly emerge as a problem. Unless the allusion to opponents who teach the law (see also Titus 3:9) is simply intended to enhance the fiction of Pauline authorship by recalling Paul's struggles with Judaizing opponents in Galatia and Philippi (see Introduction), the most likely hypothesis is that the opposing teachers used the Jewish Scripture as a basis for their speculations and perhaps even as a warrant for their ascetic practices (4:3). The author's point here, however, is not to rebut their use of the law, but to expose their ignorance and to suggest a connection between their doctrine and moral chaos. In short, he uses this brief discussion of the law to cast aspersions on the would-be teachers of the law.

The author presents as the only legitimate use of the law its application as a moral restraint on the lawless. This is far from Paul's view (see, e.g., Rom 2:12-16; 3:20-31; 8:1-8; Gal 3:19-24) and the author does not develop it carefully. Instead he lists people of various lawless categories for whom the law is lawfully (i.e., "legitimately") intended. (The wordplay is deliberate.) This is the first of several vice lists in the Pastoral Letters (see also 6:4-5; 2 Tim 3:2-5; Titus 3:3). Such lists were often coupled with lists of virtues and used in moral exhortation (see, e.g., Gal 5:19-23; Col 3:5-17; Philo *Sacrifices of Abel and Cain* 22-27, 32) or, as here, to vilify opponents (see, e.g., Rom 1:29-31; Lucian *Runaways* 16) (McEleney 1974). This particular list seems to be carefully constructed in two distinct parts. The first part describes the lawless in terms used elsewhere in these letters to define the opposing teachers and their activities. These teachers, e.g., are also described as "disobedient" or insubordinate (Titus 1:10; Gk. *anhypotaktos*), a word suggesting the resistance to authority that is anathema to this author (see 2:11; 3:4; Titus 2:5, 9; 3:1). Their actions are said to lead to godlessness or impiety (2 Tim 2:16; cf. Titus 2:12) and unholy behavior (2 Tim 3:2; cf. 1 Tim 2:8; Titus 1:8), and what they do is repeatedly described as profane (4:7; 6:20; 2 Tim 2:16). Whatever the opposing teachers were saying about the law, the author is suggesting here that its proper use is as a moral restraint just for the likes of them. The second part of the list seems deliberately to echo the Decalogue: "for those who kill their father or mother, for murderers, fornicators, sodomites, slave traders, liars, perjurers" (vv. 9*b*-10; cf. Exod 20:12-17). The effect of the combined list is to link the disobedient, godless, unholy, and profane behavior associated with the opposing teachers with actions condemned by the law they profess to teach.

Sound teaching, on the other hand, results in sound behavior. This is the presupposition of verse 10*b* and a fundamental premise of these letters (see, e.g., 6:3-5; 2 Tim 1:8-14), as is the connection between sound teaching and the gospel (v. 11; see also 4:6). The reference to the gospel allows the author to undertake a digression on Paul's appointment to its service (1:12-17).

Gratitude for Mercy Shown (1:12-17)

The paragraph begins with a statement of gratitude similar to the expressions of thanksgiving with which Paul usually opens his letters. But whereas Paul offers thanks to God for what God has done through Christ in and for the various churches (see Rom 1:8; 1 Cor 1:4; 1 Thess 1:2), here the gratitude is to Christ for what he has done for Paul. To define what this is, the author draws on traditions about Paul's call to be an apostle (see 1 Cor 15:9-10; Gal 1:13-15), though there is a new emphasis here on the intentionally paradigmatic quality of that event. Paul is not simply entrusted with the gospel, he illustrates the gospel as well.

Paul's gratitude is directed toward Christ, "who has strengthened me." The phrase echoes Phil 4:13 (see also 2 Cor 12:9), though the meaning here is somewhat different. In Philippians, Paul speaks of receiving strength to endure afflictions and deprivations (see also 2 Tim 1:7, 8; 4:17). Here the reference is to his general empowerment for service (Gk. *diakonia*) for the gospel, so that being "strengthened" is essentially synonymous with being entrusted with the gospel (1:11) or appointed to his apostolate (1:1).

To describe this appointment in terms of being judged or deemed faithful or trustworthy (v. 12; cf. 1 Cor 7:25) strikes, however, an odd note. The passage speaks of a former life that was anything but faithful (v. 13; see also Gal 1:13-17) and communicates a strong message about divine grace that confronts and transforms sinners (v. 14; see also Titus 3:3-5). Yet it is reading too much into this phrase to insist that it means that Christ's act of choosing Paul rendered him at once worthy. Instead the author hints at a period between the act of grace, which transformed the life of the former persecutor and provided the requisite faith and love (vv. 13-14), and the appointment to Christ's service, which was based on tangible evidence of that faithfulness. This drives a small but significant wedge between two events that Paul himself regarded as one: his life-changing encounter with the resurrected Christ and his commission to be an apostle (Gal 1:13-17). The wedge was necessary, however, for this author's changed circumstances, for the appointment of proven, faithful ministers was exceedingly important in the struggle with opposing teachers, and here Paul serves as a model for that process (see also 3:10-11; 2 Tim 2:2; Titus 1:9).

In the undisputed letters, Paul speaks of his earlier persecution of the church (v. 13*a*; see also 1 Cor 15:9; Gal 1:13, 23; Phil 3:6), but he does not refer to himself with the other two terms found here: "blasphemer" (Gk. *blasphēmos*) and "man of violence" (Gk. *hybristēs*). The first word refers to a slanderer or, more specifically, to one who dishonors the name or being of God, while the second, found only here and in Rom 1:30 in the NT, refers to violent, insolent, or reckless behavior. (The NJB refers, e.g., to "contemptuous" behavior.) These dramatic terms magnify Paul's sinfulness and, as a consequence, magnify also the scope of Christ's mercy in dealing with him (see vv. 15-16). The new ideas introduced here, blasphemy and violence (or contempt), stand in direct contrast with the faith and love that are the consequences of grace. They also, however, link Paul's former life with the present life of the opposing teachers, who are described as blasphemers (1:20; 6:4 [NRSV:

"slander"]; 2 Tim 3:2 [NRSV: "slanderers"]) and as engaging in insolent, arrogant, or unruly behavior (2 Tim 3:2; Titus 1:16). This underscores the necessity for distinguishing between Paul's pre-Christian life and the transformed life that served as a basis for his appointment to Christian service, but it also raises the possibility of a future act of divine mercy for the present blasphemers as well (see also 1:20; 2 Tim 2:25-26; cf. Titus 3:10).

Paul's violent, blasphemous actions are explained as stemming from ignorance (v. 13b; see also Acts 17:30; Eph 4:18) and unbelief. Since unbelief defines those outside the realm of truth and salvation (see 5:8; Titus 1:15; cf. 4:10, 12; 5:16) and thus those inside the realm of sinners, Paul is offered as an example of the sure and worthy saying cited in verse 15: "Christ Jesus came into the world to save sinners" (see also Matt 9:13; Luke 15:2; 19:10). Ignorance, however, suggests mitigating circumstances that distinguish Paul from the false teachers, who arose within the group of believers (1:19) and thus cannot legitimately claim ignorance as an excuse. Indeed, their words and actions constitute a willful and thus culpable renunciation of the faith (4:1; 6:21; Titus 3:11; see also Rom 1:18-32).

Verse 15 contains the first of five "sure" sayings cited in these letters. (The Greek word is *pistos*, which means literally "faithful" or "trustworthy"; the same word is used of Paul in v. 12.) The same formula (or a slightly shorter version of it) is found in 3:1 (probably referring to the saying in 2:15); 4:9 (referring to 4:8); 2 Tim 2:11a (probably referring to 2:11b-13); and Titus 3:8a (probably referring to 3:3-7). The phrase provides solemn emphasis to certain statements, which usually concern salvation, and links them with other faithful things that the church can rely on: Christ (2 Tim 2:13), Paul (1:12), church leaders (3:11), and their proclamations (Titus 1:9). Thus while believers (literally "faithful ones") are explicitly called to trust in Christ for eternal life (v. 16; the NRSV translates the phrase "believe in," but the nuance seems to be that of trust; see 2 Tim 1:12a), they are also implicitly encouraged to trust in the reliable words contained in these letters.

The entire passage (vv. 12-16) has a strong christological emphasis. It is Christ Jesus who has empowered Paul, judged Paul faithful (or trustworthy), and appointed him to his ministry (cf. Gal 1:15). It is the Lord's (i.e., Jesus') grace that has produced in Paul the faith and love that, with other virtues, lead to salvation (2:15; 4:12-16; 6:11-12; 2 Tim 2:22; 3:10). (To say that this faith and love are "in Christ Jesus" [v. 14; see also 3:13; 2 Tim 1:1b, 13; 2:1, 10; 3:15] indicates their source or the sphere within which they are available [Allan 1963].) It is Christ Jesus who came into the world to save sinners (cf. Rom 8:3); and it is Jesus Christ who has displayed the utmost patience in granting Paul mercy, to make him an example of the extraordinary grace available to those who come to believe. Apparently this patience is more than a demonstration of divine grace; it provides a model for human actions as well, for Paul himself also manifests it (2 Tim 3:10) and urges Timothy to do the same (2 Tim 4:2; see also 2:24).

The salvation of sinners accomplished through the coming of Christ Jesus and exemplified in his patient and merciful treatment of Paul, the foremost sinner, constitutes the "gospel of the glory of the blessed God" (a literal translation of v. 11). Thus the section that presents this gospel, though focusing on Christ's role, closes with praise to God (v. 17). This doxology is probably a liturgical fragment (see also 6:16; Rom 16:27; Jude 25); all of its elements are traditional and can be found in Jewish and Christian literature ("King of the ages," see Tob 13:6, 10; "immortal," see Wis 12:1; Rom 1:23; "invisible," see John 1:18; Rom 1:20; Col 1:15; Heb 11:27; "only God," see Ps 86:10; Isa 37:20; John 5:44; 17:3; Jude 25). The author affirms God's invisibility though he insists that God's *glory* is revealed in the gospel and through Christ's mercy and patience (cf. Exod 33:17–34:7; see also Titus 2:13; 3:4).

Charge to Timothy (1:18-20)

The direct address to Timothy resumes (see 1:3-4), creating a framework for this opening section and ultimately for the letter as a whole (see also 6:20-21). "These instructions" (singular in the Greek, but apparently intended as a collective noun) refers to the admonitions in 1:3-5. The phrase also, however, points ahead to the instructions that fill the rest of the letter (see also 3:14; 4:6, 11;

6:2*b*). Thus the passage provides an effective transition to the body of the letter and highlights its hortatory character.

The prophecies about Timothy were Christian prophecies (see 1 Cor 12:10), either spoken at an earlier time to identify Timothy as God's choice, or pronounced during the ordination ceremony to confirm it (see 4:14; 2 Tim 1:6; also Acts 13:1-3). The reference to them here confirms Timothy's appointed role as an instrument in God's plan (see comments on 1:4) and, more specifically, his role as Paul's legitimate successor. Singled out by prophecy, named as Paul's "child" (see also 1:2), and possessing the faith and good conscience that are signs both of grace (1:14; 2 Tim 1:3) and of the fulfillment of God's plan (1:5), Timothy is presented as Paul's worthy heir and his designated lieutenant in the fight for truth and virtue.

The exhortation to "fight the good fight" echoes the philosophical moral discourse of the period, which often compared life (as here) to a military campaign or to an athletic contest (see also 6:12; 2 Tim 4:7; also 2 Cor 10:3-5; Phil 1:27-30; 3:12-14). It provides a particularly apt metaphor for the struggle against opponents, and the author mentions two of them by name (cf. 1:3). It is impossible to determine whether Hymenaeus and Alexander are the names of known opponents, either of Paul, Timothy, or the author himself, or are instead part of the historical fiction of these letters. Hymenaeus is mentioned again in 2 Tim 2:17 as someone who has "swerved from the truth" and an Alexander is named in 2 Tim 4:14 as someone who did Paul "great harm," but neither Acts nor the other letters in the Pauline corpus mention such individuals. (The Alexander referred to in Acts 19:33-34 is not an opponent of Paul.) The author's purpose in mentioning them here is to provide concrete counterexamples to Timothy's faithful discipleship, a common technique in hellenistic moral exhortation and one used extensively in 2 Timothy (see 2 Tim 1:15-18; 2:15-18; 3:1-12). Identifying Hymenaeus and Alexander as "certain persons" (see also 1:3) who have "suffered shipwreck in the faith" (i.e., whose piety or fidelity to saving doctrine has been destroyed; see comment on 1:2) returns the argument to its opening emphasis on opposition to sound teaching. The author now describes a drastic corrective measure.

"Turned over to Satan" (cf. 5:15) refers on a social level to expulsion from the community of faith. The author shared with his readers the conviction that within this community one had not only the support of an extended Christian family but also the saving presence of the Holy Spirit and thus the hope of eternal life (Titus 1:2; 2:11-14; 3:4-7). For those expelled, the avenues of social support were severed and there was no divine protection against the cosmic forces of evil. One was thus "turned over to Satan" or vulnerable to "the snare of the devil" (3:6-7; 2 Tim 2:26).

The author had a clear precedent for this action in Paul's dealings with a certain man in Corinth (1 Cor 5:3-5). The action also underscores the seriousness of the opposition, here defined for the first time as blasphemy, and represents a somewhat sterner response than Timothy himself is called to make (1:3; see also 2 Tim 2:24-26). The author does not indicate how their words or actions were blasphemous, that is, irreverent toward God. The Greek word translated "to blaspheme" *(blasphēmein)* can also refer to the social act of slander (see 6:4; 2 Pet 2:10-12; Jude 8-10), but the context and the punishment here suggest the more serious religious charge, which was punishable by death (see Lev 24:11-23; Mark 14:61-64; Acts 6:11–7:60). Here the goal of the expulsion is described as instruction, training, or correction (Gk. *paideuthōsin,* translated "learn" in the NRSV), an activity that usually has a positive connotation and outcome (see 2 Tim 2:25; Titus 2:12; see also 1 Cor 11:32; cf. Luke 23:16, 22). This reduces somewhat the otherwise stark contrast between the Lord's response to Paul's blasphemy (1:13) and Paul's response to Hymenaeus's and Alexander's blasphemy, though, as mentioned earlier, the circumstances are not identical and some contrast is surely intended.

◊ ◊ ◊ ◊

In this opening chapter the author lays the theological foundation for the instructions that follow. He weaves a connection between doctrine and behavior and suggests that certain teachers are unraveling the moral fabric of the church with their false doctrines. The author does not engage in theological or ethical debate with the opponents' views, which are thus hidden from sight. Even the meager substance of the discussion of the law is not directed at rebutting an opposing position, but rather at establishing the point that doctrine and behavior go hand in hand. This connection then provides the backdrop for all that follows. When the author addresses the behavior of certain groups within the church, the threat of false doctrine hovers in the background, and when the author warns against certain teachers, moral chaos is the implied consequence.

The chapter also serves as a preface to the moral instructions that follow by presenting a strong statement about divine grace, which precedes and accomplishes all acts of human obedience and love (1:12-16; see also 2 Tim 1:9; Titus 2:11-14; 3:3-7). As in the undisputed Pauline letters, grace is a power that confronts and transforms the sinner, here by its superabundant, overflowing presence (1:14; see also Rom 5:20; 6:1; 2 Cor 4:15). According to Titus 2:12, this transforming power acts concretely through a process of training or education (*paideuein*, the same Greek verb used in 1 Tim 1:20) and the author must assume that the instructions that fill these letters cooperate in that process. Nevertheless, the human mode of response is still defined as one of trust in Christ and in God. The Pastoral Letters, however, encourage the reader also to view Paul, Timothy, appointed church leaders, the proclaimed word, and the contents of these letters as trustworthy instruments of God's saving power and will.

Paul's conversion is presented as a true conversion (i.e., from ignorance and unbelief to faith and understanding; cf. Gal 1:13-17) and as a paradigm of Christ's merciful patience (i.e., grace) toward ignorant sinners. Paul's own actions toward Hymenaeus and Alexander provide a second, complementary paradigm of the firm disciplinary action to be applied to those who willfully reject the truth (see also 2 Tim 2:24-26; Titus 1:10-11; 3:10-11). The whole chapter, indeed all three Pastoral Letters, raises the question of how to deal with theological opposition. This author's solution is to reject the very principle of debate and dialogue and to operate instead from the unassailable pinnacle of truth (2:4, 7; 3:15; 4:3; 2 Tim 2:15, 25; 3:8; 4:4; Titus 1:1, 14). With rare exception, the author does not even present the content of the opponents' teaching. Instead he dismisses it as speculation (1:4), disputes about words

(6:4), meaningless talk (1:6), and blasphemy (1:20). Against these "idle talkers" (Titus 1:10) he lines up God's firm plan, the church's sound and unwavering teaching, and church leaders—identified by prophetic insight—who preserve the Pauline gospel and faithfully follow and transmit the instructions entrusted to them.

BODY OF THE LETTER (2:1–6:19)

The body of the letter (chaps. 2–6) consists primarily of the instructions mentioned in 1:18 and is thus fairly homogeneous in content and form. A slight shift occurs, however, at the end of chapter 3, marking a minor division of the text. Liturgical or hymnic fragments (2:5-6a; 3:16) bracket 1 Tim 2:1–3:16, which focuses on issues more or less connected with worship: prayer (2:1-7), appropriate dress and behavior for women (2:8-15), and qualifications for bishops and deacons (3:1-13). These are instructions of general validity offered directly to the worshiping community and its leaders. Concern for false teachers recedes into the background, though their presence is still felt in various ways. The next group of exhortations (4:1–6:19) are given directly to Timothy, who is instructed to pass them on to the community (4:6, 11; 5:7; 6:2b). Opponents are more frequently mentioned in this portion of the text (4:1-3, 7; 6:3-5, 20-21) and many of the exhortations concern groups that seem to be sources of tension or conflict within the church. The instructions in chapters 2–6 thus tend to become increasingly focused on small groups within the church, but the opening exhortation on prayer (2:1-7) provides a reminder of the universal saving will of God that links the church community with the world outside.

Instructions to the Community and Its Leaders (2:1–3:16)

Prayers for Everyone (2:1-7)

The body of the letter opens with the command to pray for everyone (1 Tim 2:1-7). The author supports this exhortation in two ways, first by pointing out the desirable social consequences of such prayer and then by providing a theological warrant for it. For the latter, the author cites what seems to be a liturgical fragment. The brief passage then closes with another recollection of Paul's commission (cf. 1:1, 12-16), which is punctuated by an emphatic oath. Though containing various sorts of material—-exhortation, liturgical fragment, biographical information—the flow of the argument is reasonably smooth.

◊ ◊ ◊ ◊

The words "I urge" (the Greek *parakalo* repeats the verb with which the letter opens, linking the following written exhortations with the oral ones recalled in 1:3 [see also 6:2*b*; Titus 2:6, 15]). This verb is found frequently in the undisputed Pauline letters, where it falls short of being a formal command (see Phlm 8-9) yet, because of the acknowledged apostolic authority of the author, is also more than a request (see, e.g., Rom 15:30; 1 Cor 1:10; 2 Cor 5:20; 10:1). A similar nuance is present here, and the early appearance of this verb in the body of the letter signals its essentially hortatory character.

As the first exhortation in the letter, and the one of foremost importance ("first of all"), the author asks that prayers be made for everyone, with special attention to "kings and all who are in high positions." The emphasis is on the concern for "everyone" (see also vv. 2, 4, 6*a*) and the exhortation to pray for political leaders serves as a concrete example of this concern, not as its goal. The various overlapping categories of prayer do not provide an exhaustive list but are intended to suggest a completely inclusive one. All forms of prayer made in, and by, the community are to be used to pray for those outside the community of faith. Prayers for political authorities had been part of Jewish synagogue liturgy for some time (see Jer 29:7; Ezra 6:10; Bar 1:10-14; 1 Macc 7:33). Though mentioned only here in the New Testament (cf. Rom 13:1-7; 1 Pet 2:13-17; Titus 3:1), noncanonical Christian examples abound (see, e.g., Pol. *Phil.* 12.3; *1 Clement* 60-61), indicating that such prayers formed an important part of early Christian liturgy as well. In both synagogue and church they served in the first century as a sign of loyalty to the empire and as an important substitute for the prayers and sacrifices to the emperor demanded by the emperor cult.

The author encourages this prayer by mentioning its goal (which was perhaps also its content): "a quiet and peaceable life in all godliness and dignity" (v. 2). Paul advocated a quiet life in the face of what appears to have been eschatological excitement and unrest (1 Thess 4:11; see also 2 Thess 3:12). The words in 1 Timothy have a different orientation and reflect an appreciation of the fact that the way political authorities exercised their power had a direct effect on the quality of the lives of early Christians. Benevolent rule by these authorities could make possible a quiet and peaceable life (the two Greek adjectives, *ēremos* and *hēsychios,* are nearly synonymous), an external reflection of the philosophical ideal of inner tranquility (Plato *Republic* 604b-e; Epictetus *Discourses* 4.4.39-48; 4.5.17). Such a life also stands in sharp contrast to the unruly and noisy behavior of the opponents (6:4, 20).

"Godliness" (Gk. *eusebeia*) and "dignity" (Gk. *semnotēs*) are terms familiar in hellenistic moral discourse but not used by Paul. *Semnotēs* refers to a dignified and serious demeanor that encourages respect. It is especially appropriate for those in leadership roles (see 3:8, 11; Titus 2:2, 7) but here characterizes the behavior of all Christians. *Eusebeia* is the more important term. It defines Christian life in these letters in much the same way that faith defines it for Paul: a godly and pious life that includes reverence for God and behavior appropriate to that reverence (see Titus 2:11-12). It is the conduct that corresponds to sound teaching (6:3; Titus 1:1) and thus separates false teachers from true (4:7-8; 2 Tim 3:5, 12-13). In the Greco-Roman world the term also connoted respect for the divinely ordained orders of life in the domestic and political realms. It is debated whether the meaning of the word in the Pastoral Letters includes this nuance, though its use in 1 Tim 5:4 to describe familial duty seems strongly to suggest it. At any rate, it is difficult to ignore this overtone in letters that vigorously encourage respect for order in so many other ways (see, e.g., 2:11; 3:4, 12; 4:12; 6:1; 2 Tim 2:4, 21; 3:2; Titus 1:6, 10; 2:3-10; 3:1).

The exhortation to pray for everyone is bolstered by a theological warrant in verse 4: God's desire that everyone be saved. The message of God's saving grace is pervasive in these letters (see 1:15-16; 2 Tim 1:9; Titus 2:11; 3:4-7) and is also reflected in the author's extensive use of the title "Savior" for God (see 1:1). Here, as in 4:10 and Titus 2:11, the author emphasizes that this will to save extends to all, perhaps to counter a more restrictive view of salvation promulgated by his gnosticizing opponents (see Introduction). Salvation is here linked with coming "to the knowledge of the truth" (see also 4:3; 2 Tim 2:25; 3:7; Titus 1:1; Heb 10:26; 2 John 1). This phrase has a Gnostic ring (see 6:20) and is probably used in a polemical way. Indeed, the emphasis on truth found throughout these letters seems to have its genesis in the struggle with opposing teachers (see, e.g., 6:5, 20; 2 Tim 2:18; 3:8; 4:4; Titus 1:14). Thus, coming to knowledge of the truth, though a general allusion to conversion, clearly refers specifically to acceptance of the sound teaching of the church (see 2:7; 3:15; 2 Tim 2:15, 25).

In support of this theological warrant, the author cites what appears on the basis of its content and form to be a liturgical fragment (vv. 5-6a), the first of several in these letters (see also 3:16; 2 Tim 2:11-13). The existence of "one God" was a central tenet of Judaism and Christianity; references to this distinctive belief appear often in polemics against pagan polytheism (see Deut 6:4-15; 32:36-39; Isa 44:6-20; 1 Cor 8:4-6; Gal 3:20). It is occasionally found in the writings of Greek and Roman philosophers (see Jas 2:19) who, though not espousing monotheism, used the phrase as an expression, e.g., of pantheistic harmony or the conceptual unity of the divine. Marcus Aurelius, for example, clearly assumed the existence of a multiplicity of gods (*To Himself* 2.11), yet he could also say, "For there is both one universe, made up of all things, and one god immanent in all things" (*To Himself* 7.9). As in Rom 3:30 and Eph 4:6, however, the existence of one God is affirmed in 1 Timothy in order to support the author's claim of the availability of salvation to all (v. 4). Any polemic against many divine beings (as posited, e.g., by Gnosticism) is of secondary importance.

The christological clause of the acclamation is developed in more detail. It mentions Christ's role as mediator and his humanity, but the key phrase for this author is the final one, "Christ Jesus . . . who gave himself as a ransom *for all*." The concept of Christ's death as a ransom (Gk. *antilytron*, literally a redemption or buying back, as from slavery or captivity) is widespread in the New Testament (see, e.g., Rom 3:24; Eph 1:7; Titus 2:14; Heb 9:15; 1 Pet 1:18) and the phrase in verse 6*a* seems to be a clear echo of Mark 10:45 (see also Matt 20:28). It states, however, more radically than that text, or any other New Testament text, the efficacy of Jesus' self-giving death for *all* humankind (cf. Gal 1:4; 2:20; Eph 5:20). It is this statement of the universal effect of Jesus' death, more than the reference to his role as mediator, that determines the author's interest in this liturgical fragment, for his argument in this portion of the letter turns on the concept of God's universal saving will.

It is, in fact, difficult to determine what importance the concept of mediator had for the author, for there are no other references to a mediator Christology in these letters and few elsewhere in the NT. Paul affirms that the law was given by a mediator, but the mediator is Moses, not Christ, and that serves as a sign for Paul of the law's inferiority. In Hebrews, Christ is acclaimed as the mediator of a new covenant (8:6; 9:15; 12:24), but the Pastoral Letters show no interest in covenant theology. The Christology of this fragment may have been influenced by the plea in Job 9:32-33 for an "umpire" to mediate between Job and an apparently implacable God (Hanson 1982, 68), for the implied solidarity between "Christ Jesus, himself human" and humankind answers Job's requirement that the mediator share his mortal nature. The author of the Pastoral Letters, however, has a much more benevolent view of God (4:10) and thus does not share Job's need for an impartial umpire. On the other hand, the reference to Christ's humanity is repeated elsewhere (3:16) and may have functioned to counter docetic views of the opposing teachers (see Introduction). Within the framework of this opening argument (2:1-7), however, the emphasis rests on the universal benefits of Christ's self-giving death.

The final phrase of verse 6 probably resumes the author's commentary, but its meaning is difficult to determine. The phrase reads literally, "the witness (or testimony; Gk. *martyrion*) to the proper times" (Gk. *kairois idiois*; the same phrase is found in 6:15 and Titus 1:3), and seems to refer to the time determined by God, an allusion to the existence of a divine plan (see 1:4). With this phrase the author shifts the emphasis from the redeeming power of Jesus' death to its testamentary power: It serves as a testimony to the saving will and plan of God. (The REB translates the phrase loosely but aptly: "revealing God's purpose at God's good time.") The revelatory aspects of Jesus' life and death are emphasized elsewhere in the letters (see, e.g., 2 Tim 1:8-10). Here the author links Paul's work with this primal revelation of God's saving nature and will.

Paul's appointment is described with three terms: herald, apostle, and teacher (see also 2 Tim 1:11). "Herald" (Gk. *kēryx*) points to the proclamation (Gk. *kērygma*) of the gospel (see 2 Tim 4:17; Titus 1:3; see also 2 Pet 2:5), that is, to the activity of preaching. "Apostle" (literally, "one who is sent") is Paul's most characteristic designation (1:1; 2 Tim 1:1; Titus 1:1). It too is intimately linked with the task of proclamation (1:11) but connotes more explicitly than the word "herald" a special divine commission. In this context, though, the emphasis seems to be on the term, "teacher." It has the final and climactic position in the series; it is the role of teacher that is disputed in these letters; and *this* role is defined more expansively as teacher *of the Gentiles* (Gk. *ethnē,* which can also be translated "nations"; see also 3:16). Even the oath, which seems oddly out of place in this context (cf. Rom 9:1; Gal 1:20), focuses attention on Paul's role as "teacher of the nations." Thus it is the role of teacher that shows most clearly the connection between Paul's appointed work and God's desire for "everyone to be saved and to come to the knowledge of the truth."

◊ ◊ ◊ ◊

The author opens the body of the letter with a strong statement of God's universal saving will. This emphasis may derive in part from his desire to counter the opponents' doctrines (which may have included the more restrictive view of salvation characteristic of later Gnostic movements), but it does not seem to be entirely polemical. In many ways exhortations throughout these letters are affected by the fundamental conviction that God desires the salvation of all. Opponents, for example, must be dealt with sternly, but the hope is for their salvation (see especially 2 Tim 2:24-26). Church leaders and members are urged to lead lives that their pagan neighbors would approve as virtuous, and the goal seems to be not simply to improve the church's standing in the community or to forestall criticisms, but also to remove potential barriers to prose-lytization (see, e.g., Titus 2:3-10). Even the statement forbidding women to teach in church (2:9-13) needs to be read—at least in part—in this light, for the issue, as the author sees it, is precisely one of jeopardized salvation (see below).

The most striking feature of the rich Christology of this passage lies neither in the concept of mediator, nor in the emphasis on Jesus' humanity. These statements may have been originally intended to counter the plethora of mediating archons and the docetic Christology of Gnosticism, but this polemical intent is not evident in this passage. Instead the author interprets Jesus' redemptive death as a manifestation of God's saving nature and a revelation of God's saving plan. The passage thus provides an introduction to the epiphany Christology that prevails in 2 Timothy and Titus (see comments on 2 Tim 1:10; Titus 2:11; 3:4).

The passage also introduces the ideal of quiet virtues, for example, godliness and dignity. These virtues are presented here, not simply as the author's preference or as socially advantageous behavior, but as what is "right and acceptable in the sight of God." This theological assertion thus governs subsequent exhortations to quiet, peaceable, dignified, and modest behavior by various groups within the church (2:8, 11; 3:3, 11; 5:14) and stands as an implicit criticism of all unruly, contentious behavior, especially that of the opponents (5:13; 6:2, 4-5).

Men's Prayer and Women's Silence (2:8–3:1a)

The author returns in the first clause of this passage to the topic of prayer that was introduced in 2:1, but he discusses here the manner, not the content, of prayer. In particular, he discusses the manner in which *men* should pray (v. 8). In a parallel but somewhat longer clause concerning women (vv. 9-10), he deals with dress and deportment, not prayer. The focus remains on women through the rest of the passage (vv. 11-15), but the content shifts once again. Here women are exhorted to learn in silence and are forbidden to teach, and biblical warrants secure these instructions. In the end, the author provides for the women's salvation, but he includes a warning note as well and concludes somewhat enigmatically with his favorite refrain: "The saying is sure" (3:1*a*).

The passage is oddly disjointed. There are several awkward grammatical transitions, and while the setting of corporate worship ties the instructions on prayer and teaching together, the comments on women's dress and deportment do not seem limited to that setting. Though the passage opens with a statement about men, concern for women's behavior provides the strongest unifying motif. This was a fairly typical concern of the hellenistic world, but the emphasis the topic receives in this letter probably derives from the author's desire to counter the activities of the opponents who seem to have had particular success in interesting women in their teachings (2 Tim 3:6-8; see Introduction). The instructions here are ultimately intended to prevent the spread of the opponents' influence any further in the church.

◊ ◊ ◊ ◊

The author presents the instructions in 2:8-15 as a logical consequence of what was said in the preceding paragraph ("I desire, *then,* . . . "). The most immediate connection is with the biographical reminder in verse 7, for it is Paul's appointment as herald, apostle, and teacher that lends compelling weight and apostolic authority to the request ("I desire") in verse 8 (see also 5:14; Titus 3:8; the expression is not used in the undisputed Pauline letters). In addition, though, the exhortations in this passage are directed toward achieving within the community the quiet and peaceable life that was also the goal of the prayers for ruling authorities (2:1-2). Furthermore, since a worship service split by anger and argument (v. 8) belies the unifying truths expressed in 2:1-7 (i.e., that prayers are to be made for all, that God desires everyone to be saved, that Christ gave himself as a ransom for all), the author here requires that praxis in worship be conformed to doctrine. Even the insistence on women's silence and submission can be seen as rooted theologically in the author's conviction that God desires the salvation of all, though it is also rooted socially in the presence and influence of the opposing teachers (see below).

The opening verb, "I desire," governs two clauses, one dealing exclusively with men, the other exclusively with women. The first clause is relatively brief and concerns the way men should pray: "lifting up holy hands without anger or argument." Praying with arms raised and palms open to heaven (the *orans* position) was typical in antiquity (see, e.g., Pseudo-Aristotle *On the Cosmos* 400a; Virgil *Aeneid* 2.153; 1 Kgs 8:54; Neh 8:6; Ps 141:2), and the desire that these hands (and thus the petitioner) be "holy," for example, sinless and pure, was also typical (Seneca *Natural Questions* 3, pref. 14; Ps 26:6; cf. Isa 1:15-16; Jas 4:8). The weight of the injunction falls on the final phrase, "without anger or argument." Admonitions against anger and argument were commonplace (see, e.g., Plutarch *On the Control of Anger*; Epictetus *Discourses* 1.28; 4.5; Prov 15:18; Eccl 7:9; Sir 27:30–28:12; Matt 5:21-24; Phil 2:14), but their context in this letter gives them special import. With these words the author not only reinforces the desire for the quiet and peaceable life expressed in 2:2, he also insists that the disputatious activities associated with the opposing teachers (see, e.g., 6:4-6, 20; 2 Tim 2:14; Titus 3:9) be eliminated from the worship service.

The words "in every place" echo Mal 1:11, where they emphasize the universal rule of God. Here the author's desire that men raise holy hands "in every place" seems to complement God's desire that everyone be saved (2:4). The phrase may, however, refer instead to every house church in the area addressed by this letter.

The second clause, though formally parallel to the first, is surprising in its content, for instead of the expected statement concerning the manner in which women should pray, the author gives instructions concerning dress and deportment. According to the NRSV, the women are urged to "dress themselves modestly and decently in *suitable clothing*," but the Greek text could equally well be understood as urging them to "adorn themselves with proper conduct" (so NAB), a point that is then repeated in verses 9b-10a. All the significant Greek words in this clause (*katastolē, kosmios, aidōs, sōphrosynē*) connote modesty (especially when used of women), restraint, and moderation, and are typical of the quiet virtues that these letters encourage (see also 2:2; 3:2-3, 11; 6:11;

2 Tim 2:24; Titus 1:8; 2:2-8) and of the moral discourse of the period (see, e.g., Epictetus *Discourses* 2.10; Plutarch *Advice to Bride and Groom* 26).

Sōphrosynē is the most significant of these terms, both within the Pastoral Letters and in the wider culture. Nearly untranslatable by a single word (NRSV: "decently"), the Greek term suggests the prudence, temperance, discretion, soundness of judgment, and self-control that constituted the Greek ideal of behavior (see, e.g., Aristotle *Nicomachean Ethics* 3.10-12). As one of the four cardinal virtues of Stoic philosophy, the word was common in philosophical moral discourse and in laudatory tombstone inscriptions as well. Since it was a standard feature of moral exhortation, however, it yields little information concerning the actual situation that the author is addressing here. Indeed, *sōphrosynē* and related words appear frequently in the Pastoral Letters to define the behavior expected of all church members (see especially 2:15; 3:2; Titus 1:8; 2:2, 5, 6, 12).

The contrast in verses 9b-10a between women's external adornment (braided hair, jewelry, fine clothes) and their moral virtue (good works) was also typical of ethical writings (see Plutarch *Advice to Bride and Groom* 26, 48; Epictetus *Discourses* 3.1; *Encheiridion* 40; 1 Pet 3:3-4) and cannot be used with confidence to draw conclusions concerning specific behavior within the church. It probably does suggest something, though, about the socioeconomic makeup of this church, for such an admonition, though conventional, could only function credibly in circles where elaborate hairstyles and expensive jewelry were a real (though perhaps rare) possibility (see also 6:17-19). Instead of external ornaments, the women are to "wear" good works. The emphasis on works is strong in these letters (see also 5:10, 25; 6:18; 2 Tim 2:21; 3:17; Titus 2:7; 3:1, 8, 14), but it does not nullify the concept of grace. Instead the author suggests that grace produces the good works expected of God's people (see 1:14; Titus 2:11-14).

The reference to *professing* reverence for God conveys an ambiguous message. The original Greek verb, like the English word "profess," can refer to a public proclamation (see 6:12; Titus 1:3), but in polemical contexts it can have the negative nuance of pretense (cf. 2 Tim 3:7). This introduces into the text a subtle critical tone that provides an appropriate transition to the stringent restrictions that follow.

In verses 11-12 the author shifts from persuasion ("I desire") to authoritative command. Though there are several elements in this exhortation (silence, submission, teaching), they are structured in a chiastic pattern (*abcb'a'*) that establishes teaching as the central concern. Nearly identical commands to silence (Gk. *hēsychia*) frame the passage and echo the prayer for the quiet life *(hēsychion bion)* that introduces the body of the letter (2:2). The emphasis has shifted, however, from an attitude of quiet repose to verbal silence and social subordination. The requirement of subordination is stated positively in verse 11 ("with full submission") and repeated in negative form in verse 12 ("[not] to have authority"). These strictures on speech and authority thus surround and enforce the central prohibition: If a woman is not permitted to speak or exercise authority, she surely will be unable to teach.

The social context for the silent and submissive behavior enjoined here is clearly the worship service, which included teaching as well as prayers and exhortation (4:13; see also 1 Cor 14:34-35, a passage of disputed origin that may be based on 1 Tim 2:11-12). The command derives its content, however, from the household management tradition that was adapted and used by hellenistic moralists to define the proper conduct of, and relationships among, various members of a household (see Seneca *Epistles* 94.1). The author of the Pastoral Letters has transplanted these regulations from the private household to the church, which he understands to be the "household of God" (3:15; see also 3:4; 2 Tim 2:20-21; Eph 2:19; 1 Pet 4:17), and that changes somewhat their meaning and application. Wives were typically exhorted to behave in ways that reflected their subordinate status; that is, they were admonished to be silent and submissive to their husbands (Plutarch *Advice to Bride and Groom* 32-33; Josephus *Ag. Ap.* 2 §201; see also Eph 5:22-33; Col 3:18-19; 1 Pet 3:1-7; Titus 2:5). In *this* passage, however, the requirement is not that each wife must be submissive to her own husband during the worship service (*pace* Hanson 1982, 72). Understood in that way, the requirement would affect only married women, while the scriptural warrant in verses 13-14 implicates all women. Instead, the requirement seems to be that the behavior of a woman (i.e., of *any* woman) in the worship service must reflect in all its particulars the subordinate status of women; that is, no woman should exercise authority over any man, and therefore no woman should teach.

Two biblical warrants are provided for these injunctions, both derived from Genesis. The first refers to the sequence of creation that is described in Genesis 2 and rests on the widespread assumption that the first born (here the "first *formed*") has superior status and rightful authority over younger siblings (see Gen 27:29; Deut 21:15-17; Heb 1:6; cf. Gen 25:23; 37:9-11; 1 Sam 16:6-13). With this reference the author implies that women who teach and thus exercise authority over men are violating the social order established by God at creation.

The second warrant is developed in somewhat more detail and refers to the story of the fall in Genesis 3. The author ignores all aspects of this story except one. Relying on Gen 3:13 he asserts that only Eve was deceived (or "tricked," cf. Gen 3:12) and thus—here he departs dramatically from Genesis—only she became a transgressor. The verb "deceive" in 1 Tim 2:14 is a stronger variant of the one in the Greek version of Genesis (the LXX) and occasionally has the nuance of seduction. Though the author may have known the legend of the serpent's sexual seduction of Eve (see e.g., *Prot. Jas.* 13:1-5; 2 Cor 11:2-3), he does not emphasize the idea here beyond the rather common insistence on "modesty." The key for this author is the issue of deception. Deception was a stock charge frequently leveled, for example, by philosophers against their rivals and opponents (see, e.g., Dio Chrysostom *Orations* 4.33-35; Philo *Who Is the Heir* 302-6; Lucian *The Fisherman* 25). The author of the Pastorals, however, is interested in the term because it links Eve, who was deceived, with the women of the church, who are being deceived (2 Tim 3:5-7), and with the opponents, who are the contemporary deceivers (4:1; 2 Tim 3:13; Titus 1:10). The author's reasoning is that the deception of Eve and not Adam reveals this to be a weakness peculiar to women, and the particular success of the opponents with women confirms it. Thus women must not be permitted to exercise the crucial role of teacher lest their vulnerability to deception permit the spread of false teachings in the church (cf. 5:13).

The passage closes with a remarkable statement that transforms the punishment of Gen 3:16 into a means of salvation (see also 5:14; Titus 2:4). This means of salvation (childbirth) is particularly appropriate to the nature of Eve's fall, if this is understood as a seduction, but such theological niceties are not the author's primary concern. His objective in promoting childbearing is to provide an effective response to the ascetic demands of the opponents (see 4:3; Introduction), one that will protect the women from the message of celibacy and thus keep them from suffering shipwreck in the faith (1:19).

A significant proviso is attached: "provided they continue in faith and love and holiness, with modesty." The shift from a singular verb form in the first half of the verse ("she") to a plural form in the second ("they") seems to imply a change in subject, and some think that the author here introduces a new requirement that the woman's *children* exhibit good behavior. But children are not specifically mentioned and the reference to modesty (*sōphrosynē*) repeats the opening admonition to women (v. 9), so it is probable that the concern here, as in verse 9, is with women's behavior. They will be saved through childbirth *if* they continue in faith, love, holiness, and modesty. This qualification serves as a warning and also brings the startling statement concerning salvation through childbirth into some congruence with the letter's overall theology (see, e.g., 1:14).

The author seals the argument with the familiar words, "The saying is sure" (see also 1:15). Though in the NRSV the words introduce the discussion of the office of bishop in chapter 3, the Greek text is ambiguous on that point. In fact, it seems more likely that the phrase concludes the preceding argument. Every other occurrence of this formula is clearly connected with a statement on salvation, and this one is probably no exception. It underscores and certifies as trustworthy what the author has just said concerning the way that women will be saved.

In a few manuscripts, none of them early or reliable, the saying is described as a "human" one (Gk. *anthrōpinos*) rather than a "faithful" one (Gk. *pistos*). Whether understood as a reference to 2:15 or 3:2, this change was probably introduced by a scribe who was reluctant to link that prosaic statement with the more profoundly theological assertions identified as "faithful" elsewhere in these letters (cf. 1:15).

◊ ◊ ◊ ◊

This is the first of several passages in which the author addresses the conduct of women (see also 3:11; 5:3-16; Titus 2:3-5). This passage is remarkable for the stringency of the restrictions it applies to their participation in worship and for its elaborate supporting theological argument. The author is clearly reacting against the presence of the opposing teachers. It is to prevent the spread of their message that he forbids the "easily deceived" women to teach and it is to counter the teachers' asceticism that he presents the remarkable concept of salvation through childbirth. This reference to salvation picks up the earlier statement that God desires everyone to be saved and to come to the knowledge of the truth (2:4) and seems to be, in the author's view, a direct illustration of it. Salvation for everyone requires special means for some, especially for those whose salvation is being jeopardized by problems peculiar to their circumstances (see also 6:17-19). In linking salvation with childbirth, however, the author is making a mockery not only of his Pauline roots (see, e.g., Rom 3:21-26; Gal 2:16-17; Phil 3:8-11) but also of his own views concerning the abiding power of divine grace and the efficacy of the gender-neutral virtues of faith and love (1:12-14; 6:11-15; Titus 2:11-14; 3:3-8).

While the author's prohibition of teaching and promotion of childbearing derive directly from his concern to counter the success of the opposing teachers, in the remaining admonitions to women he embraces the conservative cultural norms of his day. Indeed, little separates his view from the Greco-Roman ideal as illustrated by a contemporary tombstone inscription to Turia, a virtuous Roman matron: "Why mention domestic virtue and chastity, and submissiveness, geniality, the ready loom, modesty in attire? Or your love to your kin and my kin, of my mother as your parents? This is all common with all honorable women" (Lefkowitz and Fant 1982, 209). Cultural norms control the ethical perspective throughout these letters, making it sometimes difficult to determine which admonitions were given because they were an ethical commonplace, and which reflect concrete problems within the community.

In applying the domestic expectation of silent and submissive behavior to women in the worship service, apparently thereby excluding them not only from any teaching activity but also from participating in the prayers of the community, the author is again abandoning his Pauline heritage. Even when imposing some restrictions on the Corinthian women (1 Cor 11:2-16), Paul does not deny their right to participate actively and vocally in the worship service. (The demand for silence found in 1 Cor 14:34-36 is widely—though not universally—recognized as an insertion by a later editor, probably one familiar with the strictures on women's participation presented in this passage.)

The author is not unique in placing the blame for the fall on Eve's shoulders (see also Sir 25:24; 2 Cor 11:3; cf. Rom 5:12-21). By focusing on the issue of deception, however, he is able, in good midrashic fashion, to wed the biblical narrative to his contemporary situation (cf., e.g., Paul's use of the figure of Abraham in Romans 4). The author thus shows no paucity of exegetical inventiveness; it is in the conclusions he draws that he poses the gravest hermeneutical challenge.

Qualifications for Church Leaders (3:1b-13)

The transition from the preceding discussion of women's proper dress and decorum to this list of qualifications for church offices seems abrupt, but it is not without logic. The attention given here to worship leaders continues the general focus on worship that prevails throughout 2:1–3:16. More specifically, though, the rejection of a teaching or leadership role for women because of their gullibility raises naturally the question of the qualities to be sought in those who are approved for these roles. These qualities reflect for the most part virtues lauded in the Greco-Roman world, but they also promote the "quiet and peaceable life" that is, according to this document, pleasing to God as well (2:2-3). The characteristic hellenistic concern for proper household relationships is prominent, encouraged, no doubt, by the author's understanding of the church as the household of God (3:4-5, 12, 15).

The passage consists of a straightforward listing of qualifications first for a bishop or overseer (vv. 1-7) and then for deacons (vv. 8-13). Rationales are occasionally provided that link the qualifications with the demands of the positions (vv. 5, 6*b*, 7*b*, 13), but many of the qualities sought are not specific to ecclesial duties. Some of the listed virtues do, however, acquire increased significance when read in light of the social conflict within this church.

Catalogues of virtues were common in Greco-Roman ethical teaching where, as here, they followed a relatively fixed schema and promoted a general ideal. Thus, the qualities listed in Onosander's *Strategikos* for a hellenistic military leader are nearly indistinguishable from those required here of a bishop: "temperate, self-restrained, vigilant, frugal, hardened to labor, alert, free from avarice, neither too young nor too old, indeed a father of children if possible, a ready speaker, and a man with a good reputation" (Dibelius and Conzelmann 1972, 158).

◊ ◊ ◊ ◊

Bishops (3:1*b*-7): The author first lists the qualities expected of a person the NRSV describes as a bishop. (The NJB refers to him as "president"; the NEB, as "leader.") The Greek word, *episkopos,* means literally "overseer" and was widely used in the Greek-speaking world to refer to persons in positions of general oversight (especially of financial matters) as well as to specific officials of various civil and religious organizations. It was thus a natural term to apply to those who exercised leadership roles in the emerging Christian churches. Paul, for example, addresses his letter to the Philippians not only to the congregation but also to its "bishops (or overseers) and deacons." He does not, however, give any indication that there were formal qualifications for these positions or prescribed duties. The terms were simply descriptive of the leadership roles certain people played in the congregation: oversight of the church and ministry to the needs of its members. Each Pauline house church

probably had its own leader or overseer, usually—but not necessarily—the head of the house in which the group met (see, e.g., Rom
16:3-5), but there is no evidence in Paul's letters of regional leadership, either in the form of a bishop or a council of elders.

The Pastoral Letters represent a further stage of development and
presume the existence of something more akin to a formal "office"
of bishop (Gk. *episcopē*) to which one "aspires" (v. 1) and for which
there are qualifications (Holmberg 1978, 109-21). The author does
not specify the duties of the bishop, though they obviously included
some oversight function (vv. 4-5). His goal was not to introduce an
office into the church but through the list of qualifications to
highlight the contrast between those who appropriately hold leadership positions and those who do not. He was also concerned that
church leaders be well qualified to deal with opponents, and that
the teaching responsibilities in the church be firmly tied to its
ordained leaders (see also Titus 1:9).

Because the author is discussing an extant church hierarchy, he
also does not discuss the relationship between this position and the
other leadership positions mentioned in these letters. The bishop is
clearly distinguished from the deacons, whose title suggests responsibilities of service rather than oversight, but the relationship between the bishop and the elders is more ambiguous. In some New
Testament documents, the terms "bishop" (or overseer) and "elder"
seem to be used interchangeably for the same office or function (see
Acts 20:17, 28; 1 Pet 5:1-2; see also *1 Clement* 44). In 1 Timothy,
however, the discussion of the qualifications of the bishop is entirely
divorced from references to elders (4:14; 5:17-22), as if the positions
were completely separate. Titus 1:5-9, however, mentions the two
together and suggests some overlap of membership.

The nature of that overlap is difficult to determine, especially if
1 Timothy and Titus reflect the same pattern of church leadership.
In both of these letters the bishop is mentioned in the singular while
elders, deacons, and widows (who may have had official status as
well; see below) are referred to always in the plural. Some argue
that the singular is generic and that there were actually a number
of bishops too. Yet it seems more likely, given the persistent use of
the singular form and the analogy the author develops between the

bishop and the (singular) head of a household, that there was indeed only one bishop of a given region.

There were also elders, who probably functioned, originally at least, in Christianity as they did in Judaism—as the leaders of a particular Christian community who were chosen because of their maturity and leadership qualities. There would probably have been considerable overlap between these community-wide leaders and those who still had oversight over individual house churches within the community, that is, between elders and those originally called "overseers." At the time of these letters, the leadership structure may have evolved further, with a single bishop or overseer appointed from the local elders probably having oversight over the council of elders and thus over the church of a given city or region (von Lips 1979). (The letters of Ignatius of Antioch, written about 113 CE, clearly reflect this structure; see, e.g., Ign. *Trall.* 2-3.)

The listing of qualifications follows no obvious order, save that the first on the list ("above reproach," see also 5:7; 6:14) summarizes all that follow. The significance of the requirement concerning marriage is not clear, though it is applied to deacons, elders, and (in revised form) widows (see 3:12; 5:9; Titus 1:6). The translation of the NRSV, "married only once," is an interpretation; the literal translation of the Greek is "husband of one wife." The phrase has been variously interpreted to exclude marriage after divorce (see Matt 19:9; Mark 10:11-12; 1 Cor 7:11), marriage after the death of a spouse, polygamy, or promiscuity. It is probably best interpreted very literally: the would-be bishop should have had only one wife. This corresponds to Paul's instructions urging widows and widowers to remain unmarried (1 Cor 7:8, 39-40), instructions that were retained in the second-century church (*Herm. Man.* 4.4.1-2; Athenagoras *Supplication* 33.3-6). It also corresponds to the high regard the ancient world had for women who married only once (Lightman and Zeisel 1977), though the extension of the principle here to men is unusual (cf. 5:9). The prominent position of the requirement, the first concrete item on the list, suggests some special significance for the author's church. It certainly highlights the expectation, if not the requirement, of marriage, in obvious contrast to the absolute prohibition of marriage by the opposing teachers (4:3).

The three virtues that follow are characteristic of the ideal of moderation promoted more broadly in Greco-Roman moral teaching and throughout these letters (see 2:9; 3:11; Titus 2:2-5). Hospitality was also promoted as a virtue (Epictetus *Discourses* 1.28.23), though it received special emphasis in Christianity, where it facilitated the spread of the gospel by traveling preachers (see, e.g., 5:10; Rom 12:13; Heb 13:2; Phlm 22; 1 Pet 4:9; 3 John 5-8). Its presence here on a list of qualifications for bishop thus points beyond the normal hospitality he should display as head of a household to the hospitality he should extend on behalf of the church.

The requirement that the bishop be an apt teacher is not highlighted in any way except by the context, which criticizes the opponents' teaching (1:6-7; 4:1), forbids teaching by women (2:12), and encourages "Timothy's" teaching (4:11-16). The bishop's role as teacher is more prominent in Titus 1:9, where it is explicitly linked with the need to refute opponents (see also 2 Tim 2:24-26). The qualities mentioned in 1 Tim 3:3 are repeated in Titus 1:7-8 and 2 Tim 2:24-25 and are typical items on Greco-Roman virtue lists (see above). In their present context they promote the peaceable life so admired by this author (2:2) and, more important, exclude the opposing teachers, who are characterized in several places as quarrelsome and belligerent (see 2 Tim 2:23; Titus 3:9). Absence of greed is a typical item on virtue lists, but it is a particularly prominent concern in 1 Timothy (see also 3:8; 6:9-10, 17-19), where it serves to balance the equally typical charge that the opponents are motivated by base avarice (6:5).

The author emphasizes the last three items on this list—household management, spiritual maturity, and reputation with outsiders—by attaching comments to them that clarify their relevance for church leaders. Thus the requirement that the bishop manage his household well—a common enough expectation of men in the Greco-Roman world—is linked to the need to care for the church, which is the household of God (3:15). The requirement that he keep his children subordinate and submissive (see also Titus 1:6) reflects the prevailing cultural expectations and complements the subordination of women to men required in 2:11 (see also Titus 2:5, 9; 3:1). It may have other significance as well. An inability to deal with rebellious children would foreshadow problems in dealing with rebelliousness in the church, and the opposing teachers are displaying just such a rebellious spirit (see, e.g., 1:3-4; Titus 1:10). Furthermore, he must maintain the control over his children "with all gravity" (a better translation than the NRSV's insistence that he keep the children "respectful in every way")—that is, without losing the solemnity and dignity expected of a *paterfamilias*, of a church leader, indeed, of all Christians (2:2; Titus 2:7).

The reason given for the stipulation that the bishop not be a recent convert (Gk. *neophytos,* which means literally "newly planted"; see 1 Cor 3:6-9) is presented in the NRSV as a concern that such a person "may be puffed up with conceit" (see also 6:4; 2 Tim 3:4). The Greek verb *(typhōthēnai)* also means "to be deluded or blinded," and that translation makes good sense here (see also 2 Tim 3:13-15). A recently converted Christian could easily be deluded by false teachings and, as bishop, could then lead the church astray. The meaning of the phrase, "fall into the condemnation of the devil" is disputed. The Greek word translated "devil" *(diabolos)* means literally a slanderer and could refer either to a human opponent or to Satan. A similar phrase in 2 Tim 2:26 suggests that here the author had God's archenemy in mind (see also Eph 6:11), though a few verses later the same word is used in a more mundane sense (3:11; see also 2 Tim 3:3; Titus 2:3). The "condemnation of the devil" is not, however, a condemnation that Satan inflicts (the role of ultimate judge is reserved for Christ; see 2 Tim 4:1), but either the condemnation that Satan faces (see, e.g., Rev 20:1-3) or, even more likely, the condemnation of being handed over to the devil (see 1 Tim 1:20). In any case, the threat is ominous.

The discussion of the bishop concludes with a comment on his relationship to outsiders. Because of society's latent or real hostility toward Christians and also because of Christianity's proselytizing stance (see 2:4), concern for the reaction of outsiders is often visible in the New Testament (1 Cor 14:16; 1 Thess 4:12; 1 Pet 2:11-12; 3:1-2). It is a particularly strong concern in the Pastoral Letters

(5:14; 6:1; Titus 2:5-10), which also show a pervasive and corresponding concern that Christians embody the best virtues of Greco-Roman society. Here, though, the concern is focused on the leader of the church, because he represents the church and is its most prominent member. As in the previous verse, the reason given for this requirement is ambiguous, though it also seems to involve Satan (i.e., the slanderer) in some way. The "snare of the devil" is the trap set by Satan to capture the unwary and the unrighteous (see 2 Tim 2:26; Job 2:1-5), but the connection with outsiders is not clear. Probably the idea is that anything that disgraces the church leader in the eyes of outsiders disgraces also the church, and that is the plan—and the snare—of the devil. The final verse thus summarizes the intent and content of the list: it requires behavior of a bishop that is "above reproach" (v. 2) in the eyes of God and of society.

Deacons (3:8-13): The root idea expressed by the Greek word *diakonos* (deacon) is that of the go-between, and it came to signify one who performed acts for, or in the service of, another. In many New Testament texts the word refers to the concrete service of waiting at table (Acts 6:2; see also Luke 17:8; John 12:2), though it was used in hellenistic sources to describe roles as diverse as those of the Cynic philosopher (Epictetus *Discourses* 3.24.65) and the household attendant (Collins 1990).

The word was quickly appropriated by Christians to define their leadership roles in terms of service (see Mark 10:45). Paul, for example, describes Timothy (1 Thess 3:2), Phoebe (Rom 16:1), the civil ruler (Rom 13:4), Apollos (1 Cor 3:5), himself (2 Cor 6:4), and even Christ (Rom 15:8) as *diakonoi*. In Phil 1:1, the deacon is linked with the bishop or overseer, though the relationship between these two is not spelled out (cf. *1 Clem.* 42.4-5; *Did.* 15.1). Though Paul used this word, as he did "overseer," to describe a role or function, in 1 Timothy the noun clearly refers to a position for which one is tested (3:10) and from which one derives certain benefits (3:13). What the deacons' responsibilities were is not, however, indicated, nor are we told how their testing took place or precisely what the expected benefits were (see below). As in the preceding passage, only qualifications for the position are mentioned.

The opening list of qualifications reproduces a number of those listed for a bishop (cf. 3:2-3) and enforces the cultural and ecclesial ideal of moderation. Unique to *this* list is the distinctly Christian requirement that deacons "hold fast to the mystery of the faith with a clear conscience." The phrase, "the mystery of the faith," is probably formulaic and should not be pressed for special revelatory significance (cf. Eph 1:9; 3:4; Col 2:2; 4:3). The reference seems to be to the content of the Christian faith, which is summarized a few verses below (see comments on 3:16). Deacons are thus required to hold fast to that content, and a strong contrast is surely intended with the opposing teachers, who have rejected conscience and thus suffered shipwreck in the faith (1:19; see also 1:4-6; 4:2).

The women mentioned in verse 11 present a puzzle. They have been identified by some as women deacons, by others as deacons' wives. (The Greek word, *gynaikas,* can be translated either "women" or "wives.") Though the placement of the verse—in the midst of a discussion of qualifications for men who would be deacons—lends support to their identification as wives, the other interpretation seems preferable. There were, for example, women deacons in the Pauline churches (Rom 16:1) and the moral require-ments for the women here match those for the deacons in verse 8 (though both sets of moral requirements also reflect the cultural ideal and are not specific to particular leadership responsibilities within the church; see Titus 2:2-3). There is no possessive pronoun, which would be expected if the reference were to "*their* wives" (i.e., the deacons' wives). The repetition of the word "likewise" (see v. 8) also suggests that a distinct but parallel group of people is being discussed. Once again, the text gives no indication of the responsi-bilities of these women, though the injunctions in 2:12 would seem to preclude any real leadership role. Some have suggested that the women here are the widows mentioned in 5:3-16 (implying that the "widows" had some functional role in the church; see below) or that the special assignment of the women mentioned here is defined in Titus 2:3-5 as instruction of young wives. Neither hypothesis, however, can be confirmed on the basis of the wording of this brief verse. It simply hints at an official position for women but does not emphasize it in any way. Instead the author returns quickly to the topic of male deacons and continues the list of the qualifications for them.

The final qualifications echo the domestic requirements of a bishop (see 3:4), and the assumption is that deacons, like a bishop, will be married. The final clause is odd. It provides a practical reason for seeking the position of deacon just as 3:1 provides a practical reason for seeking to become a bishop (it is a "noble task"). Because concern for social prestige was such a characteristic feature of the first-century Mediterranean world (Malina 1981), the promised good standing probably refers to standing within the community as well as to enhanced status before God.

◊ ◊ ◊ ◊

What is most remarkable about this discussion of the bishop and deacons is what is *not* present: There is no theological grounding of these positions, no list of duties associated with them, and (apart from v. 9) no spiritual requirements for them. Instead, the lists promote as qualifications for church leadership roles the moral virtues of the Greco-Roman world, though, to be sure, the very highest of these virtues. The goal of this was in large part apologetic: these church leaders represented the church to an unbelieving society and through their exemplary lives they could deflect the hostility that new cults often faced. In particular, the stable households of these men not only stood as testimony to their leadership skills but also silenced any suspicion among outsiders that the new cult would undermine family structure and thus threaten the social foundation of the orderly and stable empire. Such suspicions were common (Balch 1981).

This author assumes that the truth of the church's teaching is confirmed or denied by the conduct of its members (1:9-11), and the exemplary behavior required here of church leaders would have obvious propaganda value for the new religion by fostering a way of life that the entire civilized world would admire. Thus the goal defined in 2:4—that everyone come to a knowledge of the truth— would be in no way hindered by the behavior of the church leaders and would, in fact, be actively promoted by it.

At the same time, the requirement that church leaders must manage (literally "stand at the head of") their households excluded slaves from any of these positions. For the same reason, women would also be excluded, except perhaps from a special version of the role of deacon (3:11). This marks a significant departure from Paul's own churches, where women played various leadership roles (Rom 16:1-2; see also Pliny *Letters* 10.96) and where "slave" was an honorable epithet both for Christ (Phil 2:7) and for church leaders (Rom 1:1; Gal 1:10; Phil 1:1).

Purpose of the Letter (3:14-16)

These verses interrupt the seemingly endless exhortations with a comment on the purpose of the letter. The statement of purpose embraces the contents of chapters 2–3, but by returning the focus to Timothy as the recipient of the letter, it also provides a transition to the chapters that follow, where the instructions are given as direct address to him. Two brief comments underscore the significance of these instructions: one on the nature of the church and another on "the mystery of our religion," which the author summarizes by quoting a portion of an early Christian hymn. Taken together, these features establish again the important connection between doctrine and conduct (see also 1:8-11) and provide one of the most significant passages in the letter, one that provides a reminder of "Paul's" purpose, a definition of the church, and a summary of its faith.

◊ ◊ ◊ ◊

The author again alludes to the letter's fictional situation (see 1:3, 18) but here amplifies it somewhat by describing the absent Paul's intention to return to Ephesus and his concern over the consequences of a delay. In constructing this fiction, the author uses a familiar Pauline motif ("I hope to come to you soon," see, e.g., Rom 1:13; Phil 2:24; 1 Thess 2:18), which was also a common feature in letters of that time. The resulting scenario provides an ideal pretext for introducing the letter's exhortations, for Paul himself, being dead, will not return and the pseudonymous letter must represent the apostle in the period of this protracted "delay."

The instructions referred to here (the Greek text says simply "these things") include not only those just mentioned in chapters 2–3 but also those to come in chapters 4–6. The passage thus offers a second explanation of the purpose of the letter that complements the one given in 1:18. But whereas 1:18 speaks of equipping Timothy to "fight the good fight," referring to general moral endeavor with echoes of the struggle with the opposing teachers, here the reference is specifically to behavior "in the household of God." With this phrase the author introduces a metaphor of signal importance for the Pastoral Letters.

Paul, himself, never used this phrase to describe the church, though he once refers to "the family of faith" (Gal 6:10; see, however, Eph 2:19; 1 Pet 4:17). He used instead the image of the body of Christ when he wanted to promote diversity within the community (1 Cor 12:12-31; Rom 12:4-8) or, when he wanted to stress God's presence within it, the image of the temple of God (1 Cor 3:16-17; 2 Cor 6:16 [which may, however, be non-Pauline]; see also Eph 2:21-22). The Greek phrase found here (*oikos theou*) can mean either the *house* of God, suggesting a sacred space, or the house*hold* of God, suggesting a divinely ordered social structure. Though the phrase that follows, "the pillar and bulwark of the truth," develops the architectural image, it is the concept of the church as a social entity that dominates these letters (see, e.g., 3:5; 2 Tim 2:20-21), which show a pervasive concern for orderly behavior and appropriate relationships among various groups within the church.

When the author conceptualizes the social structure of the church as a household, he is following a familiar pattern, for Greek and Roman philosophers viewed the family as the microcosm of the empire. What strengthened the one, strengthened also the other. Therefore Aristotle devoted Book I of his *Politics* to the household and concluded this Book with the observation that "every household is part of a state, and these relationships [i.e., husband and wife, father and children, master and slaves] are part of the household, and the excellence of the part must have regard to that of the whole" (1260b). During the rule of Augustus, Dionysius of Halicarnassus made a similar observation: "every state, since it consists of many houses, is most likely to enjoy tranquility when the lives of the individual citizens are untroubled" (*Roman Antiquities* 2.24.2).

The household that these authors, including the author of the Pastoral Letters, had in mind was, of course, the patriarchal household, the norm for Greco-Roman culture. Thus the bishop managed the household of God just as the husband/father ruled the traditional household (3:4-5; see also 3:12; Titus 1:6-7), and other members of the church were assigned their proper places within a hierarchy that enveloped both the natural and the ecclesiastical family. Women, slaves, and children were subordinate and therefore were to be submissive (2:11; 3:4, 12; 6:1; Titus 2:5, 9); younger members of the community were to respect the older (5:1-2, 4); older women were to behave with due decorum (Titus 2:3); and all were to be subject to and respectful of the Roman authorities (2:1-2; Titus 3:1). So closely identified was the church with its constituent households that instructions in intimate household relationships (see Titus 2:4) are here presented as community instructions, enforced by church leaders for the well-being of the church.

This author does not emphasize God's spiritual presence in the community as Paul does, but the epithet "living God" (see also 4:10) suggests an active deity working in and through the community. The phrase was often used by both Christians and Jews to draw a sharp contrast between their God and the lifeless idols of the pagan world (Jer 10:9-10; Dan 6:20, 26; 2 Cor 6:16; 1 Thess 1:9). That particular contrast is missing here, though a contrast may be intended with the "demons" mentioned in the following verses (4:1-5).

The final phrase describes the church as the "pillar and bulwark of the truth." Here the polemical tone is more obvious, for throughout these letters the opponents are associated with falsehood and deceit (4:1-2; 6:5; 2 Tim 2:18; 3:8). Both architectural metaphors ("foundation," though, is a better translation of the Greek *hedraiōma* than the NRSV's "bulwark") contribute to the image of the church as a stable structure firmly supporting truth in the face of opposition (see also Jer 1:18).

The reference to truth prompts the author to define it, which he does in verse 16 by quoting a fragment of a Christian hymn. The christological statements contained in these lines are introduced as "the mystery of our religion." This phrase is nearly synonymous with the one in 3:9 ("the mystery of the faith"), though the Greek word here translated "religion" *(eusebeia)* suggests *both* religious piety (i.e., faith) and a way of life appropriate to that piety. It is the same word that is translated "godliness" in 2:2 and is a characteristic feature of this author's religious vocabulary. Only here and in 3:9 is the content of the Christian faith called a "mystery" in these letters. Paul himself used the word to refer to Israel's role in God's plan of salvation (Rom 11:25), to the paradox of salvation through the Cross (1 Cor 2:1, 7), and to the resurrection (1 Cor 15:51). Here "mystery" embraces the entire message of salvation summarized in the hymn fragment and underscores the importance of revelation.

The passage is easily recognizable as a hymn fragment because of the nearly identical length and structure of each line. The connection between the passage and its context is grammatically awkward, further evidence that an independent fragment has been introduced into the argument. The fragment opens with a masculine relative pronoun (Gk. *hos,* "who") that has no antecedent, for the only noun in the first part of the sentence is neuter ("mystery," Gk. *mystērion*). In some late manuscripts the pronoun is also neuter and refers clearly back to "mystery," but this represents an attempt by later scribes to correct the awkward grammar. A somewhat larger number of manuscripts have "God" instead of either pronoun, the result of misreading the pronoun (ΟΣ) as the common abbreviation for the Greek word for God (Θ͞Σ). The more difficult pronoun "who" is probably the original reading, and the awkwardness arose because the first line of the hymn (probably something like "Blessed be our Lord and Savior Jesus Christ, who . . . ") was dropped when the fragment was incorporated into the letter (see also Phil 2:6).

The structure of the hymn has been analyzed in several different ways. The NRSV prints it in two stanzas of three lines each, but it is difficult to discern any logical christological pattern with that division. The pattern is clearly not chronological, for while the first line refers to the incarnation and the sixth to the ascension (see Acts 1:11), lines four and five refer to events that occurred after the ascension. It is possible to construe lines three and six as refrains that interrupt the chronological sequence, but a more persuasive possibility is that the hymn consists of three stanzas of two lines, each stanza describing (in alternating sequence) parallel events in the earthly and heavenly realms.

Since the first line is a reference to the (earthly) incarnation, the second, understood as a heavenly complement to the first, refers to the resurrection, here described in terms of divine vindication. This view of the resurrection as God's vindication of the crucified Messiah is found in Acts (see 2:23-24; 10:39-40), though the specific word "vindicated" is not present. "In spirit" suggests that this vindication occurred when Christ entered the spiritual or heavenly realm (see also Rom 1:3-4; 1 Pet 3:18-22). Line three then describes the appearance of the resurrected Christ before the heavenly angelic powers (see Eph 1:21; Heb 1:3-4; 1 Pet 3:22; Rev 5:8-14), while line four refers to the proclamation of the message of the resurrected Christ to the earthly nations (Gk. *ethnē*, translated "Gentiles" by the NRSV). The fifth line documents the earthly conclusion of the Christ event (worldwide belief) while the sixth describes the heavenly conclusion (Christ's ascension to glory).

Stanza 1	line 1	revealed	in flesh	(earth)
	line 2	vindicated	in spirit	(heaven)
Stanza 2	line 3	seen	by angels	(heaven)
	line 4	proclaimed	among nations	(earth)
Stanza 3	line 5	believed in	in the world	(earth)
	line 6	taken up	in glory	(heaven)

The overall pattern is thus *abbaab* (*a* = earthly event; *b* = heavenly event). Moreover, each stanza has a recognizable theme: the first defines through the incarnation and the resurrection the two spheres in which the Christ-event occurred; the second documents the presentation of Christ and the message about Christ through these same heavenly and earthly realms; the third describes two parallel conclusions.

◊ ◊ ◊ ◊

This brief passage contains two of the most significant theological passages found in this letter: the description of the church and the fragmentary Christian hymn. The image of the church as the household of God has controlled the letter's structure and content in a number of ways that have been described above. It also introduces a metaphor that would have had significant psychological and social power, for in Greco-Roman society the household was the dominant social reality. To use that image for the church was to harness that power for the church. The hymn reinforces the magnitude of the truth that the church is called both to preserve and to reflect through its obedience to the instructions presented in this letter. It also contributes to certain of the letter's major themes, the most significant of which is the theme of epiphany.

The hymn presents a striking pattern of parallel events in heaven and on earth. The revelation or epiphany ("he was revealed" in Greek is *ephanerōthē*) of Christ at the incarnation and before the heavenly powers (lines one and three) is mirrored or extended by the apostolic preaching of the church, which "reveals" Christ to the nations (lines four and five). A similar pattern is found elsewhere in the letters. Not only is the incarnation presented as an epiphany (2 Tim 1:8-10; Titus 3:4), but the parousia or Second Coming is also described the same way (1 Tim 6:14-15; 2 Tim 4:8; Titus 2:13), as is the preaching of the gospel (2 Tim 1:10; Titus 1:3). An understanding of the Christ-event as an epiphany is thus the distinctive feature of the letter's Christology and is neatly summarized in the hymn. Moreover, the worldwide audience that the hymn foresees for this gospel and the worldwide faith that it will elicit echo the universal message of the earlier liturgical fragment (2:5-6a) and may, like it, be intended to counter the opponents' more exclusionary theology (see above, pp. 51-54). In the immediate context, though, the main purpose of the citation is to underscore the connection between doctrine (represented here by the hymnic fragment) and behavior. The behavior defined by the letter's instructions properly reflects the theological truth preserved, proclaimed, and protected by the church and summarized in verse 16. Indeed, this behavior itself is part of "the mystery of our religion" and constitutes one manner in which the mystery is proclaimed.

Instructions for Timothy (4:1–6:19)

The instructions in the remainder of the letter (chaps. 4–6) differ from those in chapters 2–3 in that they are addressed specifically to Timothy (see, e.g., 4:12; 5:23; 6:11, 20), who is directed to pass them on to the members of the church (4:6, 11; 5:7; 6:17). The content of these chapters is quite diverse. Some sentences are personal exhortations to Timothy (4:6-16; 5:23; 6:11-16, 20), which, it may be assumed, are also aimed indirectly at other church leaders. A large portion of this section is devoted to instructions concerning various social groups within the church that may have been the source of some friction (5:1–6:2). The section begins and ends, though, with warnings about the danger of false teachers (4:1-5; 6:3-10, 20-21). Like the similar warnings in chapter 1, these verses underscore the urgency and timeliness of the letter's reminder of "how one ought to behave" (3:15). The verses also temper the preceding celebration of worldwide faith (3:14-16) with the sober reminder of apostasy.

Prediction of False Asceticism (4:1-5)

The opening warning is introduced as a word from the (Holy) Spirit and contains both a stereotypical denunciation of the opponents (vv. 1-2) and one of the few descriptions in these letters of the actual content of their teachings (v. 3; see also 2 Tim 2:18). It also contains the author's only theological rebuttal of these teachings (vv. 3b-5), which may derive from Paul's instructions to the Corinthians but which focuses more than Paul did on the doctrine of creation to refute the opponents' ascetic demands (cf. 1 Corinthians 8, 10).

◊ ◊ ◊ ◊

References to the Holy Spirit are rare in these letters (elsewhere only at 2 Tim 1:14 and Titus 3:5-6) and the one here adds weight and solemnity to the warning that follows. Inspired Christian prophets were understood to mediate the words of the Spirit (see Rev 2:7, 11) and the author may have some such prophecy in mind. It is also possible, however, that the author, like Paul (see 1 Cor

7:40), is claiming the Spirit as the authoritative source for his own words. The Spirit's (author's) warning concerns events that will occur "in later times" (v. 1). The words have an apocalyptic ring to them, but the usual apocalyptic phrase is "in the last day(s)" (see 2 Tim 3:1; John 6:39; Acts 2:17; 2 Pet 3:3). In fact, the author's careful and detailed rebuttal of the predicted teachings indicates that the time in question was probably his own, not the future End of time, though he has employed the traditional expectation of trouble before the time of the End to shape his warning about apostasy (see Mark 13:22; 2 Thess 2:9-12; 1 John 2:18; Rev 13:14).

Here, as often in these letters, "the faith" refers to the content of faith and is almost a synonym for Christian teaching or even Christian religion (see comments on 3:16; see also 4:6; 5:8; 6:10, 12, 21). Elsewhere the author retains the meaning of faith as the decisive act of believing (1:5; 2 Tim 1:5; 3:15), though the word also appears in various virtue lists alongside other indicators of moral excellence like modesty, purity, and gentleness (2:15; 4:12; 6:11).

Because the letter is written in Paul's name (i.e., as if out of the past), the arrival of the deceitful teachers (which has already occurred in the author's time) is predicted for the future (see also 2 Tim 3:1-9; 4:3-4). In other passages "Paul" confronts false teachers himself or urges Timothy or Titus to do so (1:3-4, 19-20; 6:19-20). The author has in each case the same group in mind (the opponents his own church faces), but the letters' fiction suggests a long history of similar opponents that makes Paul's advice relevant to the current controversy (see also Acts 20:29-30).

The author's invective ("deceitful," "hypocrisy," "liars") is typical of the language used by philosophers to denounce their opponents, the sophists (see, e.g., Dio Chrysostom *Orations* 4.33-36), and thus it cannot be used to reconstruct the actual situation behind the letter. Here the goal is rhetorical: the demonic spirits and deceit linked with the opposing teachers (see also 2 Tim 2:26; 3:13; Titus 1:10) stand in sharpest possible contrast with the (Holy) Spirit and the truth that guide the author and those who follow him (3:15; 4:3). Paul, himself, occasionally used such contrastive language, especially when dealing with opponents in Corinth (see 2 Cor 4:4;

11:13-15), and it is very characteristic of sectarian writings such as those from Qumran (see also 1 John 4:1-6). The implication of the charge that their "consciences are seared with a hot iron" is not entirely clear. Burning with a hot iron (Gk. *kaustēriazein*) was done to numb or cauterize a wound, to punish, or to identify ownership (NEB, cf. 2 Tim 2:26). Any of these meanings could apply here; the essential point is one of contrast between those whose consciences are good (1:5, 19) or pure (3:9; 2 Tim 1:3) and those whose consciences are rejected (1:19), stained (Titus 1:15), or "burned."

Starkly juxtaposed to the stereotypical polemics in verses 1-2 is the following sentence that gives concrete information about the content of the opponents' teaching: "They forbid marriage and demand abstinence from foods." It is clear from this statement that these opponents are promoting an ascetic life, and it is probable from the author's rebuttal that this was rooted in a negative view of the created world as an impediment to salvation (see Introduction and comments on Titus 1:15). The opponents' views on marriage have strongly affected the community and have influenced the author's instructions at several points, especially when he insists as a countermeasure that women marry and bear children (2:15; 5:9-10, 14; Titus 2:4-5). The issue of abstinence from food, however, is far less prominent in the letter, surfacing again (and then only indirectly) at 5:23. It is odd, then, that the focus of the theological rebuttal here—the only such rebuttal in these letters—is on food, and not on marriage. The answer must lie, as several other commentators have observed, in the fact that Paul's own letters provide an outline and warrant for the author's response to the question of food (see Romans 14; 1 Cor 8:8; 10:23-31), while the apostle's comments on marriage are somewhat less helpful in this conflict (see especially 1 Cor 7:7-8, 25-40).

Like Paul, then, the author insists that food that has been received with thanksgiving can be eaten (Rom 14:6; 1 Cor 10:30) and gives as a reason for this the fact that all food has been created by God (Gen 9:3), a point Paul himself does not make. The author of the Pastorals is, however, very insistent about this, repeating it twice in this brief passage, and he is equally insistent about the need to receive the food with thanksgiving—the prayer at meals that acknowledges food as the Creator's gift. The final clause repeats and reinforces the point: food is sanctified (a strong statement—elsewhere in the New Testament only people are sanctified) by God's word at creation (see Gen 1:29-31) and by prayer (i.e., of thanksgiving). Some see in the language of thanksgiving (Gk. *eucharistia*) and sanctification an allusion to the eucharist (i.e., the rite of communion), which may have been implicated in the debate over the issue of food.

◊ ◊ ◊ ◊

This passage lifts for a brief moment the rhetorical veil that has concealed the opponents behind stereotype and invective, allowing some concrete information about their teachings to emerge. It is not much information, but it does provide a glimpse of the complexity of the issues the author was facing. The opponents' rejection of marriage, for example, had tremendous social consequences. It freed women from the restrictive bonds of patriarchal marriage and allowed them to live lives that were more autonomous (cf. 2:12; 5:13). That very style of life, however, was threatening to contemporary understandings of family and, since the family was the model and cornerstone of the Roman Empire, it was potentially threatening to that as well. Since this author's social views were closely tied to those of his culture, he, too, viewed this as a threat to family (Titus 1:11) and also to the moral foundation and hierarchical structure of the church (see 3:4-5, 15). The opponents' ascetic diet would have been less socially traumatic, but it probably had severe liturgical consequences. The negative view of the material world implied by this asceticism would have vitiated the Christian practice of grace before meals and possibly the Eucharist as well. It may even have been linked with a denial of the reality of the incarnation (cf. the emphasis in 2:5; 3:16).

Neither the author nor his opponents have captured Paul's flexibility on these issues. The apostle preferred celibacy, but he viewed this as a gift, not a doctrine, and insisted that the salvation of those with different gifts was not at risk. Paul's view on diet was that the Christian's new freedom and knowledge in Christ made food, even food that had been sacrificed to pagan idols, an indifferent matter, unless someone else were negatively affected by this practice (1 Cor 8:4-13; 10:23-31). For the opponents in these letters, though, celibacy seems to have become a doctrine that was rooted in a negative view of the material world. The author's anticelibate response has also hardened to the point of linking salvation with childbearing (2:15).

Paul's views were, of course, closely tied to his conviction that the parousia was imminent and the "form of this world" was passing away (1 Cor 7:31). Such an attitude led him on at least one occasion to express a relative indifference to the created world (1 Cor 7:26-30), though never to an outright rejection of it (cf. Rom 1:20; 1 Cor 8:6; 10:26). This author's reminder that God created the material world and his insistence on the goodness of that creation stands then as a necessary corrective not only to the opponents' negative evaluation of creation, but also to the legacy of indifference that apocalyptic views could spawn. The author responds conservatively to the social tensions generated by the opponents' views and argues against the denigration of the created order implicit in their theology.

Exhortations to Timothy (4:6-16)

The exhortations in 4:6-16 are addressed specifically to Timothy and are, in fact, the first imperatives in this letter directed to him. Superficially they concern Timothy's activities, but the author had a much wider purpose in mind. It was common in Greco-Roman ethical writings to define desired behavior through contrasting personal examples, and the author of the Pastoral Letters makes frequent use of this device (1:18-20; 6:3-16; Titus 1:5-16; and most of 2 Timothy). Here, too, this is his primary intent, for the portrait of the ideal church leader that emerges from the exhortations to Timothy is sharpened by the contrasting portrait of the opposing teachers in 4:1-5. It is verses 6-10, however, that function most effectively as positive counterexample. After a minor break at verse 11, the remaining verses begin to anticipate issues that surface in the instructions concerning widows, elders, and slaves (5:3–6:2) and are more oriented to what follows than to what precedes. It seems best, then, to deal with 4:6-10 and 4:11-16 separately, while recognizing the transitional role of the whole chapter.

4:6-10: After an opening sentence that depicts Timothy in a way that contrasts strongly with the teachers the author has just pilloried, the author lists two instructions—one negative and the other positive—that increase this sense of contrast. The rest of the passage (vv. 8-10) provides support for the second of these instructions: a comment on the relative value of various forms of training, a confirmation formula, and the theological vision that undergirds the whole.

◊ ◊ ◊ ◊

First Timothy is sprinkled with summary references to "these instructions" or "these things" that serve a transitional function within the letter (1:18; 3:14; 4:6, 11; 6:2). Here, as elsewhere, the referent is ambiguous. The words (literally "these things") certainly refer to the theological point developed in verses 4-5 to oppose the asceticism of the opponents, but they also embrace the totality of the letter's instructions. The Greek text does not suggest as strongly as the NRSV's translation implies ("*If* you put these instructions . . . ") that there is some question about compliance. The point is to define a "*good* servant" (as opposed to a hypocritical liar [v. 2]). In this verse the Greek word *diakonos* is translated "servant" in the NRSV because here the author of this letter probably had in mind general ministerial service (1 Cor 3:5; 2 Cor 6:4), not specifically the "deacons" mentioned in chapter 3. The verse establishes a clear connection between a *good* (Gk. *kalos*) servant (i.e., minister) and adherence to the good (Gk. *kalē*, translated "sound" by the NRSV) teaching preserved in the church. Elsewhere in these letters, Timothy is presented as nourished on, or trained in, the faith by Paul (2 Tim 1:13; 3:10) and by his mother and grandmother (2 Tim 1:5). Mere training, however, is inadequate. The "good servant" must also follow such teachings closely. (The Greek word used here *[parakolouthein]* suggests not merely obedience, but careful attentiveness that yields understanding.)

The two instructions that follow are motivated in large part by the threatening presence of the opponents. The first instruction is to avoid their teachings. Earlier the author had discredited these teachings as myths (see comments on 1:4); here he also dismisses them as "old wives' tales," that is, as unreliable gossip. The rhetorical point is the contrast with the "words of the faith and of the sound teaching" (v. 6) and the sure and reliable saying about godliness (v. 9).

The second instruction—a positive one to complement the first—concerns this "godliness" (see comments on 2:2; 3:16). The image of physical or athletic training (Gk. *gymnasia*) was, like that of warfare (see comment on 1:18), frequently used by hellenistic moralists to describe the effort required to attain moral or spiritual perfection (see, e.g., Epictetus *Discourses* 1.26.3; Philo *Migration of Abraham* 199; Heb 5:14). By adding a comment on the relative value of physical training and training in godliness (similar to the arguments of the moralists), the author turns the metaphor against his opponents. The physical training that is of "some" value (literally, "for [only] a little") must be, in this context, a disparaging comment on the opponents' ascetic demands. In contrast, training in godliness—for example, in the religious life the author advocates—is profitable "in every way."

The letter's third "sure saying" formula appears here in the expansive form of 1:15 (cf. 3:1a). There is some debate as to whether it refers to the comment in verse 8 or to the theological assertion in verse 10. The former seems more likely since the word "for" in verse 10 introduces that verse as a comment on what has preceded, not as the central point of the passage. That central point is the superior value of godliness over profane myths and dubious asceticism, and the "sure saying" confirms it.

Verse 10 picks up the imagery of physical training again ("we toil and struggle") and expands the theological rationale for it. Because this section of the letter is a personal address to Timothy, not instructions to the church as a whole, "we" seems to refer to Paul and Timothy in their struggle against the opposing teachers and on behalf of the gospel, not to the common struggle of all believers to win salvation. The reference to the "living God" is appropriate here (cf. 3:15): It is only such a God that can offer the real promise of life (v. 8). The next clause, which describes God as "the Savior of all people," picks up the consistent inclusive emphasis of these letters (2:4, 6; 3:16; 6:13) and highlights the contrast with the opponents, who apparently restricted salvation to an ascetic few. The final clause, though, is puzzling ("especially of those who believe"), for, linked with the preceding clause, it seems to imply salvation of some sort for all, even those who do not believe. Such a concept goes beyond this author's views, inclusive though they may be (see, e.g., 1:20; Titus 1:16; 3:10-11). The clause has therefore been understood to mean that God is potentially the Savior of all people, but only actually the Savior of those who believe. Some evidence has been found to suggest that the Greek word translated "especially" *(malista)* means in this context something like "that is to say," in which case the final clause corrects the theological exuberance of the preceding one (Skeat 1979).

4:11-16: This passage is an extensive list of instructions to Timothy, all couched in the second person singular imperative. Some instructions concern his responsibility to provide an ethical role model for the members of the Christian community (v. 12, see also Titus 2:7), but most address his special duties as worship leader of the church, and teaching receives particularly prominent attention (vv. 11, 13, 16). Motives or warrants for obedience are occasionally inserted (vv. 15*b*, 16*b*) and a fairly extensive reminder of Timothy's ordination (v. 14*b*) serves as the theological anchor for the whole passage.

◊ ◊ ◊ ◊

The opening summary statement (v. 11) can just as easily be regarded as the conclusion of verses 6-10. The reference to "these things" (Gk. *tauta*) echoes 3:14 and 4:6. In each place the specific referent of the words is unclear—and unimportant. The repeated refrain ties the somewhat disjointed exhortations together and provides a sort of thematic unity to the letter. A very similarly worded statement is found at 6:2*b*, and the two sentences bracket and emphasize instructions that seem to be of particular importance (4:11–6:2).

The reference to despising Timothy's youth comes somewhat as a surprise, for the letter has thus far projected an image of him as a mature, responsible church leader. It may simply be one of the numerous personal references that increase the verisimilitude of these letters (see, e.g., 1:3; 6:12; 2 Tim 1:5). Timothy was known to have been Paul's younger coworker (Phil 2:22), and Paul himself had instructed the Corinthian church not to let anyone "despise" him (1 Cor 16:10-11), though he did not link this problem to Timothy's age. On the other hand, the words may reflect a difficult issue that the church faced in its early years. The bishops and deacons, unlike the elders (see comments on 5:17), did not have implicit or explicit age requirements (3:1-13). The "natural" subordinate relationship of youth to age could thus be overturned by the appointment of a youthful church member to one of these leadership positions. It is not clear if this was an actual problem in the author's church. It was just this sort of situation, though, that led Ignatius of Antioch to admonish the church in Magnesia (Asia Minor) in the early decades of the second century "not to presume on the youth of the bishop, but to render him all respect" (Ign. *Magn.* 3.1). Within 1 Timothy, however, the reference to Timothy's youth seems to serve a more literary function, for it anticipates the next section where issues related to groups defined (in large part) by age are addressed. There the natural deference of youth to age is generally upheld (5:1-2) and while older widows are honored (5:9), younger ones are viewed as dangerously flighty (5:11). At the same time, however, "elders" are not beyond rebuke (5:19-20) and, as this verse signals, leadership categories can supersede age categories in defining the social order of the church (5:22).

The expression of concern about reactions to Timothy's youth leads most immediately, however, to a bit of advice on how to garner respect, using the common ethical motif of example (Gk. *typos*; see also Phil 3:17; 2 Thess 3:9; 1 Pet 5:3). The categories of exemplary actions listed here can be divided into two parts. First, the two all-embracing categories of speech and conduct are paired; then a triad of virtues are mentioned—love, faith, purity. This triad recalls Paul's famous one (1 Cor 13:13), but purity replaces hope as the third member. Purity (Gk. *hagneia*) can refer to sexual chastity (see 5:2) but often, as here, it has the diluted meaning of morally blameless actions. Often in public inscriptions it referred to the blameless discharge of an office, and thus it provides a transition to the exhortation of verse 13, which focuses explicitly on Timothy's responsibilities as church leader.

The three activities listed in verse 13 constituted a significant part of the worship service, which also would have included hymns, prayers, and the Lord's Supper (see 1 Cor 11:17-31; 14:26). Teaching climaxes this list and, along with exhortation (or preaching), reappears in the description of the work of elders (5:17) and in further instructions to Timothy (6:2b). This emphasis (see also v. 16) results from the author's concern over abuse of teaching by his opponents (4:1; 6:3).

These admonitions concerning worship leadership provide the context for the author's reference to the gift (Gk. *charisma*) that Timothy has received and help define it specifically as the gift for ministry. There follows a clause that, by reminding Timothy of the origin of his gift, highlights the significance of the ordained ministry in this church. Not everything, however, about the event mentioned here is clear. The prophecy, for example, can be interpreted either as a proclamation by Christian prophets before the ordination service (identifying Timothy as God's candidate) or as their exhortation to him during the ordination service itself (see comments on 1:18). The nature of the rite of laying on of hands is somewhat clearer. It has roots in the ancient conviction that the human hand could transmit blessings (Gen 48:14). In rabbinic Judaism there developed a rite in which the teacher would pass on his authority to his students at the end of their course of studies by laying his hands on their heads (see, e.g., *b. Sanh.* 13b-14a). Something of that notion of an unbroken succession of teachers is present in this passage, though the main emphasis of the Christian rite is different.

The most immediate Christian antecedent of the rite described here was probably the baptismal laying on of hands after the candidate's immersion (see Acts 8:14-17; 19:1-6), for the transmission of the Holy Spirit (or the Spirit's gifts) was central to both (see 2 Tim 1:6-7). This passage presents the elders as the ones who laid hands on Timothy and thereby transmitted to him the gift of

ministry (or the gifts necessary for ministry), and the elders themselves were apparently ordained by the same rite (see 5:22; see also
Acts 6:6; 13:3). In 2 Timothy, however, only Paul is mentioned as
taking part in the laying on of hands (2 Tim 1:6). The explanation
for this apparent discrepancy is to be found, however, in the second
letter's special emphasis on the close personal relationship between
Paul and his disciple.

The final verses add no new content to the exhortations; they
simply reinforce the ones just given. They do add, however, the
notion of progress (Gk. *prokopē*), a central concept in Stoic philosophy and one also congenial to this author's view of the importance of diligent effort (see 4:7; 2 Tim 2:3-6, 22; Plutarch *Progress
in Virtue*; Epictetus *Discourses* 1.4). The opponents also progress,
but only like gangrene, from bad to worse (2 Tim 2:17; 3:13).
Timothy's progress, however, is toward full, effective use of his gift
of ministry, which will be both visible and salvific for himself and
for the members of his church.

◊ ◊ ◊ ◊

The verses in this central section of the letter stand out from the
surrounding exhortations because they contain instructions
meant—apparently—for Timothy alone. Yet the author's real message is communicated at a different level and to a wider audience.
The flattering portrait of Timothy created by the instructions
addressed to him serves as a foil for the denunciation of the
opposing teachers in 4:1-5 and vice versa. The author expected his
community to be edified by these contrasting personal examples.

The instructions themselves highlight godliness, exemplary conduct and speech, and effective teaching, issues that are emphasized
throughout these letters. At the heart of the instructions stand two
complementary theological assertions: one defines the saving nature
of God (v. 10), the other describes the vehicle of that salvation, for
example, a properly ordained ministry that is loyal to its origins
(v. 14) and attentive to its responsibilities, especially that of good
teaching (vv. 6, 16).

Much is revealed about the author's theological concerns here in
what he does and does not mention concerning the service of

ordination. He makes no direct reference to the Spirit, though the concept of gift or *charisma* clearly implies the Spirit's role (see 1 Cor 12:4-11). Even God is not mentioned in connection with the rite here (cf. 2 Tim 1:6), though the reference to prophecy alludes to divine participation in it. The focus instead is on the imparting of a gift by direct contact with established church leaders. (By contrast, the passages in Acts where a similar ritual is depicted make no mention of the imparting of a gift [Acts 6:6; 13:1-3; 14:23]. There the edifying focus is on the role of prayer.) This essential gift, which enables and empowers for ministry, is carefully controlled through the rite of laying on of hands (see 5:22). In these letters there is no indication of spiritual gifts apart from that of ordained ministry, and those who have not participated in this rite are not divinely acknowledged or gifted for that ministry. Moreover, the rite guarantees the continuity of the church's leadership (see also Titus 1:5) and thus the reliability of the church's teaching (6:20). In the letter's context of opposing teachers and teachings, these are important points.

Though the Greek word *(charisma)* is the same, the way spiritual gifts are construed in this passage differs sharply from the way Paul described them. Here there is only one gift—that of ministry—not many, and the gift is inextricably tied to the rite of ordination. Whereas Paul thought of these gifts in terms of their dynamic manifestations through various acts of service to the community, the author of these letters views the gift more objectively as something that is "in you" (4:14) or "within you" (2 Tim 1:6). It can be present as only a latent power that must be rekindled (2 Tim 1:6) and can be neglected (4:14). It seems to be a permanent, but not always activated, presence.

This author thus agrees with Paul that divine gift and human endeavor work together. Though it is through the laying on of hands that the gift is imparted to, or implanted within, a candidate, it is the individual's responsibility to activate and utilize this divinely given potential. The rite is essential for imparting the gift, but the rite does not, according to this author, guarantee responsible use of it. Indeed, the final admonition in this section indicates that neither the rite nor the presence of the gift guarantees a person's salvation, though active exercise of the gift transforms a person into an agent of God's salvific will.

Instructions Concerning Various Groups (5:1–6:2)

This extensive passage contains instructions concerning three groups within the church—widows (5:3-16), elders (5:17-25), and slaves (6:1-2). The transition to it is effected by 5:1-2, which is grammatically part of the personal instructions to Timothy (4:6-16), is theologically rooted in the understanding of the church as the household of God (3:15), but has content that anticipates the verses that follow (5:3–6:2).

The author's rationale for treating these three groups together is not immediately clear. Other church leadership positions—bishop and deacons—were discussed together in chapter 3, but elders are considered here in rather odd company, that of widows and slaves. The latter group is also isolated from its natural context, which would be a discussion of other members of the household (cf. Titus 2:1-10; Eph 5:22–6:9). Widows appear nowhere else in these letters. Discussion of the three groups is superficially linked by the keyword "honor" (Gk. *timan;* see 5:3, 17; 6:1), but it is a more fundamental issue that has led the author of these letters to treat *these* three groups in the same context.

It is clear from the author's comments concerning the widows and the elders that certain problems have arisen in conjunction with these groups. The admonitions concerning slaves are very brief, but some indications of a problem can be discerned there as well. The section thus derives its unity from the fact that the author is addressing groups that have generated problems in the church, and the problems seem to have some connection with the opposing teachers. Thus this passage gives way to a final section that castigates these teachers and warns of their destruction (6:3-10).

The author uses a wide variety of material in this section of the letter. Exhortations abound. Some are addressed directly to Timothy and only implicitly involve the church; others (particularly those beginning with "Let . . . ") are presented to Timothy as instructions for the church. Included also are a list of qualifications similar to those for the bishop and deacons (v. 10), quotations of scripture (v. 18), and an aphorism typical of the Wisdom literature (vv. 24-25). The instructions to slaves clearly had their origin in the household management tradition that also lies behind Eph 5:22–6:9 and Col 3:18–4:1. Some parts of the passage are obscure; nevertheless, the problems the author addresses seem real and concrete.

Widows are given the most extensive treatment (fourteen verses); slaves, the least (two verses). Presumably, the sequence in which the groups are addressed says something about the relative severity of their problems.

◊ ◊ ◊ ◊

Age Groups (5:1-2): In Titus 2:2-8 the instructions concerning various age groups are more fully developed. Here they simply provide a reasonably smooth transition to the issues that form the heart of this passage. At the same time, though, they introduce an element of confusion into the text, for the Greek word translated "older man" in verse 1 in the NRSV *(presbyteros)* can designate simply an older person (as here) or someone who, by virtue of his age, was regarded as a leader (as in verse 17, where it is translated "elder"). In the NEB the word "elder" is found in both places, but the content of verses 1-2 makes it highly unlikely that the author had only church leaders in mind there. Elders could be among the "older men" referred to in verse 1, but they did not constitute or define by their leadership position the whole of the group. The passage simply anticipates the later instructions concerning elders (and older and younger women) and places those instructions under this general advice on how to speak to (literally "exhort" or "urge," see 6:2) various age groups in the church.

The advice given in these two verses is very conventional. Similar instructions can be found in the writings of Plato (*Republic* 463c) and frequently in the Wisdom literature of the Old Testament (e.g., Prov 15:28; 30:11-12; Sir 3:8; 8:6) and it became a standard piece of moral instruction throughout the ancient world. The author of this letter, though, applies conventional advice concerning relationships among household members to the church as the household of God. To ensure respect and cohesion within this community,

"Timothy"—and by extension any church member—is to relate to other church members as he would to members of his own family (but see the comment on 6:2). The particular form of the instructions found here draws on the fiction of Timothy's youth and on the letter's overarching concern for exhortation ("Speak to . . . "). It also provides a concrete example of how Timothy is to model love and purity in his behavior (4:12; 5:22).

These brief verses speak first of men and then of women. The instructions that follow take up these groups in the opposite sequence: first women (widows, vv. 3-16), then men (elders, vv. 17-25).

Widows (5:3-16): The passage opens and closes with instructions to "honor" or "assist" real widows (vv. 3, 16). The word "honor" thus has in this context clear economic implications (see also 5:17, though a different meaning is found in 6:1), but the significance of calling a widow "real" (Gk. *ontōs*) is not as obvious. Verses 4-8 highlight the destitution and ongoing piety of those "real" widows who are to be assisted by the church, but verses 9-15 provide quite different criteria for putting them "on the list" (literally, "enrolling" them): age, being a "wife of one husband," and having an established record of good deeds both in the church and in their families. The two sets of criteria are so different that it raises a question about whether the real widows and the enrolled widows constitute the same group.

Because the qualifications for putting widows "on the list" are similar to those mentioned earlier for the bishop and deacons (see 3:2-3, 12), it has been suggested that these widows held some sort of official position within the church, while the "real" widows were simply *real widows*: women whose husbands had died, who had no family members willing or able to support them, and who were thus dependent on the benevolence of the church for their survival. An office of widows certainly existed by the third century and the regulations for that office draw heavily on this passage (see *Didascalia Apostolorum* 14-15), but it is difficult to find in 1 Timothy evidence that "real" widows and "enrolled" widows were two distinct groups. The passage opens and closes on the same note of concern for real widows, and the intervening instructions contain no obvious breaks (cf. 3:11). It is likely that there was a single group, referred to either as "real" or as "enrolled" widows. In his effort to reduce the membership of this group, the author used material of various sorts, giving rise to the perception of separate groups (Bassler 1984). There were, however, widows in the church who were not members of this designated group.

Two separate problems were generated by the group: first, it strained the church's financial resources and, second, some younger members of the group were acting in ways that the author found disturbing. The second problem seems to be linked to the presence of the opposing teachers (see below) and the author's solution is a radical one. He wraps his discussion of it in the more traditional issue of limited resources, rhetorically linking them together.

The responsibility the Christian churches felt to provide assistance to women whose widowhood had left them without adequate means of support had roots deep in Jewish custom and law. Widows (and orphans) in Israel were understood to be under God's special care (Exod 22:22-24), because they were the most vulnerable persons in this patriarchal society, lacking a husband or father. More secure members of society were obligated to provide them with food and justice (Deut 24:19-22; Isa 1:17). The story of the church's early years indicates that from the beginning Christians retained this commitment to widows (Acts 6:1; 9:36-41), but at the time 1 Timothy was written, that commitment was obviously putting a financial strain on the church.

Part of the reason for this strain was that the meaning of "widow" had apparently shifted, allowing an increase in the number of women who could be included in this group. The Greek word (*chēra*) refers at the most basic level to a woman who is living without a husband. Its most common meaning, but not its only one, was a woman whose husband had died. In this passage, however, the author refers to a "pledge" (Gk. *pistis*) that the widows took, a vow that would be violated by marriage (v. 12). Clearly something more than support for bereaved women is involved here. In fact, the passage suggests that celibacy, not the death of a spouse, was the defining feature of the group, for the young widows are criticized for their desire to marry, not to *remarry* (v. 11). Apparent confirmation of this can be found in Ignatius's letter to the Smyrneans, written at about the same time, in which he sends greetings to "the virgins who are called widows" (Ign. *Smyr.* 13.1). The widows' circle thus probably consisted of virgins (see 1 Cor 7:25-38) as well as divorced women (see 1 Cor 7:10-11) and "real" widows, all of whom, it seems, had taken a vow of celibacy and were supported, at least in part, by the church.

Membership in the widows' group was obviously an attractive option for women, for its numbers had grown beyond the church's ability and willingness to support them. Part of this attractiveness was probably linked to the fact that it permitted a life free from the restrictions of patriarchal marriage and closer to the ideal that Paul had expressed (1 Cor 7:8; see also Gal 3:28). Whether the group should be construed as an "office" or not would depend in part on whether the widows had official duties, and the author does not address that question. He focuses on the problems generated by the group.

Not only did the widows impose a high financial burden on the church, they also lived a celibate life closely resembling that of the opposing teachers (4:3). In fact, the comment that some widows had "turned away to follow Satan" (v. 15) probably refers to defections to the opponents (see 4:1). Moreover, the visible activities of the widows, castigated by the author as "gadding about from house to house" (v. 13), had the potential of creating a negative reaction in the wider society, which expected women to follow a more domestic and less public pattern of behavior (see, e.g., Plutarch *Advice to Bride and Groom* 9, 30, 32). The "adversary" that the author fears will revile the church (v. 14b) is probably a suspicious and hostile outsider (see Titus 2:8). The author therefore takes steps to address all these problems. In doing so he mentions the financial strain on the church, but his words betray a deep concern to limit the opponents' influence on this group and to forestall any criticism it might generate for his church.

Verse 4 is a central piece of the author's instructions concerning the widows, but its meaning is disputed because of an odd shift in the grammatical structure of the sentence. The first clause of the sentence has a singular subject: "If a widow has children. . . . " The sentence continues, however, with a plural verb whose subject is not specified: "they should first learn. . . . " The plural verb may signal that the children and grandchildren mentioned in the previous clause are the ones who should learn, but the unheralded change of subject is awkward. Alternatively, the author may still have had widows in mind as the subject, even when shifting to the plural verb form in the second clause ("they [i.e., the widows] should learn . . . "). In this case, too, the grammar is awkward, but it is not without precedent (see 2:15).

If the first interpretation is correct, and most commentaries accept it, the author is attempting to reduce the church's financial burden by reminding Christian children of their responsibility to support their own widowed mothers. The vigor with which this author pursues this argument, denouncing anyone who does not "provide for relatives" as "worse than an unbeliever" (v. 8), points to the severity of the problem. It would appear that natural families were too willing to let the church family, the "household of God" (3:14), take over the familial responsibility of caring for destitute female relatives. Children were therefore reminded that care for their parents was a "religious duty" (Gk. *eusebein;* v. 4). The language comes from hellenistic moral discourse (see comments on 2:2), but the sentiment derives from the Decalogue (see Exod 20:12). The author picks up this concern for financial matters again in verse 16, where he expresses his desire that other people shoulder the care of widows so that "the church not be burdened."

If the second interpretation is valid, however, widows are reminded that their religious duty is first to fulfill their duties to their own families, and only secondarily to enter the widows' circle. This is promoted as the appropriate way to honor their deceased ancestors (the usual meaning of *progonoi,* translated "parents" here in the NRSV; see, however, 2 Tim 1:3). The stern reproach of verse 8 then loses the predominantly financial cast it had with the previous interpretation and is now directed against the widows themselves, to encourage them not to neglect their own natural family duties ("whoever does not *take thought for* [Gk. *pronoei*] family members . . . "). Both lines of interpretation thus match concerns of this author (i.e., economic matters and proper family relationships), but the second seems preferable, if only because it keeps the focus throughout the passage on the widows' behavior.

The author does, however, approve alternative arrangements to relieve the financial burden on the church: Christian women who were supporting widows in some way were encouraged to continue this support (v. 16). The NRSV's translation of this verse is misleading. The Greek text makes no reference to "*relatives* who are really widows," but only to "any believing woman who has widows." (It was later scribes who inserted a reference to believing *men* into the text [see NRSV textual note].) The author gives no details of the nature of the arrangement, but the story of Tabitha in Acts 9:36-42 may reflect a similar practice. We can surmise that Christian women of means, perhaps themselves widows, provided material support— food, housing, or clothing—to other widowed women in their congregation.

The author also invokes moral criteria to eliminate abuse of the circle (vv. 5-6). The constant supplications and prayers could be a reference to the duties of the widows. It emerges as the primary responsibility of the third-century widows' office (see *Didascalia Apostolorum* 15), and here it is presented as a defining trait of a "real" widow, a demonstration that she has truly "set her hope on God" (v. 5). It is not clear if these prayers were done alone or in the company of other widows; they were probably not done in the worship service, for women's participation there was restricted (2:8).

In verses 9-10 additional criteria are introduced to restrict further the membership of this group. A number of these criteria seem to be pointed both at severing the unhealthy connection between the celibate widows and the equally celibate teachers and at reducing the potential offense of the group. The author does not challenge the legitimacy of the widows' vow of celibacy, but he introduces requirements for enrollment that made membership in the group a reward for having given active service to the church *and* for having lived the domestic life expected of women. To be enrolled, a woman had to have been the wife of one husband (NRSV: "married only once," see comments on 3:2) and "one who has brought up children." Thus even as it permitted celibacy, requirements for membership in the group promoted the contemporary ideal of marriage and childbearing. A woman could only qualify for membership if she had led a life that, on the one hand, conformed to the expectations of Greco-Roman society and, on the other, was antithetical to the demands of the celibate teachers.

Advanced age was also a requirement, clear evidence that the purpose of the group was not to meet the material needs of vulnerable women, for true widowhood was no respecter of age. The age limit imposed—sixty years—was regarded in antiquity as the point of transition to old age. It was also an age at which marriage would be an improbable option.

The other requirements are activities recognized as Christian works of love. Hospitality, for example, was deeply rooted in ancient Mediterranean customs but was also widely encouraged as a Christian virtue (see 3:2; Titus 1:8) because of its theological and social implications. It reflected God's hospitable grace (Rom 12:13; 14:1; 15:7), encouraged interaction between Christian communities, and facilitated the movements of traveling Christian preachers and thus the spread of the gospel. Washing the feet of visitors was usually the responsibility of a slave. In this church the women (and perhaps also the men) performed the service for other Christians (i.e., "saints") probably as both a concrete demonstration of hospitality and a gesture of humility. Its prominence as a Christian virtue may rest on the traditions of foot washings by Jesus (John 13:1-17) and by an unnamed woman (Luke 7:44).

Younger widows—their actual age is unclear, certainly it was less than sixty—have obviously generated serious problems and they are rejected out of hand for membership in the group. The first problem lies in their inability to sustain the celibate life required of them. The way the author links alienation from Christ, a desire to marry, and violation of "their first pledge" suggests that the vow of celibacy was part of a spiritual union with Christ that was construed on the analogy of marriage. Since ordinary marriage is regarded very positively in these letters, the condemnation or judgment (Gk. *krima*) of those widows who desire to marry indicates the uniqueness and gravity of their vow. Though not specified here, this condemnation would certainly come from God (see comments on 3:6; 1 Cor 11:29-34), not simply from the community.

The second problem involves activities of the young widows, which the author defines with language reflecting harsh stereotypes of his age. Some have linked the activity the author describes as "gadding about" to house calls that were a part of the widows' duties. This is unlikely, however, for here, as in the later *Didascalia,* the visitations are identified exclusively as an abuse, not as a responsibility. What is clear is that this activity violated the prevailing ideal of a secluded domestic life for women. Indeed, the author's view is close to that of Juvenal, who condemns women who flit "from one home to another, . . . rushing boldly about the entire city" (*Satires* 6, lines 224-26, 398-99).

Additionally, the women were "saying what they should not say," indicating some problem with the content of their speech. The author does not indicate what that was, but a similar charge is leveled against the opposing teachers (Titus 1:11). Since both groups lived celibate lives, both may also have been verbally promoting this. The author's solution to all these problems was to restore the women to a patriarchal household and to a noncelibate way of life (v. 14; see also 2:15; Titus 2:4-5).

Elders (5:17-25): It is difficult to determine how much of this passage directly concerns elders. Some argue that in verse 20 the author turns to a new issue, sin and repentance, but most agree that he has elders in view throughout the passage. Some of the admonitions, however, are vague and disjointed, and it is only the context that suggests an application to the situation regarding the elders.

It is not entirely clear what that situation was. In fact, the relationship of the elders to other leadership positions mentioned in this letter is also not entirely clear. Their roots lie in the institution of synagogue elders, a group of adult men who provided general oversight of the Jewish community, especially in regard to the interpretation and application of the law. Jewish Christian churches probably retained some form of this institution. The book of Acts, for example, refers to Christian elders and apostles sharing leadership responsibilities in the Jerusalem church and participating jointly in legal decisions (Acts 15:1-29; 16:4; see also 1 Pet 5:1, where Peter, an apostle, refers to himself as an elder). It also contains references to elders in the Pauline churches (Acts 14:21-23; 20:17), though Paul's own letters do not ever mention them.

In Titus, elders are linked with the bishops (Titus 1:5-9; cf. 1 Pet 5:1-2), but here in 1 Timothy the two positions are treated separately, though there is some overlap in function. Both, for example, are expected to rule or manage the church well, to preach, and to teach (see 3:2, 5; 5:17; Titus 1:9). It is likely that these letters represent a period of consolidation of various types of leadership positions—elders from Jewish Christianity and bishops and deacons from the Gentile churches. The issue here, though, is not consolidation *per se*, but recompense and correction.

Elders who rule well are to be given "double honor," and the scriptural warrants given in verse 18 indicate clearly that here, as in 5:3, "honor" includes financial recompense. The promise of "double" honor raises the question, however, of the intended point of comparison. Is it to be double that of the widows or is the recompense of one group of elders to be double that of another?

At least two groups of elders seem to be indicated by the passage, but the line of demarcation between the groups is disputed. Some place the emphasis on "rule" and see an implied contrast between "ruling elders," who receive double recompense, and inactive elders, who receive a single share. The adverb "well," however, cannot be overlooked; it is a significant part of the author's argument, just as it was in 3:4, 12, where he insisted that the bishop and deacons must manage their households *well*. Here the author seems to assume that all elders rule but proposes double recompense for those who rule *well*, with a particular focus on their teaching and preaching skills and an intentional contrast to those who not only do not rule well but have even fallen into sin (vv. 19-20). Since the latter would hardly receive any recompense at all, the widows' allotment seems to be the standard of comparison (von Lips 1979, 110), but the text is unclear on this point.

As a warrant for his suggestion that certain elders deserve double recompense, the author cites two texts. The first is Deut 25:4, cited also by Paul in 1 Cor 9:9 to support his argument that apostles have a right to receive payment for their work, though he himself refused to make use of that right—at least in Corinth. The second is a saying of Jesus quoted in the form found in Luke 10:7 (cf. Matt 10:10). Paul also alludes to this saying—but does not quote it—as part of the argument mentioned above (1 Cor 9:14). This suggests that the author of 1 Timothy probably knew Paul's letter to the church in Corinth and borrowed his warrants from it.

Unlike Paul, though, this author introduces *both* sayings as scripture (Gk. *graphē*). This is the only place in the Pastoral Letters where the Jewish Scripture is cited *as scripture* (cf. 2 Tim 2:19), even though elsewhere the author professes an exceedingly high regard for these sacred writings (2 Tim 3:16).

This is also one of only two places in the New Testament where a Christian writing is cited as "scripture" (cf. 2 Pet 3:15-16). It is not clear if the writing in question is the Gospel of Luke or a collection of sayings that served as a source for that Gospel. Much depends on the dating of 1 Timothy and the dating of Luke's Gospel, and both are widely debated points. Some noncanonical writings of the early second century begin tentatively to refer to Christian writings as scripture, or use with them the standard formula for introducing scripture, "it is written" (see *2 Clem.* 2.4; *Barn.* 4.14). It is only later in that century, however, that the term came into widespread use for New Testament writings. The use of the word here does not imply the existence of a formal New Testament canon. It is much more likely that it reflects the liturgical practice of reading Christian writings alongside Jewish Scripture in the worship service, so that the term for the latter came to be associated with the former.

Having argued for providing financial "honor" for elders who rule well, the author moves to an issue that seems of even greater importance to him: procedures for dealing with elders who have been charged with certain unspecified sins. First, however, he protects the elders from irresponsible accusations by invoking the Old Testament rule (though not identified as such) of two or three witnesses (Deut 19:15; see also Matt 18:16; John 8:17; 2 Cor 13:1). Next, though, he calls for public rebuke or exposure of those who persist in sin (v. 20). Elders are not explicitly mentioned in verse 20, and some argue that the author begins here a general discussion of how to deal with sinning Christians (see vv. 20, 22, 24). The context, however, indicates otherwise, for 5:3–6:2 seems to be devoted to special groups. The exhortations in verses 20-25 are, however, somewhat disjointed and acquire coherence only by subsuming them under the topic of elders.

Rebuking—especially rebuking opponents—is the clear responsibility of the bishop (Titus 1:9), and these instructions to Timothy (see also 2 Tim 4:2), like those to Titus (see Titus 1:13; 2:15), serve also as guidelines for regular church leaders. The sorts of offenses that should be met with a rebuke are nowhere given. The elders are simply described as "sinning," a word used to describe actions of Paul before his conversion (1:15), of the "silly women" deceived by the opponents (2 Tim 3:6), and of the opponents themselves (Titus 3:11). It is possible, but unprovable, that elders who are "sinning" are those who have joined these opposing teachers. Problems with these teachers form a recurring theme in these letters, and they are scathingly attacked in the passage that follows (6:3-5). This hypothesis would also account for the author's strong interest in rewarding those elders who have performed their teaching responsibilities *well*.

There is an apparent contradiction between the instructions given here ("rebuke" the elders who are sinning) and the opening instruction (5:1) *not* to speak harshly to an older man (literally "rebuke," though a different verb is used). The author probably views verses 17-25 as an elaboration of the opening exhortation, though, for the constraints he places on the punishment of the elders (vv. 19, 21) can be construed as avoiding excessive harshness. The positive pedagogical value of the rebuke is emphasized (see also 1:20; 2 Tim 2:25), though it is not clear whether "the rest" who will be instructed by the disciplinary process are the rest of the elders or the rest of the church. The former seems more likely.

The author introduces the next instructions with an impressive vow, which probably had liturgical origins (see also 6:13; 2 Tim 4:1). The reference to "elect angels" to round out the triad is odd; the nearest parallel can be found in Rev 1:4-5, where the seven spirits are archangels (see Rev 8:2). The presence of the angels also evokes the concept of apocalyptic judgment (see Mark 13:26-27; Rev 14:6-11), which, though muted in these letters, would be particularly appropriate for this warning. The vow thus lends strong emphasis to the warning against prejudice or partiality, which would include both excessive harshness or undue leniency.

Some interpret verse 22 as a warning not to restore a penitent sinner too quickly, an interpretation that fits the view that verses 20-25 concern sinners in general. However, the action referred to is literally a laying on of hands, and this is not documented as a rite of restoration before the third century. In these letters, laying on of hands consistently refers to ordination (4:14; 2 Tim 1:6), and that is the meaning here as well. In light of the problem of "sinful" elders, the author encourages a period of testing or investigation of candidates before ordination (see also 3:10). A couple of general exhortations follow that are probably meant to suggest that a church official is in some way responsible for sins committed by anyone he has too hastily ordained.

The relevance of verse 23 is a mystery. It reflects the philosophical ideal of moderation, eschewing the extremes of total abstinence and drunkenness (see Aristotle *Nichomachean Ethics* 3.10.1-12.10), but it seems unconnected with the surrounding argument. The reference to purity in verse 22 may have suggested this warning against overzealous purity. On the other hand, if the problem with the elders was in any way connected with the presence of the ascetic teachers (4:3), this bit of advice may be a jab at the teachers' abstinence. The medicinal use of wine was widespread (cf. Luke 10:34).

The passage closes with a pronouncement about the inevitable surfacing of both sin and virtue. Though general in nature, the content of these verses places the exhortations about sinful elders within the shadow of the final judgment. These verses also provide support and rationale for the warning about not ordaining with undue haste: It may take time for some sins to emerge. The verses serve equally well as a rationale for the instructions concerning widows, where the issue was also to some extent one of recognizing sinners and distinguishing them from the virtuous (vv. 6, 10, 15).

Slaves (6:1-2): The brief admonitions concerning slaves that conclude this section of the letter seem oddly out of place. They do not concern an "official" church group (cf. the discussions of widows and elders); they employ the key word "honor" in a very different way (i.e., without any financial overtones; cf. 5:3, 17); and they bear no obvious relationship to the age groups that provide the general rubric of this section (see 5:1-2). They appear, then, almost as an afterthought following on 5:24-25, which in a way summarized the preceding argument. The only possible connection between these verses and those that precede is that here too instructions are given to a group within the church that has been the source of some tension or discord.

Instructions to, or about, slaves are found in Christian writings, both canonical and noncanonical, dating from the later decades of the first century and the beginning of the second. The tone of these instructions is consistently conservative: Christianity did not understand itself to be a revolutionary movement even though its teachings had clear reformatory implications. Thus slaves were exhorted to be obedient to their masters, while masters were themselves often instructed not to be harsh with their slaves (Eph 6:5-9; Col 3:22–4:1; 1 Pet 2:18-25; *Did.* 4.10; *Barn.* 19.7).

The background for this formulation lies in the discussions of household management that were common in philosophical writings since the time of Plato and Aristotle. These discussions often included references to specific household duties in which the proper relationship of various members of the household to other members was defined, usually in paired groupings (Balch 1981). The widespread interest in domestic responsibilites in early Christianity reflects the particular social circumstances of that movement.

Most social groups in Greco-Roman society (e.g., clubs, guilds, and associations) were fairly homogeneous. Christian groups, on the other hand, were composed of members from various levels of society—Jew and Greek, slave and free, male and female—but they met in circumstances in which social standing was to have no significance (Gal 3:28). They ate together at table, and they called each other "brother" and "sister," though they may have been, in fact, master and slave. This ethos of equality within the church was in some tension with the social realities of their lives outside the church, especially in the extended family, which was hierarchically defined. It created real problems for church members who had to move between these social worlds or deal with other church members in terms of both social worlds.

To compound the problem, Roman magistrates were highly suspicious of foreign cults for a number of reasons, including the widespread conviction that such cults—and Christianity was considered one of them—disrupted proper social relations and customs. Thus, to silence such criticism and to address the social tensions within the church, Christian writers reinforced the patterns of social behavior that the wider society expected of all its members.

Slaves are instructed to honor their masters. Honor is not, of course, a reference to financial recompense in this context (cf. 5:3, 17) but to the social attitude and behavior that, with shame, constituted the "pivotal values" of the Mediterranean world (Malina 1981, 25-50). The author calls on slaves to acknowledge through their attitude and behavior the higher social rank of their masters and to show them respect.

The advice to slaves in 6:1-2 does not have any accompanying instructions to masters (see also 1 Pet 2:18-25). Part of the reason for this is that the author is not interested simply in the slave's relationship to the master and vice versa, but in the effect of slaves' behavior on the community, especially on the way the community was perceived by outsiders. Thus slaves are treated along with elders and widows, where the significance of the actions of these groups for the community is of paramount importance. One cannot discount, however, the possibility that this author is simply not sensitive to the slaves' perspective and so does not include the usual admonitions to masters for fair treatment.

The exhortation in verse 1 matches that in Titus 2:9-10, and the presupposition in both is that insubordinate behavior by Christian slaves can bring the Christian message into disrepute, while the slaves' properly submissive behavior will enhance it. The second verse, however, addresses the specific problem of Christian slaves who have Christian masters and who feel very keenly the tension between their subordinate social status and their equal religious status. Thus they object to having to serve as slaves to those who are their Christian "brothers" (NRSV: "members of the church"). The author counters by mentioning two other names for Christians:

"faithful" (NRSV: "believers") and "beloved." The point is not well developed, but it seems to be that since the masters are faithful to, and beloved by, God, slaves should also be faithful in their service to those who call them by the name of (beloved) "brother."

The NRSV further describes the masters as "those who benefit by their (i.e., the slaves') service," but the Greek word translated "service" *(euergesia)* usually defines the benefaction rendered by a social superior to those below, not the other way around. The title *Euergetēs* ("Benefactor") was, for example, often adopted by hellenistic rulers. Thus the clause should refer to the work of the master, and the alternative NRSV translation, which presents the masters as those "who devote themselves to good deeds," seems preferable even though it gives a highly optimistic description of their behavior. The logic of the sentence is weak in either case, and the author's discussion of the topic is too brief to provide real clarity about his meaning.

◊ ◊ ◊ ◊

The conservative and conventional social ethics of this author are particularly prominent in this passage: younger women are barred from participating in the form of spirituality nurtured by the widows' group and restricted instead to domestic roles; slaves are exhorted to serve their masters—whether Christian or pagan—with proper honor and respect. The author clearly feared—with some cause—that dramatic changes in the status or behavior of women and slaves would bring opprobrium on the church, and he zealously sought to avoid that.

Paul, too, expressed concern for the opinions of outsiders when admonishing the Thessalonians to live quietly (1 Thess 4:11-12) or the Corinthians to restrain their ecstatic spiritual outbursts (1 Cor 14:23-24). Giving no offense to others was a basic feature of his apostolic work—and he encouraged his churches to do likewise—for his ultimate goal was to facilitate the conversion of outsiders and so to spread the gospel message (1 Cor 10:31–11:1). Yet Paul's apocalyptic conviction that the "present form of this world is passing away" (1 Cor 7:31) tempered somewhat the conservative thrust of this concern. Thus he promoted the gift of celibacy in spite of its radical social implications (1 Cor 7:8-11, 32-35) and even challenged—in a very circumspect way—the compatibility of slavery with Christian love in his letter to Philemon. However, the author of the Pastoral Letters, beset by celibate opponents and suspicious outsiders and less convinced than Paul was about the passing of the present form of the world, radically restricts the availability of the option of celibacy, though he does not eliminate it altogether. He also advocates a more conservative position on slavery.

Slavery supported the economic structure of the entire Roman Empire and with few exceptions the New Testament writings passively presuppose or actively endorse it. The arguments in support of the institution, however, vary widely. Paul, for example, draws on Stoic thought to argue that the condition of external slavery is of little concern to those who "belong to the Lord" (1 Cor 7:21-24), a position that permitted him some flexibility in dealing with the concrete case of Onesimus and Philemon. In other writings, slaves are encouraged to view their service to their masters as a form of service to God or to "the Lord," an argument that provided firm theological support for the institution (Eph 6:7; Col 3:23; *Did.* 4.10). The author of the Pastoral Letters, on the other hand, rests his argument on pragmatic grounds: The slaves' obedience promotes the success of the Christian message, not because it is in any way a reflection of Christ's obedience (1 Pet 2:18-25), but because it is a pattern of behavior approved by Roman society. It will not cause offense. Behind the pragmatism, though, there is a deeper theological issue: God's desire that everyone be saved (2:4). Compliance with the social mores of the hellenistic world (where this was not thought to compromise the gospel) increased the acceptability of the Christian message and thus promoted God's ultimate goal of salvation for all.

The extended patriarchal family is thus the norm for the letter's social exhortations. The family or household is also the model for the church (3:15) and there is, in fact, a remarkable interchange of church and family roles in these exhortations. The family position and responsibilities of widows have, for example, been eclipsed by their official status and role within the church, though the author views this situation as one in need of some correction. Nevertheless, the qualifications for membership in this group remain a mixture of deeds done in and for the family and those done in and for the church. Slaves' obedience, though clearly a domestic concern, is treated in terms of its impact on the church's mission, so that the church as a whole acquires a stake in their behavior.

There were, however, points at which the church as the household of God and the individual households that constituted it coexisted in some tension. As members of God's household, all Christians were siblings and addressed one another with the kinship language of "brother" and "sister," but as members of real households these Christians had different roles. They were fathers or husbands or masters; they were children or wives or slaves. When conflict arose between roles in the two "households," one system had to prevail. Paul, for example, drew heavily on the Christian kinship language of "brother" to convince Philemon to modify his family role enough to accept the runaway slave Onesimus back without reprisal (Phlm 15-16), and perhaps even to free his "brother" (the probable intent of Phlm 21). The author of 1 Timothy takes the opposite approach, rejecting the slaves' appeal to Christian kinship to modify their servile social status and insisting instead on obedient submission as their Christian duty.

The author's instructions concerning slaves and women thus reflect a serious problem, one faced by any religious group seeking to make converts: how to maintain the distinctive (but, to outsiders, sometimes offensive) theological and social features of the group while building enough bridges to the outside world to make conversions possible. The author of the Pastoral Letters consistently chooses a conservative social route.

Opposing Teachers and the "Man of God" (6:3-16)

As he moves toward the letter's close, the author returns to the topic of the opposing teachers and gives his longest and sharpest polemic against them in this letter (vv. 3-5). As before, the author includes a contrasting portrait of the faithful church leader, communicated in this instance through a series of instructions to Timothy (vv. 11-16; see also 4:11-16). Many themes from the opening chapter surface again here: the contrast between sound teaching and empty speculations or controversies (vv. 3-4; 1:4, 10); similar vice lists (vv. 4-5; 1:9-10) and doxologies (vv. 15-16; 1:17); reminders of Timothy's ordination (vv. 12-14; 1:18); the motif of the good fight or struggle (v. 12; 1:18). The new element in this passage is the accusation that greed is what motivates the opponents and the corresponding development of instructions on the proper attitude for a church leader to take toward money. In between these two passages, the author has insisted that "real" widows and elders who "rule well" be "honored" with monetary support. The polemic against the greed of the false teachers thus serves simultaneously as a warning to these other groups, or to those who might join these groups, not to abuse the church's generosity.

The passage falls naturally into two parts: the attack on the opponents with its supporting teaching on the dangers of greed (vv. 3-10), and the exhortations to Timothy with their supporting reminder of his ordination charge (vv. 11-16). The two parts can be discussed separately, though as in 1:18-20 and 4:1-10, the author intended maximum edification and warning to come from pondering the contrasting portraits of faithful and false church leaders together.

◊ ◊ ◊ ◊

Vices of the Opponents (6:3-10): The author moves from an admonition to Timothy to "teach and urge these duties" (a summary reference to the preceding instructions; see also 3:14; 4:6, 11) to a warning about anyone who "teaches otherwise," signaling the contrast that will be developed in the following verses. These words also recall the letter's opening warning, repeating the same Greek verb *(heterodidaskalein)* found in 1:3. Much of the content of verses 3-5 repeats or echoes that earlier warning: the presentation of the correct teaching as "sound" or healthy (1:10; see also 2 Tim 1:13; 4:3; Titus 1:9; 2:1); the charge that opponents lack any trace of understanding (1:7; see also Titus 1:15-16); the description of their activities as senseless, speculative verbal disputes (1:4; see also 6:20;

2 Tim 2:23; Titus 3:9); and the use of a vice list to indicate the moral consequences of such activities (1:9-11; see also 2 Tim 3:2-5).

The author also repeats, but more clearly this time, his double emphasis on the connections between correct teaching and the religious and moral way of life defined as "godliness" (Gk. *eusebeia;* see 2:2) and between "other" teaching and moral chaos (see especially 1:8-11; also Titus 1:16). This "chaos" appears almost exclusively as antisocial attitudes and activities that destroy the social cohesion of the household of God (cf. Rom 1:29-31). The opponents themselves, those who "teach otherwise," are dismissed as people who are "sick" (NRSV: "morbid craving"), deluded (a better translation of *tetyphōtai* than the NRSV's "conceited"; see also 3:6), and depraved (see also Titus 3:11).

On the other hand, the "teaching that is in accordance with godliness" is paired with "the sound words of our Lord Jesus Christ," though the meaning and significance of the latter phrase is disputed. Some take it to be a reference to the basic Christian message, for example, the gospel concerning Jesus, so that the two paired phrases are essentially equivalent (Fee 1988). Yet the author of these letters prefers the singular "word" for this usage (see 2 Tim 2:9; 4:2 [NRSV: "message"]; Titus 1:9). The plural here seems to indicate actual "words" of Jesus, probably known to the author from a pregospel collection (see comments on 5:18).

The climax of the polemic, and (as the subsequent argument reveals) its obvious goal, is the charge that the opponents' actions are motivated by greed. It is difficult to assess the accuracy of this charge. It was a standard piece of the philosophical polemics from which this author borrows so heavily. As such it may be rhetorical window dressing, another device by which the author defames his opponents. On the other hand, though, it is a nearly constant motif in these letters, anticipated in the qualifications for bishop and deacons (3:3, 8; see also Titus 1:7) and repeated in subsequent attacks on the opponents (2 Tim 3:2; Titus 1:11), and the charge may in fact have substance. If so, it is impossible to know precisely how the opposing teachers hoped to acquire "gain" (Gk. *porismos*) through "godliness" (Gk. *eusebeia*), though the church's willingness to provide financial support to some groups (5:3, 17) suggests possible avenues for reward.

The remainder of this section (vv. 6-10) develops at some length the theme of appropriate and inappropriate gain, marking that as the centerpiece of the author's warning in verses 3-5. The whole has been nicely structured: After the warning about the opponents' greed or desire for "gain" (v. 5b), the meaning of true "gain" is explained and defended (vv. 6-8), followed by a graphic description of the consequences of greed (vv. 9-10a). The author then returns the argument to its starting point by mentioning the concrete example of the greed (and apostasy) of his opponents.

The actual gain that comes from godliness is not specified, for the author has already defined it earlier in the letter as "promise for both the present life and the life to come" (4:8), that is, as something that both enhances the present life and leads to eternal life. The mention of "contentment" adds a requirement that sounds very Stoic, for the Greek word (autarkeia, usually translated "self-sufficiency") represents a favorite virtue of this philosophical school and of the Cynics as well (Marcus Aurelius To Himself 6.16; Epictetus Discourses 3.13.7). The author's very strong Pauline sense of grace precludes, however, the Stoic notion of total self-determination (see, e.g., 1:12-16), and the concept of "contentment" with one's present (financial) circumstances captures better the author's meaning here, as his subsequent argument shows (see also Phil 4:11).

The author supports his claim about contentment (which supplants godliness as the focus of attention in this portion of the argument) with two popular maxims. The first (v. 7) is best known in the form found in the book of Job: "Naked I came from my mother's womb, and naked shall I return there" (Job 1:21), but it is well documented throughout the Wisdom literature (Eccl 5:15; Wis 7:6) and appears in the writings of Seneca as well (Epistles 102.25). The form in 1 Timothy is somewhat odd, for the two parts of the saying are linked by the Greek word hoti, which means "because" (not "so that," as the NRSV translates it). Though later scribes made modifications to improve the sense of the text (adding words that change the meaning to "it is true [or clear] that . . . "), the basic meaning of the original is clear enough.

The second saying (v. 8) is even more widely attested, with versions of it found in Israel's Wisdom literature (e.g., Sir 29:21), hellenistic philosophy (e.g., Plutarch *Dinner of the Seven Wise Men* 12), and the sayings of Jesus (Matt 6:25-34; see also Heb 13:5). The rigor of the saying—limiting one's necessary possessions to food and clothing (literally "covering")—is striking in this letter, for elsewhere its author attacks the asceticism of his opponents, which could not have been much more rigorous than this, and celebrates the enjoyment of all gifts of creation (4:4), including wine (5:23). Moreover, a few verses later in this chapter the rich are advised on how to conduct their lives, and while this does involve generosity with their possessions, it does not involve reducing them to mere food and covering.

Some of the apparent discrepancy is eliminated by recognizing that at this point in his argument the author probably has the behavior of church leaders in mind. In contrast to the greed that motivates the opponents, the life of the true church leader should be characterized by an attitude of contentment. It is the presence of this trait rather than the absence of material possessions that is significant. The qualifications for bishop and deacons show, for example, that men aspiring to these positions were expected to have considerably more than food and bare shelter. They managed extended households and were expected to extend hospitality to visitors. The maxims cited here are thus not intended to promote radical self-denial as a normative way of life. Instead they encourage an attitude that is the prerequisite for a life free from corrupting greed.

In the final verses the author uses dramatic metaphors to describe the fate of the one who is motivated by greed. Such persons fall into a snare (a favorite metaphor, see also 3:7); they pierce or impale themselves with many woes; they plunge like sinking ships (see also 1:19) into ruin and destruction, by which is meant not financial or moral ruin but eschatological, that is, final ruin (see 1 Thess 5:3). The author closes the argument with another maxim that summarizes the philosophical view of greed ("the love of money is the root of all kinds of evil," cf. Dio Chrysostom *Orations* 17.6; Diogenes Laertius 6.50), and then returns to the concrete case of the opposing teachers, the obvious referent of the "some" who have wandered away from the faith (see 4:1).

Exhortations to Timothy (6:11-16): The significance of this passage is widely debated. It appears to many that it interrupts the discussion of proper Christian attitudes toward wealth contained in verses 6-10 and 17-19, thus creating a disjointed and somewhat ineffectual conclusion to the letter. Others, however, see in these verses a carefully crafted complement to the argument of verses 3-10, a positive example of church leadership that stands in stark and deliberate contrast to the negative behavior of the opposing teachers (see 2 Tim 3:14; 4:5; Titus 2:1, which also open with the words, "but you . . . "). This positive portrait is communicated through exhortations to Timothy, in which a virtue list replaces the vice list that described the moral consequences of the opponents' teaching, the promise of the reward of eternal life replaces the threat of ruin and destruction, and the good confession replaces crass greed as the driving force for behavior. The exalted, formulaic language indicates that much of this passage derives from Christian liturgy, but there is some dispute over which liturgy is reflected: baptism or ordination.

The language of the passage, especially the words of verses 11-12, seems well suited to a liturgy of baptism. The opening exhortation for Timothy to separate himself from sinful ways is appropriate to this rite (see, e.g., 1 Cor 6:9-11), as is the call to "take hold of the eternal life." The "good fight of the faith" suggests the rigors that the newly baptized Christian will face in the world (see 2 Tim 3:12). Here and in 2 Tim 4:7, the image is one of competitive sports. In 1:18, on the other hand, different words are used that suggest a hostile military engagement (Pfitzner 1967).

Though the words suggest baptism, the context points to the rite of ordination. The author's point is to set the "man of God," his behavior and his motivation, against the behavior and motivation of the one who "teaches otherwise" (v. 3). Competing church leadership roles are envisioned here, and a reminder of the ordination liturgy is most appropriate to the author's argument.

The epithet, "man of God," confirms this hypothesis. It is used in only one other place in these letters, where the "man of God" is assumed to be engaged in the tasks of teaching, reproof, correction, and training in righteousness (2 Tim 3:16-17). These, however, are the tasks of the church leader, not the newly baptized Christian (2 Tim 2:24-25; Titus 1:9). (The Greek words, *anthrōpos theou,* are not as gender specific as the English translation would suggest, but since church leadership, especially public teaching, was almost exclusively reserved for men [see above, pp. 59-63, 70], the NRSV's translation is appropriate.)

The origin of the title lies in the OT, where it refers to those engaged in special leadership roles in Israel: Moses (Deut 33:1), David (2 Chron 8:14), Samuel (1 Sam 9:6), and various prophets (1 Sam 2:27; 1 Kgs 13:1). In later usage, Philo of Alexandria refers to Israel's priests and prophets as "men of God," though he uses this term to emphasize their transcendence over the corporeal world rather than their roles as leaders of Israel and spokespersons for God (*Giants* 61; *Unchangeableness of God* 139). In the *Letter of Aristeas,* all Israelite men are called "men of God," yet they are given this title only insofar as they function as priests, devoted to the worship of God and separated from the concerns of the world. It is doubtful that the author of the Pastoral Letters intends the spiritual overtones of these later writings, for otherworldliness is far from the center of his concern. The persistent link, though, between this title and leadership roles in Israel strongly suggests a similar link in 1 Timothy, which has a pervasive concern for qualified, orthodox leaders.

Other aspects of the passage support this interpretation. Variations of the phrase, "fight the good fight," appear in several places in these letters, but always in the context of a discussion of church leadership (1:18; 2 Tim 4:7). Though a baptism may have many witnesses, the author of the Pastoral Letters emphasizes elsewhere the witnesses to Timothy's ordination (2 Tim 2:2; see also 1 Tim 4:14). In fact, baptism is nowhere else mentioned in these letters, while references to ordination are frequent (1:18; 4:14; 5:22; 2 Tim 1:6; 2:2).

Thus it seems that the author refers here to Timothy's ordination confession, that the wording of the passage is influenced by ordination liturgy, and that the single "commandment" that Timothy is charged to keep (v. 14) is not (as some argue) the whole Christian tradition or the ethical demands of verse 11 but his specific ordination charge. The ordination liturgy may have included elements of the earlier baptismal liturgy, thus accounting for the baptismal perspective in verses 11-12. The context, though, places the emphasis on the ceremony that defined the public charge, the model behavior, and the religious convictions of the one who was ordained properly to lead and teach the church.

The virtue list in verse 11 does not focus on behavior peculiar to Christian leaders, nor does it focus specifically on the conflict with the opposing teachers. It simply lists common Christian virtues that stand in general contrast to the vices ascribed to the opponents. A similar list appears in 2 Tim 2:22, headed, as here, by "righteousness." Righteousness in these verses is upright conduct (as in Matt 3:15; 5:6; 1 Pet 3:14), one of the cardinal moral virtues (see Plutarch *Chance* 2), not God's gift (cf. Rom 4:5; 10:3-4). In Greek philosophy and especially in hellenistic Judaism, it was often paired, as here, with godliness in order to cover all aspects of behavior: that appropriate to one's relationship to other humans and that appropriate to one's relationship to God or to the gods (Aristotle *On Virtues and Vices* 1250b; Josephus *Ant.* 6 §265; 8 §121; see comment on 2:2). Faith or faithfulness (Gk. *pistis*) also appears on virtue lists in philosophical writings, but when paired with love and endurance it also echoes the familiar Pauline triad (Rom 5:3-5; 1 Cor 13:13). Throughout the Pastoral Letters faith and love are nearly inseparable virtues (see, e.g., 1:14; 2:15; 4:12; 2 Tim 1:13). Gentleness is an attribute particularly prized in these letters (3:3; 2 Tim 2:25; cf. Titus 1:7) and noticeably lacking in the opponents (6:4; 2 Tim 3:2-4).

The double acclamation in verse 13 transcends in style and content the demands of the immediate context, marking it as a fragment of established liturgy. God's creative or generative activity is acclaimed, echoing the thought both of Paul (Rom 11:36; 1 Cor 8:6) and of contemporary philosophers (see Acts 17:28). Though on one level this refers to God's primeval creation, on another level it refers to God's eschatological giving of life, and it is this second meaning that the context highlights (4:8; 6:12, 19). The acclamation of God is developed further in the doxology of verses 15-16.

The acclamation of Jesus focuses more narrowly on the "good confession" given before Pontius Pilate. The content of this confession is not mentioned, though presumably the author had something like Matt 27:11 or John 18:33-37 in mind. What is significant, however, is the fact that Jesus models the act of courageous confessing in circumstances of real or potential affliction. At the same time Jesus is also the content of subsequent Christian confession, which would invariably include the words, "Jesus Christ is Lord" (see v. 14; also 1:2; Rom 10:9; 1 Cor 12:3).

The author moves from the confession of the earthly Jesus to the return of the Lord Jesus, but he does not use the usual term for this event (Gk. *parousia*). Instead he refers to the "manifestation" or epiphany (Gk. *epiphaneia*) of the Lord, and thereby introduces a characteristic emphasis of his Christology. Indeed, epiphany language defines the Christology of these letters (Oberlinner 1980). Here it is the second coming that is called an epiphany (see also 2 Tim 4:8), emphasizing the fact that that event, which constitutes God's decisive intervention on behalf of the faithful, will make manifest the divine glory of the risen Jesus (Titus 2:13). Elsewhere, however, Jesus' first appearance on earth is also called an epiphany, for through it God's saving will is made manifest (Titus 3:4-5). Here it is not the content of the epiphany that is stressed, but the fact that it will occur at a God-determined time (see also 2:6), which marks the outer limit of Timothy's commission (cf. 3:14). The nearness of that time is not stressed (cf. Rom 13:11-12), but this epiphany will bring with it the fulfillment of the promise of eternal life (v. 12) and the public confirmation of Timothy's good confession (v. 12). In the meanwhile, this good confession will proclaim, and thus in its own way make manifest, both the glory of Christ and the saving will of God.

God, of course, is the one who brings about the epiphany of Christ; the giving of life, both temporal and eternal; and the provision of all good things (6:17). The author thus concludes this portion of the letter with a solemn doxology, which may have been part of the ordination liturgy but which is ultimately derived from the hellenistic synagogue. It contains typical monotheistic emphases ("only Sovereign," "he alone who has immortality"; see also 1:17; Rom 16:27) and biblical epithets like "Lord of lords" (Deut 10:17; Ps 136:3). "King of kings" originated as a title of eastern monarchs (see Dan 2:37), but it was taken over for God—with a polemical thrust against ruler cults—in the Jewish synagogues (see 3 Macc 5:35). While Greeks and Romans claimed immortality for their heroes and emperors (Dio Cassius *Roman History* 56.41.9), this doxology insists that God *alone* is untouched by death. The notions of the invisibility and inaccessibility of God have both Greek and Hebrew roots (Exod 33:18-23; Pseudo-Aristotle *On the Cosmos* 399a). Together with the very similar doxology in 1:17, this acclamation keeps the letter's theology firmly focused on God. God's total sovereignty is proclaimed as the foundation of Christian obedience and hope and God's absolute inaccessibility is the necessary precondition of the epiphany function of the Christ-event. This triumphant and exalted liturgical language stands in sharp contrast to the prosaic philosophical maxims that dominated verses 3-10 and turns the argument back to its theological foundation.

◊ ◊ ◊ ◊

The second portion of this passage (vv. 11-16) is rich in theological assertions whose meanings are discussed above, but these assertions are apparently cited as part of the liturgy of an ordination service. It is the implicit reminder of the moral and theological consequences of the service itself that is of real importance to the author's argument. He has charged the opposing teachers with greed: They are not only willfully ignorant of the truth, they are also motivated in their actions by the desire to reap some financial gain from their religious posturing. By this allusion to the ordination service, the author indicates what motivates the true "man of God": a call to faith and to ministry (see also 1:18); a public confession in imitation of Jesus' own confession, intimating a life of hardship rather than immediate gain; a solemn and sacred commission; and an understanding that the second manifestation of Jesus will require an accounting of how well one has fulfilled that commission (see

2 Tim 4:1-8). At that time the true "gain" that comes from godliness will be realized (6:6; see also 4:8). The doxological conclusion defines the theological power behind the commission, and its reverent listing of divine titles and attributes contrasts sharply with the depraved theological disputes of the opponents (6:4-5).

The author develops this argument secure in the conviction that truth has been fully established and perfectly preserved in the church, and that this truth warrants no dissension or discussion. As in earlier passages of this sort, it is impossible to penetrate behind the author's stereotypical polemics to determine exactly what his opponents were doing and saying. We see their activities only through the lens of his hostile interpretation. In other less hostile contexts, the Greek word translated "controversy" in verse 4 (*zētēseis*) means little more than discussions or investigations. What to the opponents might have seemed legitimate and necessary investigations into the truth of the Christian witness are pilloried by this author as "sick" and depraved wranglings. His refusal to engage their ideas in sustained debate deprives us of the evidence necessary for rendering a judgment on the validity of his charges and thus on the ethical probity of his tactics.

The attack on greed, however, raises an issue that has plagued Christianity almost from its inception. The churches saw early the necessity of giving financial support to their leaders, but this created an opportunity for abuse that was quickly exploited (see, e.g., Matt 7:15; *Did.* 1.5-6; 11.6, 12; Lucian *The Passing of Peregrinus*). Add to that the widespread denunciation of the sophists who taught philosophy for money, and the door was flung wide to charges and countercharges of greed. Even Paul faced such charges in his dealings with the Corinthian church (2 Cor 8:20-21; 12:14-18). Thus whether or not the admonitions given here reflect the concrete behavior of the opponents, they accurately depict a widespread and enduring problem in the church.

Instructions Concerning the Wealthy (6:17-19)

After the doxology in verses 15-16, which seems to provide a resounding conclusion to the letter (see Rom 16:25-27; Jude 24-25), the calm resumption of exhortations in these verses is somewhat jarring. Some see it as a continuation of the instructions concerning money in 6:9-10, after what must then be regarded as a digression in verses 11-16. Yet, as we have seen, verses 11-16 are not a digression but a complement to verses 3-10. Moreover, verses 17-19 do not continue the topic of verses 9-10 (i.e., the danger of greed) but introduce a new one: the proper use of wealth. Others dismiss these verses as a later addition, but lack any evidence for doing so beyond their own sense of incongruity. Arguments that the verses have been displaced from their original position in the letter (e.g., after 6:1-2 or before 6:9-10) are equally groundless. The transition is simply rough (not the first such transition), but the content of the exhortations is quite appropriate to this letter.

Throughout this letter the author has addressed various aspects of church management: instructions for worship (chap. 2); qualifications for leadership roles (chap. 3); admonitions to, and about, certain groups within the church (5:1–6:2), including the opposing teachers (chaps. 4, 6). Yet the author understands the church to be the household of God (3:15), so his instructions concerning church management are really a variant of the instructions concerning household management that were a familiar topic in philosophical writings (see also pp. 103, 192). A standard feature of this topic, however, was the subject of money and property: how to acquire and use money for the support of the household (Balch 1981, 40). It is not strange, then, that the author should deal with the question of the proper use of riches by members of the household of God. It is only strange that he should introduce the topic so abruptly. The references to eternal life (v. 12), to the manifestation (second coming) of Jesus (v. 14), and to God's eternal dominion (v. 16) may, however, have turned the author's thought to the importance of actions in the present age, which then led to these remarks (v. 17).

The passage is straightforward in form. Various commands of both a negative (v. 17b) and a positive (vv. 17c-18) nature are listed, together with a statement of their intended goal or result (v. 19). The content is also not remarkable. Close parallels to the various admonitions can be found in Israel's Wisdom literature, the sayings of Jesus, and Greco-Roman philosophy.

◊　◊　◊　◊

The word "rich" ties the admonitions together with an elaborate wordplay: Those who are rich are warned to mistrust the uncertainty of riches, to rely instead on God who richly provides, and to be rich in good works. The uncertainty of riches is a widespread motif in the Wisdom literature and in the sayings of Jesus (Prov 11:28; Eccl 5:13-17; Luke 12:16-21), as is the view that God is a generous provider (Ps 104:27-28; 145:15-16; Matt 6:25-33). With this last notion, the author's basic anti-ascetic stance reappears strongly (see also 4:4) after an earlier argument that seemed seriously to compromise it (6:6-8).

The concept of God as generous provider undergirds the author's admonitions concerning the proper attitude toward, and use of, riches. The wealthy are not admonished to rid themselves of their riches (which God has provided), but to rid themselves of their reliance on them and to use God's rich generosity to enable rich generosity of their own. The ethic encouraged here reflects the tenets of hellenistic and Roman philosophy, which, drawing on Aristotle's teachings, promoted liberal generosity as the ideal mean between profligate spending and close-fisted miserliness (Aristotle *Nicomachean Ethics* 4; Cicero *On Duties* 2.15). Like this author, the philosophers claimed the greatest benefit of wealth was the opportunity it afforded to do good or noble deeds (that is, to be a benefactor), and its greatest danger was its ability to corrupt a person's heart (Seneca *On the Happy Life* 21.2). Different, of course, in this letter is the appeal to God's generosity and the reminder of the potential for eschatological reward. Generosity in the form of giving alms to the poor was also a very important aspect of Jewish piety, and in that context the practice acquired the theological arguments missing in the philosophical treatment of the subject (see Tob 4:5-11). It seems likely that this author was influenced by both strands of thought.

◊ ◊ ◊ ◊

It has been clear from a number of comments in this letter that the author envisioned a church whose membership included at least some with comfortable financial resources (2:9; 3:2-7; 5:8, 16; 6:2). Here he gives instructions directly to these wealthy Christians, and his comments are striking for their moderation. He has denounced greed as the "root of all evil," but he does not view wealth itself as inherently evil (cf. Matt 6:19-21, 24; Luke 12:33-34; James 1:9-11), and he does not insist that one choose between God and "Mammon." In fact, he sees wealth as offering a means to secure one's salvation, a source of religious security, for while the wealthy *as wealthy* face special ethical challenges, they also have special opportunities for good deeds. They are thus encouraged to be benefactors, a familiar role in Greco-Roman society (Danker 1982), but the reward for the benefaction is given in eschatological rather than social terms. Instead of cultivating useful social connections by their actions, they will receive "life that really is life." Grace is not mentioned in this argument, though elsewhere the author strongly affirms its role (1:14; Titus 3:4-7). Here the author's interest is in the ethical possibilities for wealthy Christians, and the influence of his conviction that God desires *everyone* to be saved can clearly be seen (see also 2:4, 15).

CONCLUDING EXHORTATION AND WARNING (6:20-21)

The letter ends as it began—with a stern warning about the activities of the opponents. This warning, together with the exhortation to "guard what has been entrusted to you," sums up the thrust of the entire letter: preservation of the Pauline gospel in the face of a competing message. Missing are the personal greetings that usually concluded Greco-Roman letters, especially those in the Pauline corpus (see, e.g., 1 Cor 16:19-20; cf. Gal 6:17-18). A brief benediction closes the letter.

◊ ◊ ◊ ◊

This is only the second place in this letter, outside the opening salutation, where Timothy is addressed by name. The earlier instance appeared at the end of the first chapter, the letter's "preface" (see pp. 45-49), and thus just before the opening of the body of the letter (1:18-20). The instructions and warnings that constitute the letter's core are thus framed and personalized by these direct addresses.

The admonition to "guard what has been entrusted to you" is repeated in a longer form in 2 Tim 1:12-14, which sheds some light on its meaning here. Commands to "guard" or "keep" or "hold to" or "continue in" abound in these letters. This is the first time, however, that the object of the guarding or keeping is called a *parathēkē*. This Greek term reflects the legal concept, found throughout the ancient Mediterranean world in Greek, Roman, and Jewish writings, of goods left in trust to another's keeping. Though originally applied to material goods, usually in the context of an extended absence by an owner or of underage heirs to a bequest (see Exod 22:7-8, 10-13; Philo *Special Laws* 4.30-38), the concept was also widely used of less tangible treasures: words, teachings, and spiritual goods (Plutarch *Letter of Condolence to Apollonius* 28; Philo *Who Is the Heir* 103-8). Here it is "Paul"—the Paul of the pseudepigraphical fiction—who has entrusted some goods to Timothy, as both the connection with 1:18 and the parallel text in 2 Timothy indicate.

What is it, though, that Paul has entrusted to Timothy? Paul himself was entrusted by God with the gospel (1:11), but what "Paul" entrusts to Timothy seems to be more specifically the Pauline traditions, which include, of course, the gospel (as formulated by Paul) but also the Pauline teachings that derive from this gospel, which would include the contents of these letters. Evidence for this can be found in 2 Tim 1:13-14, where two exhortations stand side by side, apparently addressing the same issue. The first exhorts Timothy to "hold to the standard of sound teaching that you have heard from me" (v. 13) and the second encourages him, as here, to "guard the good treasure entrusted to you" (v. 14).

The legal roots of the concept suggest that the instruction to "guard" this body of material means to preserve it unharmed and unchanged (Philo *Special Laws* 4.33). The guarding has future generations in mind, and thus Timothy is also instructed to identify faithful people and to entrust to them what he has received from Paul (2 Tim 2:2), passing on the traditions, secure and intact, for the instruction and benefit of other believers (see 1 Tim 4:16). This task takes on special urgency, however, because of the presence of the opposing teachers, whose message, the author believes, stands in sharp contradiction to the Pauline gospel.

The warning about the opponents contains elements found elsewhere in these letters. Timothy is to "avoid" (literally, "turn away from") the opponents, not engage them in discussion or debate (see also 2 Tim 2:16; 3:5; Titus 3:9). Their own teachings are dismissed as "profane chatter" (see also 1:9; 4:7; 2 Tim 2:16), which leads them away from, rather than toward, the true faith. Here, as often in these letters, "the faith" refers to the content of the Christian teaching or to the Christian religion in general (3:9; 4:1; 5:8).

The opponents apparently regarded what they taught as saving knowledge (Gk. *gnōsis*), a claim the author repeatedly refutes both directly (2 Tim 3:7; Titus 1:16) and indirectly in his characterization of their teachings as "myths" and "contradictions." This self-understanding of the opponents points to a connection between them and the Gnostic movement that emerged within early Christianity. It is likely, however, that the opponents represent a nascent phase of the movement, and attempts by early investigators to link the "contradictions" (Gk. *antitheseis*) mentioned here with a known work (*The Antitheses*) by the late-second-century heretic Marcion were surely wrong (see Introduction).

The closing benediction is typical of the Pauline letters, but exceedingly brief. Oddly, though the letter is addressed to a single individual, the benediction is addressed to a group. In Greek, the pronoun "you" is plural. This could reveal the intended corporate audience of this pseudepigraphical letter, or it may simply reflect the liturgical origin of the benediction in the worship service, where the plural pronoun was standard. In later manuscripts this pronoun has been replaced by a singular form, creating a more logical, but clearly secondary, ending.

◊ ◊ ◊ ◊

The overtones of the Greek word *parathēkē* are very important to this author. The more familiar Pauline noun *paradosis* (translated "tradition") and its verbal counterpart ("to hand over") emphasize the notion of reliable transmission of a body of material recognized and accepted as authoritative by a community (see 1 Cor 11:2; 15:3;

Gal 1:14). The word used here, especially in conjunction with the command to "guard" it, retains the notion of reliability (see also 1:15; 3:1; 4:9) but emphasizes more the fact that there was a depositor of the tradition (i.e., Paul) and a trustee (Timothy). That is, this terminology highlights, in ways that the word "tradition" does not, the Pauline origins of the material preserved in these letters. Furthermore, because it was a fundamental feature of the legal dimensions of the term, the faithfulness or trustworthiness of the recipient is assumed. Thus the term *parathēkē* in the conclusion of the letter does what the words "loyal child" in the salutation do: It indicates that the apostolic traditions have been transmitted through faithful, reliable hands. Moreover, it contains an implicit charge to the church to continue to hold these traditions in trust, without distortion or modification, until the final epiphany of the Lord.

Faced with the serious distortions he sees in the opponents' teachings, the author insists on faithful preservation of the Pauline traditions. Nevertheless, his unfettered use of philosophical language and concepts to present and interpret these traditions reveals that he himself has already modified the entrusted material in ways that he either does not recognize or does not acknowledge. His own handling of the Pauline deposit thus reveals a clear truth that stands in conflict with his words: The traditions must be interpreted for subsequent generations or become a lifeless fossil.

COMMENTARY: 2 TIMOTHY

SALUTATION (1:1-2)

The letter's salutation contains the three features common to hellenistic letters: the name of the sender, the name of the addressee, and a greeting formula. Each, however, has been slightly expanded with Christian content.

◊ ◊ ◊ ◊

The salutation of 2 Timothy, though closely resembling those of 1 Timothy and Titus, differs from them in several ways (see comments on 1 Tim 1:1-2; Titus 1:1-4). Paul is, for example, an apostle by the *will* (Gk. *thelēma*) of God, not by God's command. God's will is no less compelling than God's command, but this particular phraseology is more characteristic of Pauline salutations. It repeats verbatim, in fact, the opening words of 2 Corinthians, Ephesians, and Colossians (see also 1 Cor 1:1).

The second difference is that Timothy is called Paul's "beloved child" (Gk. *agapēton teknon*), instead of his "loyal" one (1 Tim 1:2; Titus 1:4), highlighting Paul's relationship to Timothy rather than Timothy's (or Titus's) relationship to Paul. This phrase picks up the language of 1 Cor 4:17 and defines in familial terms the intimate bond between the apostle and his disciple that is reflected throughout the letter's exhortations (1:4; 2:1; 3:10-11; 4:9, 21).

The association of Paul's apostleship and "the promise of life" (i.e., eternal life) repeats in more concise form the message of Titus 1:2 (see also 1 Tim 4:8), though the nature of this association is only loosely defined here. The Greek preposition *(kata)* could indicate the purpose of Paul's apostleship (NRSV: "for the sake of") or its norm (NJB: "in accordance with"). Either way, the important point is the connection between Paul's apostleship (and thus his gospel) and life.

This life is further described as being "in Christ Jesus," a phrase that appears a number of times in this letter (1:9, 13; 2:1, 10; 3:12, 15). There is nothing to suggest that the author had in mind the Pauline sense of mystical union with Christ (cf. Gal 2:17-20; Phil 3:7-14). Here the phrase seems to indicate instead the source of life (see 1:10), just as in 2:1 it indicates the source of grace (Allan 1963).

Finally, the blessing formula is similar to those found in all the Pauline letters and identical to the one in 1 Timothy.

◊ ◊ ◊ ◊

Though following closely the Pauline formula for salutations (itself a modification of hellenistic usage) and though comprising stereotypical phrases, the opening verses nevertheless establish some important points. First, Paul's apostleship and thus God's will are identified with the eschatological promise of life. This is a theme repeated with many variations throughout this letter, including Paul's role in proclaiming the message of life (1:10-11; 2:10-11) and his own confidence in that promise (4:7-8). Second, the reference to Timothy as a "beloved" rather than "loyal" child signals the different ethical focus of this letter. It is Timothy's own behavior that is the center of the author's attention in this letter, not the behavior of various (possibly disloyal) groups within the church. Following a widespread convention, the author builds his exhortations on a personal relationship (Stowers 1986, 95; see also Prov 1:8; Sir 2:1): Paul writes as an apostle, but also as father to a beloved child.

BODY OF THE LETTER (1:3–4:8)

It is difficult to divide this letter into discrete sections, for it deals throughout with two closely interrelated themes: suffering for the gospel (1:8, 12; 2:3, 9-10; 3:11-12; 4:16-18) and preservation of the tradition (1:13-14; 2:2, 15; 3:14; 4:1-5). Paul is repeatedly presented as a model for both activities (1:11-12; 2:9-10; 3:10-13;

4:6-8, 16-18), while various opponents, both named and unnamed, serve as counterexamples (1:15; 2:17-18; 3:1-9; 4:3-4, 9-15). The argument falls roughly, however, into three main parts: an opening section that roots exhortations in liturgical material, popular maxims, and especially the example of Paul's life (1:3–2:13); a middle section that emphasizes the need to avoid certain people and certain types of behavior (2:14–3:9); and a final charge to Timothy, rooted once again in the example provided by Paul's own life and faithful endurance (3:10–4:8). The letter then closes with a long list of personal instructions, greetings, and travel plans, all of which reinforce the preceding directives (4:9-22).

Exhortations to Timothy (1:3–2:13)

The first section is unified on a rhetorical level by repeated references to remembering and reminding. "Paul," for example, remembers Timothy and his faith and reminds him to rekindle the gift of God within him (1:3-6). Timothy is urged to remember the gospel of Jesus Christ and to remind others of it (2:8, 14; see also 1:15, 18). The connections between the various portions of the argument are clearly identified, establishing a chain of logic that reaches from 1:3 through 2:13. The argument is interrupted briefly by some biographical remarks concerning certain faithless and faithful companions, but it resumes in 2:1 with a series of exhortations that summarize the preceding material. For convenience this section can be analyzed in three units (1:3-14; 1:15-18; 2:1-13), but the overall coherence and integrity of 1:3–2:13 must be kept in mind.

Thanksgiving and Exhortation: "Do not be ashamed" (1:3-14)

Like most of the Pauline letters, but unlike the other two Pastorals, 2 Timothy opens with a statement of gratitude for the faith of the letter's recipient (vv. 3-5; see Rom 1:8-15; 1 Cor 1:4-9; Phlm 4-7). The first exhortations (vv. 6-14) flow directly from this thanksgiving, buttressed by a liturgical fragment (vv. 9-10) that summarizes the gospel for which Paul and Timothy are called to suffer.

◊ ◊ ◊ ◊

Opening the body of the letter with an expression of thanksgiving to God (1:3-5) reflects the apostle's usual practice, but the wording in 2 Timothy differs slightly from the rest of the Pauline corpus. Whereas Paul (and most other NT writers) uses the Greek verb *eucharistō* to express thanks, this author uses an idiom (Gk. *charin echein;* literally, "to have gratitude") found in only a few other verses of the New Testament (Luke 17:9; 1 Tim 1:12; Heb 12:28). The basis for the thanksgiving—Timothy's faith—emerges only in verse 5. Before stating it, the author reinforces in a variety of ways the extraordinary emotional bond linking Paul with Timothy: Paul prays for him "constantly," remembers him and his tears, and "longs" to see him. Phrases similar to these can be found throughout the Pauline letters (Rom 1:9; Eph 1:16; Phil 1:3; 1 Thess 1:2), and they express ideas common in hellenistic letters of friendship and exhortation (Stowers 1986). The striking concentration of them here resembles most closely Rom 1:8-11, but the pathos in 2 Timothy—augmented by the reference to tears—is considerably stronger. The tears—probably reflecting the sadness of separation (see Acts 20:37-38)—stand in sharp contrast, especially in the Greek, with the anticipated joy of reunion. The theme of reunion is pursued in 4:9, 21, but at a less emotional level.

Paul is described not only as worshiping with a clear conscience—a leitmotif of these letters (1 Tim 1:5, 19; 3:9; cf. 1 Tim 4:2; Titus 1:15; see also Acts 23:1; 24:16)—but also worshiping as his ancestors did. The discontinuity between Paul's Jewish past and his Christian faith, highlighted particularly in Gal 2:15-21 and Phil 3:4-9, is replaced here by a perspective that assumes unbroken continuity between the two. A similar perspective is found in Acts 24:14-15; 26:6, 22, but the context and purpose are different. In Acts, Paul has been arrested on charges of teaching things contrary to the Jewish law (21:28), and in response he insists that everything he has taught is grounded in the law. In 2 Timothy, however, the emphasis is not on the continuity *per se* between Paul's Jewish roots and Christian faith. Indeed, this passage does not really acknowledge a change of any sort. Instead it stresses the stability and especially the antiquity of Paul's faith.

Greco-Roman society respected "traditional piety" (Diodorus Siculus *Library of History* 4.8.5) and was, as a consequence, suspicious of new religions or new religious customs that might undermine it (Balch 1981). The seamless link established here between Paul's faith and that of his ancestors presents Christianity as a religion with creditable antiquity. The reference to Timothy's faithful mother and grandmother does the same thing (see also 3:14). The opponents, however, are described in this letter as people of very recent appearance (3:1; 4:3), whose activities threaten to corrupt the sound (traditional) doctrine of the established church.

The book of Acts describes Timothy as "the son of a Jewish woman who was a believer" (16:1), but it does not mention the woman's name. This letter does, but it is uncertain how reliable the information is. By referring also to Lois (his grandmother), the letter pushes Timothy's faithful ancestry back another generation. The author's primary purpose in mentioning her was to indicate that, like Paul's, Timothy's religious heritage has stability and antiquity. Such a heritage of piety from Timothy's mother (Eunice), grandmother (Lois), and "father" (Paul!) undergirds the letter's exhortations to loyalty and perseverance.

Having mentioned his confidence in Timothy's sincere—and traditional—faith, the author draws from it the first of three interrelated exhortations, presented in the form of a reminder (v. 6). The Greek text does not necessarily imply that Timothy had let the gift of God—that is, the gift of ministry (see comments on 1 Tim 4:14)—completely expire, for the present tense infinitive suggests continuous action, something like, "keep on fanning into flame." Nevertheless, the image of Timothy that emerges from these verses is of someone whose spirit is weak and whose fortitude is flagging. Speculations about Timothy's personality, however, are not to the point. Within the pseudonymous corpus of the Pastorals, the exhortations of this letter serve to define in some detail the appropriate role and behavior of the Christian church leader, especially his role as teacher. In this way 2 Timothy complements 1 Timothy and Titus, which portray the church as endangered by teachers with bad theology, corrupt morals, and disruptive tactics. To motivate the instructions that define appropriate leadership, however, the author presents Timothy as in need of Paul's advice.

Dissonance with the portrait of him in 1 Timothy as a competent leader is thus inevitable and not historically significant.

The rite of laying on of hands was performed, according to 1 Tim 4:14, by the council of elders. Consistent with this letter's focus on the close relationship between Paul and his disciple, however, the author here highlights Paul's personal role in the event. At the heart of the rite was the imparting of the gift (or gifts) of ministry to the church leader. It is not the Holy Spirit itself that is transmitted (cf. NJB, GNB), for the Spirit was bestowed on every believer at baptism (Titus 3:5). Rather, the gift imparted or awakened through the laying on of hands was an aptitude—here defined as a spirit of power, love, and self-discipline—for the special tasks associated with church leadership.

Like Paul, the author of these letters understands love to be the defining Christian virtue (1:13; 1 Tim 1:5; 1 Cor 13:1-13). The concern for self-discipline (Gk. *sōphronismos*), on the other hand, is more closely linked to this author's distinctive interest in the moderation and self-control prized by the Greco-Roman world (1 Tim 3:2; Titus 1:8; 2:12). In this particular context, however, it is the strength or power (Gk. *dynamis*) bestowed on the church leader that is of central importance. This power, which is actually God's power at work in him (1:8; see also 2 Cor 12:7-10), enables the church leader to discipline opponents (2:24-25), to preserve and proclaim the message (4:2), and to endure the suffering that necessarily befalls a follower of Christ (3:12) and especially a leader of the church (1:8). The reminder of the power of God imparted at ordination also leads directly to the second exhortation, "Do not be ashamed," for recognition of the presence of God's power imparts an eschatological confidence that is incompatible with shame (4:6-8).

Shame was a powerful force in the first-century Mediterranean world, one with which Christianity, with its low status and crucified redeemer figure had always to contend. Here, as in Rom 1:16, shame is initially, at least, linked to the message of the gospel, but it is also and especially linked to the low status of the herald of that gospel. The author does not develop the connection between these two issues as Paul does in 1 Cor 1:18–2:5, where the apostle argues that the "foolish" message of the cross is directly reflected in his own implausible apostolate. Indeed, the author does not explicitly mention the death of Jesus until 2:11, and even then he does not mention the cross, which gave to Jesus' death its distinctive social stigma and to Paul's suffering its distinctive theological meaning. In fact, the summary of the gospel that follows immediately, with its emphasis on God's eternal purpose and Christ's revelation of it, contains no elements that could be considered "shameful." The author's strategy is different from that of Paul in 1 Corinthians, for his goal is not to correct boastful arrogance but to encourage bold proclamation of the gospel—in spite of the potentially "shameful" consequences—among an honor-sensitive people. Thus he infuses the shame-linked items with new categories of honor: the role of proclaimer is a "holy calling" (v. 9), the gospel brings life and immortality (v. 10), and Paul's imprisonment and suffering are absorbed into the concept of God's power (vv. 8, 12). With this new "honor" system, the author can urge Timothy to join in suffering for the gospel (v. 8).

The suffering is suffering with Paul, not suffering with Christ, and the emphasis is on the power of God to rescue from suffering (3:11) or to provide help to endure it (4:7). This emphasis has solid Pauline roots (2 Cor 1:3-11; 4:7-12; 12:8-10; Phil 1:30), yet it lacks (save for the single reference to dying with Christ in an obviously liturgical piece [2:11b]) the profound grounding that Paul provided by linking Christian suffering explicitly with Christ's own suffering, a consequence of participation in the mystical body of Christ (Rom 8:17; Phil 3:7-11; Col 1:24; 1 Thess 3:2-4).

The exhortation to rely on the power of God (v. 8b) is buttressed by a passage that rehearses the way this power has been demonstrated in the Christ-event (vv. 9-10). The passage combines accurate summaries of Paul's thought with some unusual and unPauline phrases and the epiphany language characteristic of these letters. Because the content of the passage goes considerably beyond the needs of the argument, it is probably a fragment of the church's liturgy, one of several cited by this author (see also 2:11-13; Titus 2:11-14; 3:4-7).

The language of verse 9—with its emphasis on salvation (a past event) given by grace, according to God's purpose (or council), and not according to works—resembles most closely Eph 2:8-9 and

1:11. New is the language of a holy calling, which is somewhat different from Paul's phrase, "called to be saints" (or "holy ones") (1 Cor 1:2). The wider reference is to the holy calling of all believers, but the context suggests a more specific calling to church leadership. "Grace" refers here to God's preexistent (literally "before eternal times," see Titus 1:2) will to save (see also Titus 2:11), not to the acquittal of individual sinners (Rom 3:24). This saving will was both revealed and accomplished through Jesus, who is thus called Savior here (see also Titus 1:4; 2:13; 3:6).

Apart from the Pastoral Letters, the term "Savior" is rarely applied to God in the NT, but the usage obviously has deep roots in hellenistic Judaism (see comments on 1 Tim 1:1-2). It is more difficult to determine the origin of its more common application to Jesus. In the OT a few individuals in the time of the judges are called savior or deliverer (Judg 3:9, 15; Neh 9:27), but "Savior" was not a messianic title. Paul uses the word only once, in a rather politically charged passage (Phil 3:20). On the other hand, inscriptions indicate that it was a fairly frequent epithet for hellenistic deities and even hellenistic rulers. One inscription, for example, refers to Isis as "the greatest goddess, the mighty savior," and another refers to Ptolemy I as "the savior and god" (Wendland 1904). The strong appearance of the word "Savior" in the later documents of the New Testament may be influenced by this usage, though it acquires new and specifically Christian content there (Acts 5:31; 13:23; Eph 5:23; 2 Pet 1:1, 11; 2:20; 3:2, 18). In 2 Timothy, for example, it is associated with Christ's role in bringing to light and fruition God's own saving will.

In defining this role, however, the author makes no direct reference to Jesus' atoning death. He speaks only of Jesus' "appearing" (Gk. *epiphaneia*), a word he uses elsewhere for the parousia or Second Coming (1 Tim 6:14; 2 Tim 4:1 [?]; Titus 2:13). This word also appears frequently in descriptions of hellenistic gods and goddesses to refer to their helpful interventions—in battle, in sickness, or in other dangers—on behalf of their devotees (Dionysius of Halicarnassus *Roman Antiquities* 6.13.2-4; Plutarch *Themistocles* 30). The author of the Pastoral Letters, however, interprets Jesus' appearance in a much broader way as a revelation of God's eternal saving purpose which had, until then, been hidden. In fact, he can speak elsewhere simply of the appearance of God's grace and loving-kindness, omitting any reference to the vehicle of that revelation (Titus 2:11; 3:4). Jesus' epiphany, however, is not simply revelatory. There is also an element of intervention, though this is oddly described as abolishing death—presumably the *power* of death, and presumably accomplished through his own death and resurrection (see Rom 8:31-39; 1 Cor 15:35-57).

The revelatory aspect of Jesus' advent reappears in the next phrase, "[he] brought life and immortality to light." Immortality is, of course, God's unique attribute (1 Tim 1:17; 6:16), but Jesus' resurrection reveals that, in the form of eternal life, it is a possibility—a hope—for humankind as well (Titus 1:2-3). The author links this revelation, however, not directly to Jesus' resurrection, but to the gospel message about it. For all except the original disciples, it is the proclamation of the resurrection that brings to light the hope and promise of eternal life, and as long as the revelatory aspect of the Christ-event is stressed, the act of proclamation is put almost on a par with the event itself.

With the importance of proclamation established, the author returns to Paul's role as proclaimer of the gospel. The language of verse 11 reproduces that of 1 Tim 2:7, but without the latter verse's emphasis on the Gentile mission. (A large number of manuscripts, by far the majority, do include the words, "a teacher *of the Gentiles*," in verse 11, but these are late manuscripts in which words have been added to the verse to bring it into even closer harmony with 1 Tim 2:7.) The author's point here, however, is not that of 1 Tim 2:7 (God's universal saving will), but Paul's willingness to suffer for the gospel to which he was given a three-fold appointment. Thus the author returns to the issue of shame, presenting Paul as a model of the attitude encouraged in Timothy (v. 8, see also v. 16), and grounding Paul's lack of shame in his confidence in God's ability—that is, God's power (v. 8)—"to guard until that day what has been entrusted to me" (or, "what I have entrusted to him").

The interpretation of verse 12*b* is widely disputed. The Greek *(tēn parathēkēn mou)* can refer either to what Paul has entrusted to God (his life or soul, in the face of dangerous opposition to the gospel; so NRSV, NJB, NIV) or, as above, to what God has entrusted to Paul (the gospel itself; so NEB, REB, RSV, NAB). The argument preceding this verse supports the first interpretation (see also 4:7-8); the exhortations to Timothy that follow support the second. In these exhortations, Timothy is urged to guard the good treasure (*tēn kalēn parathēkēn*) entrusted to him (v. 14; see comments on 1 Tim 6:20) and then to pass it on with care to others (2:2). The focus here is on the careful preservation and transmission of the gospel and the apostolic teachings, and verse 12, read in this light, expresses the confidence that God has the power to watch over that important process. The apostolic delegates are not relieved of their responsibility to protect this material, but, as verses 7 and 14 make clear, they will have divine help in doing so.

The third and final set of exhortations (vv. 13-14), then, rests on the earlier two (vv. 6, 8). With the gift of ministry burning brightly in him, experiencing no shame concerning the gospel message, but confident of God's powerful help, Timothy is to adhere to the sound or healthy teaching (see 1 Tim 1:10) he received from Paul (v. 13). Verse 14 repeats the message, using the wording of verse 12 and reiterating the promise of divine oversight (v. 7). The final clause of verse 13 ("in the faith and love that are in Christ Jesus") is formulaic and characterizes in a general way the Christian life (see 1 Tim 1:14) and in a special way the life of the church leader.

◊ ◊ ◊ ◊

The central theological theme of this section of the letter is the theme of confidence. Beginning with a statement of confidence in Timothy's faith (v. 5), the author exhorts Timothy to show his confidence in the gospel by not being "ashamed." This is followed by a strong affirmation of Paul's own apostolic confidence (v. 12). The section's two central exhortations are both related to this issue: join in suffering for the gospel, confident of the eschatological reward (vv. 8-10); and preserve and protect the gospel, confident of God's help (vv. 11-14).

A liturgical passage (vv. 9-10) supports this theme by presenting the gospel as a demonstration of God's power. This power, revealed in both the manifestation of grace and the abolition of death, is the ultimate ground for confidence. Paul has already displayed his confidence in God's power and Timothy is urged to do so as well.

The particular arena in which this confidence is to be demonstrated is that of church leadership. Though many of the exhortations have potential relevance for the Christian life *per se,* they are applied here to the situation of a church leader. The gift of God, the holy calling, the entrusted treasure all refer to the spiritual equipment of the minister of the church.

A striking feature of this section is the refusal to acknowledge any discontinuity in Paul's or Timothy's religious heritage. Even Timothy's grandmother is presented as if she were a Christian, though the point may not be her religious affiliation, but a family tradition of faithfulness that transcends religious boundaries. In this letter, the significant break does not reside in the past, but in the present, in the activities of opponents who have swerved, or are swerving, from the truth. A full description of them is not presented until 2:14–3:9, but in the next short section (1:15-18) the author indicates their presence.

Finally, the passage raises the question of the meaning of suffering. The author does not give it the christological grounding that Paul does, nor does he seem to root it in a vision of a hostile or sinful cosmos. He presents suffering as inevitable for any Christian and essential for any church leader. Through suffering, a church leader identifies himself with Paul and manifests his confidence in the fundamental Christian promise of life. Failure to endure suffering suggests shame—not shame in the cross of Christ, but a lack of confidence in God's power to save. The author does not seem to envision a situation for the church leader that is free of the opportunity to suffer. This suffering does not necessarily involve imprisonment or persecution (Paul's paradigmatic suffering) but, as 2:3-7 indicates, the daily struggle on behalf of the gospel. Participation in that, confident of God's watchful oversight and trusting in God's eternal promises, is the model of ministry promoted here. There is some warrant for associating this model with Paul's name (1 Cor 9:12-23; 2 Cor 11:21–12:10).

Examples of Shame and Confidence (1:15-18)

In what appears to be an abrupt shift in content and tone, the exhortations to Timothy are interrupted by some personal comments about the behavior of certain named individuals. This letter contains a number of these passages (1:5; 2:17; 4:9-21) but they do not, in fact, interrupt the letter's admonitions. Rather, they provide concrete examples, both negative and positive, of the behavior encouraged of Timothy. This is particularly clear in this passage, which illustrates the message of 1:8: "Do not be ashamed."

Some see in the very personal character of these passages evidence that the author has used fragments of genuine Pauline letters (see Introduction). The Socratic Letters show us, however, that personal-sounding passages were often constructed to provide context and content for pseudonymous material (Fiore 1986). It is likely that the author of the Pastorals has also created this material, perhaps relying on oral traditions, though this is far from clear.

◊ ◊ ◊ ◊

The motif of abandonment is strong in this letter. Here it is "all" those in Asia (a Roman province in western Asia Minor that included the city of Ephesus) who have turned away from Paul (v. 15; see also 4:10, 16). Since Paul is presented as imprisoned in Rome (v. 17), it is not entirely clear how one is to understand this comment. The author could intend to imply that the churches in that province failed to send any aid to Rome for the imprisoned apostle (cf. Phil 2:25-30; 4:15-18). It could equally well imply that Paul was arrested in Asia and at that time received no help or support from the local churches. Such a scenario has, however, no support from the book of Acts. Whatever the historical scenario, the important thing is the concrete negative example offered by the Asians, and especially by Phygelus and Hermogenes. (These men are otherwise unknown.) Their actions reflect shame, for in turning away from Paul they have demonstrated their lack of confidence (trust) in his gospel (1:8-9).

The positive, honorable example of Onesiphorus (also unknown apart from this letter) is developed in considerably more detail. The author presents a picture of someone repeatedly showing his devotion to Paul and to the gospel. He "often" refreshed Paul in prison (a different Greek verb conveys a similar meaning in 1 Cor 16:18; Phlm 7, 20); he searched "eagerly" for him (the Greek adverb suggests an energetic and serious search); and he rendered much service in Ephesus, whether to Paul or to the church is not clear. (The same Greek verb is used in 1 Tim 3:10, 13 to describe the work of deacons, but here it seems to refer to a more general level of service.) All of this attests to his lack of shame over the apostle, in spite of the fact that Paul has been publicly humiliated by being chained and thereby reduced to the status of a slave. Onesiphorus thus presents a powerful example to buttress the exhortation of 1:8 (see also 1:12), one that is well suited to the context, since Timothy is urged to come to Paul in Rome, as Onesiphorus did (4:9, 21).

It seems likely that the author intended to imply that Onesiphorus had died since rendering service to Paul, for the prayer is for mercy for his household, not for Onesiphorus himself (v. 16; see also 4:19). The prayer for Onesiphorus to find mercy "on that day" (v. 18) refers to the day of judgment (1:12; 4:8) and is not incompatible with the hypothesis of his death. On the other hand, his death is certainly not stressed and one cannot necessarily infer from this verse that his death resulted from persecution (cf. Phil 2:25-30). *Paul* is the model of martyrdom; Onesiphorus is the model of faithful discipleship that is not ashamed of that martyrdom. The vague hints of Onesiphorus's death are not sufficient to blur that clear and important picture.

The prayer-wish for eschatological mercy on Onesiphorus is ambiguously framed by two references to the Lord: "May the Lord grant that he will find mercy from the Lord." Either the first "Lord" is Jesus (1:2) and the second, God (1 Tim 6:13-16); or both refer to Jesus (4:8, 18). Regardless of the awkward wording, the meaning is clear: Because Onesiphorus found and refreshed Paul for the sake of the gospel, the author prays that he might find mercy in fulfillment of that gospel (4:8).

◊ ◊ ◊ ◊

This short passage provides concrete illustrations of what it means to be ashamed, and not ashamed, of Paul and his gospel. It is not a passive mind-set that is depicted, but an active turning away (in the negative example) or a zealous seeking out (in the positive example). Though the bulk of the illustration involves the exceptional circumstances of Paul's imprisonment, and though there are hints of Onesiphorus's death, the final verse expands the activities that reveal the required "shameless" confidence to include, it would seem, day-to-day service to the church.

Continued Exhortation: "Share in suffering" (2:1-13)

In these verses the author returns to direct exhortation to Timothy, repeating in verses 1-3 the three points made in 1:6-14. The emphasis is on the last one, "share in suffering" (see also 1:8), and three maxims are cited to support this exhortation (vv. 4-7), vaguely recalling Paul's own use of the examples of soldiers, athletes, and farmers.

A brief summary of the gospel, somewhat different from the one presented in 1:9-10, leads again to a statement about Paul's willingness to suffer for this gospel (vv. 8-10; see also 1:11-12). A hymnic fragment provides a theological basis for this willingness (vv. 11-13), confirming the promise of eternal glory but also introducing a harsh note of warning before closing with an enigmatic affirmation of divine faithfulness.

Though dealing throughout with the issue of suffering, the argument of this section can be divided easily into two parts. The first consists of exhortations to Timothy (vv. 1-7); the second supports these exhortations with the model of Paul's suffering and undergirds the whole with a liturgical reminder of eschatological reward and the possible loss thereof (vv. 8-13).

◊ ◊ ◊ ◊

The Exhortation Proper (2:1-7): The author resumes his exhortations with the phrase "*You* then . . . " (Gk. *Sy oun*), drawing a conclusion concerning Timothy's behavior from the preceding negative and positive examples. Timothy is addressed as "my child," invoking the intimate relationship between apostle and disciple as further motivation for an appropriate response (1:2; see also 1 Tim 1:2, 18). The first exhortation is to "be strong" or be strengthened (Gk. *endynamou*) by the grace that has its source "in Christ Jesus" (see comments on 1:1). As in so many things, Paul is a model for Timothy here, for he, too, has been strengthened by

God (4:17; 1 Tim 1:12). The NRSV's (and NIV's) translation ("be strong *in* the grace") assumes that grace is the sphere within which one is to be strong (1:9). The Greek preposition *en,* however, can express means as well as location (i.e., "be strong by means of the grace . . . "), and elsewhere this author refers to grace as an active divine power (see comments on Titus 2:11-12). This understanding suits this context well and yields a translation that matches the content of 1:6-7, where Timothy is urged to keep burning within him the power or strength (Gk. *dynamis*) that God has given (so also REB, NEB, NJB). The tense of the imperative verb (present), like that of the infinitive in 1:6, indicates continuous action: "keep on being strengthened." The point is not to suggest or correct Timothy's spiritual weakness but to provide a rhetorical foundation for the subsequent exhortation to manifest this strength by sharing in suffering.

The second exhortation, to entrust "what you have heard from me" to faithful people, expands the exhortation of 1:13-14, where Timothy was urged to keep and guard "what you have heard from me." Making provisions for careful transmission is, of course, an aspect of keeping and guarding. It was thus a common feature of testamentary literature, many traits of which are found in this letter (see, e.g., comments on 3:1-9 and the Introduction). The NRSV suggests that Timothy received this material, not directly from Paul, but "through many witnesses." This contradicts, however, the message conveyed elsewhere in the letter, where the personal contact between the apostle and his disciple is stressed (1:6; 3:10, 14). The Greek preposition *dia* can, however, mean "in the presence of" as well as "through," yielding a translation consistent with the picture of direct reception of the apostolic traditions from Paul (so RSV, REB, NEB, NIV). The author probably had an ordination ceremony in mind, one that included not only witnesses (1 Tim 4:14; 6:12) but apparently also a summary of the apostolic traditions (3:14).

The focus is on preservation of the traditions through careful transmission, not on a chain of succession *per se* (cf. *1 Clem.* 42.1-4; Irenaeus *Adv. Haer.* 3.3-4). Thus the author does not present here, as he does elsewhere in these letters, an extensive list of qualifications for those who are to receive the materials, though it is likely that he had bishops and elders in mind (see 1 Tim 3:1-13; Titus 1:6-9). Instead he mentions only the need for faithfulness (see also 1 Tim 3:9, 11; Titus 1:9) and an aptitude for teaching (see also 2:24; 1 Tim 3:2; Titus 1:9). At several points later in this letter, the author describes in more detail the qualities that define a competent teacher: strict adherence to the word of truth, gentleness, patience, persistence, a solid grounding in scripture (2:14-15, 24-25; 3:14-17; 4:2). He also repeatedly warns against the activities of other teachers, whose false doctrines and methods are a parody of good teaching (2:14–3:9).

The final exhortation, "share in suffering," repeats the wording of 1:8 (Gk. *sygkakopathēson*, a compound word possibly coined by this author). This exhortation receives amplification, and thus emphasis, through three maxims that draw on stereotypical models of diligent work: the soldier, the athlete, and the farmer. These figures were popular in philosophical moral discourse, and Paul himself used them at several points in his letters as examples or metaphors (1 Cor 9:7, 9-12, 24-27; Phil 2:25; Phlm 2). They were amenable to various applications, and the author of 2 Timothy makes them part of his exhortation concerning suffering (Pfitzner 1967).

Epictetus likened the calling of the Cynic philosopher, who needed to be free from distractions and wholly devoted to the service of God, to that of a soldier (*Discourses* 3.22.69). His subsequent comments highlight the issue of distractions and the need for the Cynic's exclusive devotion to his task of overseeing humankind. The context of the similar comment in 2 Timothy, however, places the emphasis elsewhere, on the need to please the "enlisting officer." The preceding definition of a "good soldier of Christ Jesus" as one who is willing to share in suffering indicates rather clearly who the "enlisting officer" is and how he is to be pleased.

The figure of the athlete was usually used to emphasize either the struggle of the contest or the prize awaiting the victor. Paul occasionally developed the second point (1 Cor 9:24-25; Phil 3:12-14); moral philosophers tended to highlight the first, using it to illustrate the struggle for virtue (Epictetus *Discourses* 3.22.51). In verse 5 the athlete's crown is mentioned, anticipating the description of eschatological rewards in verses 10-13, but the immediate context places the emphasis on "competing according to the rules." These rules, of course, prescribe suffering for the church leader (1:8; 3:11-12; 4:5).

The comments on the farmer include the familiar point about enjoying the fruits of one's labors (Deut 20:6; Prov 27:18; 1 Cor 9:7, 10; cf. John 4:35-38), but the context in 2 Timothy places the emphasis on "doing the work" (Gk. *kopiōnta,* a word that connotes wearying toil and struggle rather than just getting the work done). The consistent factor in the three examples, then, is the suffering endured by the soldier, the athlete, and the farmer in the course of their labors. The motif of reward appears in the second example, and even more strongly in the third, and this message is emphasized in verses 8-13. Here, though, the main point is the struggle that necessarily precedes the reward. These points, however, must be teased from the examples, for the author does not offer an explicit application to his argument (cf. 1 Cor 9:24-27). In fact, they are treated rather like parables, left for the reader (in this case "Timothy") to interpret. Like Jesus' disciples, however, Timothy is promised some assistance with the task (Mark 4:9, 11; see also Prov 2:6).

Example of Paul's Suffering (2:8-13): The intended purpose of this passage is clear: It reinforces the preceding exhortations, especially the one in verse 3, by presenting the model of Paul's own suffering and by confirming the promise of eschatological reward. Aspects of the passage, however, are obscure and details of its interpretation are widely debated: the significance of the puzzling summary of the gospel (v. 8); the meaning ascribed to Paul's suffering (vv. 9-10); the identification of the sure saying (v. 8, v. 10, or vv. 11-13); and many aspects of the hymnic fragment in verses 11-13, especially the meaning of the last line of the quatrain (v. 13a). Many portions of the passage echo the undisputed Pauline letters, but it is not clear how much of Paul's own theology can be applied to their interpretation here. The exhortation to "think over" what is said (v. 7), though intended for the metaphors of 2:4-6, is apt for this material as well. It requires careful thought to identify the author's meaning here.

The injunction to "remember" Jesus Christ continues a theme introduced in 1:3, but here the author appeals to the gospel tradition instead of personal memories (cf. 1:3, 5, 15, 18). The summary of the gospel contains the same two elements found in Rom 1:3-4, but they appear here in an odd sequence: first resurrection, then Davidic descent. The emphasis clearly falls on the resurrection (cf. vv. 11-12), and it is not obvious what significance, if any, the author sees in the reference to David. The letters show no other evidence of an interest in Jesus' royal messiahship, and while the reference to David may confirm Jesus' humanity (see 1 Tim 2:5; 3:16), it does so only indirectly. Certainly it does not communicate a message of lowliness analogous to Paul's imprisonment. It is probably best understood as a fixed part of the tradition, cited as such, but not contributing actively to the argument. It is the eschatological hope contained in the good news of Jesus' resurrection that undergirds the admonitions to suffer.

This good news is identified emphatically as "*my* gospel" (see also Rom 2:16; 16:25), that is, the gospel with which Paul was entrusted (1:11-12) and for which he is willing to suffer. The passage does not suggest that in his suffering Paul is somehow identified with Christ or the message of the cross (cf. 1 Cor 2:2-5; 2 Cor 4:7-12; Gal 6:17; Phil 3:10; Col 1:24). Rather, the point (made with considerable rhetorical skill) lies in the *contrast* between the chained apostle and the unchained word (v. 9). Paul develops a similar contrast in Phil 1:12-14, which may have provided the model for this passage. The author of 2 Timothy has already presented the basic message of the text (1:8, 12): God is able to protect and promote the gospel, so that even when those entrusted with it suffer setbacks, the word itself does not.

The next verse suggests, however, a more direct connection between the suffering of the apostle and the advancement of the saving word. It suggests that the message, and thus the possibility of salvation, goes forth not simply in spite of the apostle's suffering (here defined more broadly as enduring "everything"), but somehow *because of it*. But how does the apostle's endurance promote the salvation of the elect? It is reading far too much into the verse to assume that Paul suffered in place of the elect, or that his suffering filled up a measure of cosmic suffering as a necessary prelude to salvation (Rev 6:11), or that it somehow completed or perfected Christ's own atoning work (Col 1:24). It is also a mistake to assume that this author intended to say that Paul endured suffering in order to embody the message of the Cross and thus to proclaim it, for these letters contain no message of the Cross. The only interpretation that seems consistent with the emphasis of this letter is that the call to suffer hardship for the gospel is also a call to work hard for the gospel (1 Tim 6:12). The shift in language from "being chained" to "endure everything" is significant, for Paul's imprisonment is an extreme example, not the only legitimate manifestation, of suffering for the gospel. Relying on God's power (1:8) does not imply passivity in the face of adversity, but empowerment to deal with it (1:6-7, 14). Likewise, awareness that the word of God is not chained implies increased effort on its behalf (4:2).

The beneficiaries of this are the "elect" or "chosen" (v. 10; Gk. *eklektoi*), an Old Testament term for Israel that was appropriated at an early stage by Christians to designate their honorable status before God (Ps 105:6; Isa 43:20-21; Rom 8:33; Titus 1:1; 1 Pet 2:9). Here, as often in the NT, Christians are designated the "elect" in the context of an eschatological promise, thus reinforcing the firm hope of salvation that is theirs (Matt 22:11-14; Mark 13:20-27; Rev 17:14). Though the concept of election is sometimes associated with predestination (Rom 8:28-33; Eph 1:4), that is not the case here, and the "sure" saying that follows in verses 11-13 describes salvation as a conditional hope, not a secure possession.

The "sure saying" formula, one of five in these letters (see comments on 1 Tim 1:15), is almost universally taken to refer to the poetic passage that follows. That passage, however, is introduced by the Greek word *gar* ("for," omitted in most English translations), as if it confirms the faithfulness of a saying located earlier in the text. The gospel saying of verse 8, however, is too remote to be the intended referent. The statement in verse 10*b*, the most likely alternative, does not have the earmarks of a traditional "saying" even though it concerns the promise of salvation, which seems to characterize all the accredited sayings (see comments on 1 Tim 3:1*a*). *Gar* may, however, be part of the quoted text and not a significant feature of the argument here. In this case, the NRSV would be correct in associating the sure saying formula with the verses that follow (Knight 1968), but the issue cannot be regarded as settled.

Verses 11*b*-13 are usually identified as a portion of a hymn because of the carefully balanced length and parallelism of the clauses. The passage consists of four lines, each containing a conditional clause ("if . . .") followed by a result clause ("then," understood). A coda, usually seen as the author's addition, is attached to the passage (v. 13*b*), clarifying to some extent its surprising final pronouncement. The first two lines are closely parallel: Similar conditional statements concerning faithful human suffering are followed by similar promises of salvation. Line three establishes a new pattern: A negative human action (denial) is followed by a matching negative divine response. The fourth line begins the same way, but then breaks the newly established pattern: A negative human action is followed by a positive divine response ("if we are faithless, he remains faithful"). The meaning of this line and its relationship to the preceding lines is widely debated. The interpretation of the passage is complicated by the fact that the author has obviously appropriated, but probably reinterpreted and possibly even reworded, traditional material. It is no longer possible to recover the original wording of the hymn. It is necessary, however, to distinguish between its probable original meaning and the meaning the author gave to it by incorporating it into his argument.

Several aspects of the wording of the hymn are puzzling. The first line of the Greek text does not contain the personal pronoun "him," though the English translations all add it. Literally, however, the text reads, "if we have died together, we will also live together." Without the pronouns, it is not immediately clear if the hymn speaks of dying and living *with Christ,* or simply of dying and living together. The closest verbal parallel seems to be the friendship formula of 2 Cor 7:3, which also has no pronouns, instead of the baptismal promise of Rom 6:8 (Furnish 1984). Nevertheless, baptismal incorporation into Christ is usually cited as the original inspiration of this text.

The author has just identified salvation as having its origin "in Christ Jesus" (v. 10), which encourages a christological interpretation of the first line, especially if the logic of the connective word *gar* ("for") is taken seriously (see above). Moreover, the past tense indicative verb ("if we have died") points to an action that has already occurred. This too supports the metaphorical understanding of dying as incorporation into Christ's death through baptism (Rom 6:3), though without the pronoun "him" in the text, the christological element is oddly subdued. Paul understood the new life that followed baptism to be the ongoing moral life of the believer, followed, in the future, by resurrection life (Rom 6:4, 8). Here only the latter seems to be intended, as both the future tense of "live" and the parallel statement about reigning imply.

The second and third lines also lack the pronoun "him," though here, too, the English translations are consistent in inserting it into the text. The conditional clause of the second line, though parallel to the first, speaks of present-tense enduring, not of past-tense dying. This changes the message from the baptismal promise of salvation to the eschatological reward for endurance, including (perhaps primarily) the endurance of martyrdom (Rev 14:12-13; 20:4). At the same time, though, it adds a new layer of meaning to the reference to dying in the first line.

The peculiar absence of pronouns and the wider context of the passage permit another transferal of meaning. Without the pronoun, the text resembles a formula of friendship or loyalty: "I will choose to die or live with you" (Euripedes *Orestes* 307-8; see also Horace *Odes* 3.9.24; 2 Sam 15:21). Such a formula admirably fits the situation envisioned in this letter—the encouragement of Timothy to join with Paul in "dying," that is, in suffering, for the gospel. The context strongly encourages this application. Nowhere in these letters is Christ's death directly mentioned. There are two references to his act of self-giving (1 Tim 2:6; Titus 2:14) and one to his resurrection from the dead (v. 8), but the act of dying itself is not stressed, and nowhere is he described as "enduring" or suffering. But Paul has endured (v. 10; 3:10-11), has suffered, and is presented in this letter as someone apparently facing death (4:6-7). Moreover,

Paul looks with certainty to his own victor's crown (4:8). And throughout the letter Timothy is urged to emulate Paul in all of this.

The third and fourth lines differ in format from the first two. The conditional clauses describe negative instead of positive actions (denial and faithlessness) and the result clauses are formulated in terms of what "he" (literally "that one") will do. (The roles of God and Christ are so blurred in these letters that it is difficult to assign the pronoun exclusively to one. Christ will function in God's role as end time judge [4:1, 8], and God's saving nature is manifested in Christ [1:9].) Whereas lines one and two speak of eschatological reward, line three describes eschatological punishment, a form of measure-for-measure retribution that probably rests on the saying tradition found in Matt 10:33 ("whoever denies me . . . I will also deny"). A future indicative verb is used in both clauses of the third line, giving this warning a highly contingent quality.

The fourth line opens with a condition based on behavior apparently equivalent to denial ("if we are faithless . . . "), but the expected statement of retribution is not present. Instead, faithless human behavior is met with a faithful divine response, apparently in complete contradiction to the message of the preceding line. The relationship between lines three and four depends on what it means for God—or Christ—to "remain faithful." The final coda suggests that the faithfulness is to God's own self, but to what aspect of the divine nature? Various interpretations are possible.

The final line could be intended to overturn the previous message of judgment with the message of grace; God is faithful to God's gracious nature and will not punish. On the other hand, the faithfulness of God or Christ can be understood in terms of faithfulness to divine justice, which *demands* the retributive response described in the previous line (see also Rom 2:2). The message could also be that the failure of a few will not nullify God's fundamental covenant faithfulness (Rom 3:3-4). All of these interpretations tend to reach outside the letter for the operative definition of divine faithfulness. It is important to look within the Pastoral Letters, and especially within the surrounding argument, to determine how this author understands the concept. Also, lines three and four need to be considered together.

In the Gospel tradition, denial is identified with feeling shame (Mark 8:38; Matt 10:32-33). Concern for shame is also strong in this letter, and the third line supports the exhortations to Timothy not to be ashamed of the gospel's message or its proclaimer (1:8; 2:3). The author also connects the hymnic passage to a warning about other people whose teachings and deeds are a form of denial of, and faithlessness to, the truth (2:14-19; 3:5-8; see also Titus 1:16). His description of God's response to these people thus reveals his understanding of divine faithfulness.

This response, and thus divine faithfulness, has several dimensions. First, it is clear that faithfulness does not preclude rejection. God denies these people, for denial of those who are not God's people is implicit in the recognition of those who are (2:19). Yet God is the source (and Jesus is the revealer) of the universal promise of life (1:1; 1 Tim 2:4), and the treatment of opponents, especially as it is encouraged in this letter, shows ongoing faithfulness to that promise. Thus opponents are to be gently corrected to facilitate God's saving will (2:24-26). God also shows fidelity to the elect, even when their faith is being upset by the teachings of the opponents. Indeed, God's faithfulness to "those who are his" is a "firm foundation" in times of uncertainty (2:19). Finally, God shows faithfulness to the gospel, which God will preserve in the face of either weakness of resolve on the part of the church's designated leaders (1:12; 2:9), or moral or doctrinal weakness on the part of the opponents (2:18; 3:9).

◊ ◊ ◊ ◊

The central theological issue raised by this passage is the author's understanding of human suffering, an issue that also surfaces in 1:3-14 and 3:10–4:8. The author alludes here to a number of Pauline texts that address this issue, but it is not clear that he appropriates the full range of the apostle's understanding of suffering. The traditional baptismal language of dying with Christ that is found in the hymn is not, for example, reinforced in any way in the text of the letter. The author does not explore the ethical implications of this incorporation into Christ's death and, apart from the hymnic piece itself, there is no evidence that he understands suffering to be in any way a result of that incorporation, or a reflection of the Cross.

Again apart from the hymnic piece, the call to Timothy to share in suffering is a call to share with Paul in suffering, not specifically to share with Christ. Even the hymnic piece seems radically reinterpreted by its context, so that in this letter it mirrors back the message of cosuffering with Paul. Furthermore, it is the suffering of Paul and Timothy as church leaders that occupies his attention here, not their suffering as baptized Christians. Thus it is not the passive endurance of persecution or martyrdom *per se* that defines this suffering, but the active struggle to proclaim the gospel and to teach the truth. Christ is not the model for this suffering, but the source—with God—of the power to engage in it.

The summons to suffering is thus not directed (through Timothy) to the church as a whole, but to the leaders of the church. The hymnic piece was probably originally intended for a baptismal service, where it reminded neophytes of the promise of salvation and warned them of the consequences of apostasy. In this new context, however, it speaks primarily to the situation of the church leaders, who are to endure everything for the sake of the elect and to demonstrate their confidence in, and faithfulness to, the gospel by engaging daily in the struggle to proclaim it.

When Paul asks Timothy to join him in suffering (1:8; 2:3), he is not insisting that Timothy join him in martyrdom but in proclaiming the gospel, which is itself a struggle (4:5; see also 1 Tim 4:10) and which may lead to persecution (3:10-12). The primary struggle, however, is with coworkers who are ashamed, opponents who are faithless, and an audience that is unresponsive—not with the Roman Empire. Paul's imprisonment forms the backdrop for this message. It is more a metaphor for this struggle than a dominant aspect of it. And just as his imprisonment will end with a crown of righteousness for him (4:8), so too nothing he (or Timothy) encounters will "chain" the gospel. The exhortation to join in suffering is thus at heart an exhortation about confidence in God. This captures the essence of Paul's own understanding of suffering, though the application is somewhat narrower.

Warnings About Opposing Teachers (2:14–3:9)

The central section of the letter, from 2:14 through 3:9, focuses on the presence of opposing teachers within the church. The material is logically connected with the preceding section with its summons to Timothy to join Paul in suffering (1:3–2:13, especially 1:8), for it describes in some detail how the struggle for the gospel is to be conducted in the face of opposition. The basic instruction to Timothy remains constant throughout the passage: Avoid these people and their controversies (2:14, 16, 22, 23; 3:5). A natural break occurs, however, at 3:1, for the opponents of 2:14-26 are presented as a current threat within the church, whereas the opponents of 3:1-9 are predicted (initially at least) as a feature of the "last days." The two sections can thus be treated separately, though they work together in presenting the picture of a church seriously threatened by teachers with false doctrine (2:18) and corrupt tactics (3:6-7).

Exhortations to Avoid Controversies (2:14-26)

Within 2:14-26, instructions to avoid debates with the opponents, whose teaching is degraded as "wrangling over words" (v. 14), "profane chatter" (v. 16), and "senseless controversies" (v. 23), are paired with advice to Timothy to engage in some substantially more profitable activities. He is to "rightly" explain the word of truth (v. 15), "pursue righteousness" (v. 22), and correct opponents with gentleness (vv. 24-26). By juxtaposing negative and positive exhortations in this way, the author is able to use the destructive wranglings of the opponents as an effective foil for the constructive actions encouraged of Timothy.

The core of this section consists of these instructions to Timothy. They are buttressed, however, by some quasi-biblical quotations (v. 19), enlivened by the concrete examples of Hymenaeus and Philetus (vv. 17-18), and elucidated by the image of the large house (vv. 20-21). In these three passages the author seems to draw upon traditional material to enhance his argument.

◊ ◊ ◊ ◊

The section opens with a transitional statement linking the preceding section, with its illustrations of diligent work (2:3-7), its

Pauline example of a willingness to "endure everything" (2:8-10), and especially its hymnic reminder of eschatological reward (2:11-13), with the warnings and exhortations that follow. This is one of the few places in this letter where the author seems explicitly to direct his comments beyond Timothy to others within the church: "Remind them . . . to avoid wrangling over words." These words are usually taken as a reference to the "faithful people" who are to be entrusted with the gospel (2:2), that is, other church leaders and not the whole of the elect (2:10). The elect (i.e., the laity), on the other hand, seem to be those who listen to the harmful debates and are harmed by them. The point, however, is not important, for the Greek text lacks the pronouns included in all modern English translations ("them"). A better translation focuses on the act of warning, not the recipients thereof: "Mention these things again and again, protesting against wrangling over words. . . . "

The activity of the opponents is here described as fighting or battling over words (Gk. *logomachein;* see also 1 Tim 6:4), a common charge in philosophical disputes (Karris 1973, 553). This battle image is picked up again in verses 23-24 in the reference to "quarrels" (Gk. *machas,* a word often used of military battles) and in the directive to the Lord's servant not to be "quarrelsome" (Gk. *ou machesthai*). These directives clarify the nature of the struggle that Timothy has been urged to undertake. In spite of the military imagery of 2:3-4, this struggle is not to involve verbal battles with opponents.

Two complementary reasons are given in verse 14 for avoiding word battles. They are not useful, a criterion characteristic of this author's pragmatism and of philosophical polemics as well (1 Tim 4:8; Titus 3:8-9). More to the point, they destroy (literally, "overturn") listeners by undermining their faith (v. 18), especially when it is weak (see 3:7). The positive advice to Timothy in verse 15 highlights the difference between the opponents and the ideal "worker." (In the Pauline churches, "worker" [Gk. *ergates*] was a technical term for a church leader; see 2 Cor 11:13; Phil 3:2; 1 Tim 5:18; also Rom 16:3, 6, 9.) Such a worker is approved by God (see also 2:4), not ensnared by the devil (v. 26), and is not ashamed (v. 15). The last point ("no need to be ashamed") echoes the concern raised earlier and here too indicates confidence in the power of God that manifests itself in active and energetic ministry (see comments on 1:8). The final clause in verse 15 defines the concrete shape this ministry should take in the face of destructive word battles, though the Greek phrase found here is more vivid than the NRSV suggests. It contains a rare Greek word (*orthotomein*) that means literally "to cut a path in a straight line" (Prov 3:6; 11:5). In some contexts this verb may have the diluted meaning of doing something "rightly," but the literal image of cutting a straight path is an effective part of the warning against getting sidetracked into word battles.

Verse 16 repeats the message of verse 14 but highlights the empty content of the opponents' teachings ("profane chatter," see also 1 Tim 6:20) instead of their disputatious tactics. From such empty chatter flows impiety, while virtue is the natural companion of sound teaching (1 Tim 6:4, 11; Titus 3:8-9). This edifying point is suggested by the constructive advice to Timothy in verse 22. Before getting to that point, however, the author describes the situation in more detail. He names some opponents, uses a vivid image to clarify the status of the church, and cites some scripture-based texts to provide assurance—and exhortation—to those buffeted by conflicting claims of truth.

The named opponents (see also 1:15) include Hymenaeus, who was also mentioned in 1 Tim 1:20, and an otherwise unknown Philetus. There is no way to determine if these were men known through the tradition to have been opponents of Paul, men who were threatening the church in the author's day, or purely fictitious names. The image of spreading gangrene suggests, however, that they represented a serious threat to the church. The use of medical imagery to depict the danger of opponents was common in philosophical discourse; Plutarch, for example, likened the talk of flatterers to gangrene and cancer (*How to Tell a Flatterer from a Friend* 24). This author uses similar language (3:8; 1 Tim 6:4; Titus 1:15) and also develops the counterimage of the church as the repository of "healthy" (NRSV: "sound") teaching (1:13; 4:3; 1 Tim 1:10; 6:3; Titus 1:9, 13; 2:1) (Malherbe 1980).

Rarely does the author reveal the content of his opponents' teaching. His brief statement here on their view of the resurrection is only the second time he provides concrete information (see also 1 Tim 4:3) and the only time that he divulges their *theology*. He does not indicate, however, how they understood the resurrection. Some significant manuscripts describe them as teaching that *a* (not "the") resurrection has taken place, leaving open the possibility of another future one and reducing (but not entirely eliminating) the disagreement with Paul's own teachings (see below). With the definite article, though (the reading preferred by most commentators), the text probably reflects a form of the overrealized eschatology that Paul encountered at Corinth. This eschatology was rooted in an understanding of baptism as a participation both in Christ's death and in his resurrection. Baptized Christians, then, could conclude that they too had been resurrected, though it was necessarily a spiritual resurrection that they experienced (the probable implication of 1 Cor 4:8). In Corinth they seem also to have denied any necessity of a (future) bodily resurrection since they regarded the flesh (Gk. *sarx*) as irrelevant (1 Cor 15:35-55).

Paul was careful to avoid these conclusions, at least in his letter to Rome, and interpreted the new life of the baptized Christian as a new moral life of obedience that carried the promise of future resurrection life (Rom 6:3-11). The author of the Pastoral Letters has captured this distinction (2:11-12; Titus 2:11-13; 3:6-7), but the authors of Ephesians and Colossians, if different from Paul, were not so careful (Eph 2:4-7; Col 1:13; 2:11-14), and neither were the opponents in the Pastoral Letters. They not only seem to have shared the Corinthians' view that the resurrection was a past—and purely spiritual—event, but they also seem to have embraced the spirit-body dualism that facilitated that view. Thus they promoted an ascetic life similar to one Paul encountered in Corinth and linked it to a rejection of the created world (1 Tim 4:3; cf. 1 Cor 7:1-16).

Clearly the opponents were having some success in promoting their view and the author offers reassurance in the face of the spreading defections. The identity of the "firm foundation" (literally, "firm foundation stone") is not indicated, nor is it terribly important. The image is drawn from Isa 28:16, a passage that elsewhere in the New Testament has been applied to Christ (Rom 9:33; 1 Cor 3:10-12; 1 Pet 2:6). Here the probable referent is the church, but the important thing is the stability of this foundation stone in the face of the opponents' faith-overthrowing message and thus the reliability of the messages it bears. The words are "sealed" on the stone, an incongruous image, but one that emphasizes the concept of ownership conveyed by the first quotation (see 2 Cor 1:22; Eph 1:13).

This quotation (v. 19a) is drawn nearly verbatim from the Greek version of Num 16:5 ("the Lord" replaces "God" in the original text). The context of the original quotation, which concerns a rebellion against the leadership of Moses and Aaron, is apt. The correspondence with the situation reflected in this letter may, however, be coincidental, especially if the author received the two quotations already linked together, perhaps as part of a baptismal liturgy, and no longer associated with the original texts. The second quotation is, in fact, not a biblical quotation at all but a freely composed saying drawing only loosely on the wording of some biblical texts (see Job 36:10; Isa 26:13; 52:1; Sir 17:26).

The sayings carry several layers of meaning. In a baptismal setting they would have referred to the church as a whole. In *this* letter, however, the first saying points either to those within the church who are not swayed by the opponents' teaching or, more fitting to this letter's emphasis, to the church leaders who are "rightly explaining the word of truth" (2:15). The second saying is then a summons to turn away from the wickedness promoted and exemplified by the opposing teachers. The image of the two kinds of vessels further develops this idea (vv. 20-21). It also introduces some confusion into the picture, for it seems to be only partially suited to the situation defined in this letter.

The image introduced in verse 20 may have its origin in some of Paul's illustrations (Rom 9:19-24; 1 Cor 3:11-15; 12:12-26), which were themselves influenced by Old Testament precursors (Isa 29:16; 45:9; Jer 18:1-11; Wis 15:7-13). The application here is, however, distinctive and somewhat surprising. The image does not involve the destruction of the utensils meant for usage lacking high honor (Gk. *eis atimian*; translated variously as "ordinary use" [NRSV], "ignoble" [RSV], "held cheap" [REB], or "humble" [NAB]); nor does it call for their removal from the "large house" (clearly a metaphor for the church). Instead it presumes the continued existence within the "house" of both types of utensils and focuses solely on the need for those intended for honor (Gk. *eis timēn*) to separate themselves from the activities or (less likely) from the persons mentioned above.

The Greek phrase, *apo toutōn*, can mean either "from these things" (NRSV, REB, RSV, NJB) or "from these persons" (see NEB textual note), but the development of the thought in verse 23 indicates that the author had activities in mind. Though the image is capable of interpretation in terms of the lives of ordinary Christians, the goal of the cleansing—to produce utensils "useful to the owner"—reflects the letter's specific interest in shaping "Timothy" as a useful church leader in the struggle for the gospel (2:3-4, 15; 3:16-17). The two kinds of utensils thus seem to represent, on the one hand, approved workers (v. 15)—the Lord's servants (v. 24)—and, on the other, the treacherous opposing teachers (3:2-9).

In verse 22 the author returns to direct exhortations (see v. 16). The admonitions to Timothy are, for the most part, positive. They complement the earlier message concerning the opponents (whose idle chatter and impiety are to be avoided) by focusing attention on the virtues expected of the ideal teacher. Timothy is first enjoined, however, to shun (literally, "flee," see also 1 Tim 6:11) some passions described in the NRSV as "youthful." A reference to Timothy's age seems surprising here (but see 1 Tim 4:12). The Greek adjective *(neōterikas)* can mean "natural to a youth" (Josephus *Ant.* 16 §399), but it is closely related to a verb that means "to make innovations" *(neōterizein)*. Though this nuance is not clearly attested elsewhere for the adjective until the third century C.E., it makes much better sense of this exhortation than a reference to age and is the likely meaning here: Flee the passions for (theological) innovation seen in the opposing teachers (Spicq 1969). Pursue instead "righteousness, faith, love, and peace." The list of virtues is familiar (see 3:10; 1 Tim 4:12; 6:11), but a certain emphasis falls on the last item, peace.

In the third and final admonition to avoid debates with the opponents (v. 23; see also vv. 14, 16), the author dismisses their discussions as "stupid" (Gk. *mōras*) and boorish or uninformed (Gk. *apaideutos;* see also 1 Tim 1:6-7; 6:4; Titus 3:9). As in verse 14, the opponents' contentiousness is highlighted, and this leads here to a description of the ideal church leader as one who promotes the opposite, that is, peace. The characteristics of this leader, who bears the traditional title, "the Lord's servant" (see also 2:15; Titus 1:1; Rom 1:1; Gal 1:10; Phil 1:1), match in many ways the attributes expected of the bishop (1 Tim 3:2-3), but here attention is given to the purpose of the required gentleness.

The hope is expressed here that through gentle education or correction opponents may be led to a knowledge of truth. (The Greek word *paideuein* can also imply discipline, but that does not fit the emphasis on gentleness; see also 1 Tim 1:20; Titus 2:12.) This is clearly rooted in the author's conviction that it is God's will to save all (1 Tim 2:4; see also Titus 1:13), for in these letters knowledge of truth is equivalent to faith (1 Tim 2:4; 4:3). The hope for change is also expressed in terms of escape from the devil's snare (see also 1 Tim 1:20; 3:6-7), but the Greek word *(ananēphein)* actually suggests the more vivid image of returning to one's senses (so REB) as from a drunken stupor (see 4:5). The "snare," then, is the delusion perpetrated by the myths and wordy debates of the opponents.

The meaning of the rest of the verse is widely disputed. Two different pronouns are used in the comment about being held "captive by *him* (Gk. *autou*) to do *his* (Gk. *ekeinou*, literally, 'that one's') will," leading some to conclude that they refer to two different agents, the devil and God (see NRSV textual note). Even if the two pronouns refer to a single agent it is not entirely clear whether God or Satan is meant. The Greek word translated "held captive" in the NRSV is an unusual one *(zōgrein)*, which means literally "to save or take captive *alive,*" or even "to preserve alive" (with some emphasis on "alive"). If the positive nuance of preserving alive prevails, the agent could well be God. The preceding reference to the devil's snare seems to place the emphasis, however, on capture and thus on Satan as the agent. Whose will is accomplished is less clear. An allusion to God's will, if intended, could have been more clearly expressed and the devil is the most proximate of the two possible references. However, the idea of the opponents ultimately doing God's will makes sense of the image of preserving both kinds of vessels in God's house (vv. 20-21). Even the opponents can be cleansed and transformed into utensils useful for God's purposes. The exact meaning of the verse remains, however, unclear.

◊ ◊ ◊ ◊

Though composed primarily of exhortations to Timothy, this section reveals the rather complex social situation that, we may presume, characterized the author's own church. There were, it seems, at least two factions struggling for influence and leadership within the church: one represented in this letter by Hymenaeus and Philetus, the other by Timothy. The opposing faction seems to have been rather strong. The energy with which the author combats it and the image of spreading gangrene both suggest this, though the author is confident that ultimately the movement will be curtailed (3:9). Both factions existed within the church and the author does not foresee, nor does he advocate, the expulsion or departure of either one. The Lord's house, he suggests, contains both useful and disreputable utensils, leaders who rightly explain the word of truth and others who do not even know it, some who are the Lord's servants and others who (on one reading of the text) do the will of the "devil."

The theologies of the two groups are clearly different, but the author's refusal to engage the opponents in substantive debate does not permit us to see exactly how different they were. Certainly their disagreement on the fundamental question of the resurrection implies other areas of theological dispute as well. The author's primary concern, however, is with praxis, not theory, especially with their debating and arguing. The repeated exhortation in this chapter is to avoid such activities (see also 1 Tim 6:3-5, 11, 20; Titus 3:9). The author has a rich vocabulary for avoidance and uses it fully to emphasize his point. The very act of engaging in such arguments is viewed as destructive to the rest of the church. Instead of entering into discussions, Timothy is to pay attention to his own teaching

(v. 14) and actions (v. 22), confident in the knowledge that God can see into the heart of the matter (v. 19) and will reward those who remain faithful (v. 12).

This suggests a radical understanding of what it means to suffer for the gospel. One endures the presence of opponents within the church. One even endures the painful experience of their apparent success. One does not engage in hostile debates with them, but corrects them gently, knowing that they are utensils in God's house for which God may have some use. This treatment of opponents is correlated with God's firm foundation: "The Lord knows those who are his" (2:19). This statement promotes confidence in the face of apparent defeat, but it also promotes an attitude of patience and gentleness. Even the bellicose opponent may prove, by repentance, to be one of God's own. One must therefore treat everyone kindly. Confident possession of the truth does not lead to arrogance or abuse because this truth includes the truth of God's mercy. As an instrument of God, the author suggests, the church leader must treat everyone in a way that promotes God's merciful purposes and respects the mystery of God's election.

This benevolent tone does not prevail throughout these letters. Indeed, the author can use exceedingly harsh language when speaking of opposing teachers (Titus 1:12-16; 3:9-11). Benevolence, however, is particularly appropriate to the theology expressed by this author. Here, at least, the author seems to recognize that his message of God's desire for the salvation of all (1 Tim 2:4; 4:10; Titus 3:11), of God's evident mercy (1 Tim 1:16), and of God's goodness and loving-kindness (Titus 3:4-5) is promoted by church leaders who embody those traits in their own words and deeds.

Prediction of the Last Days (3:1-9)

The core of this passage (vv. 2-4) is an extensive vice list, the longest, after Rom 1:29-31, in the entire New Testament (see comments on 1 Tim 1:9-10). It appears here as a description of the moral decay that will occur "in the last days." The graphic depiction of violent moral rebellion accentuates the gentle and righteous behavior enjoined of Timothy in the preceding verses (2:22-26) and the righteous and steadfast portrait of Paul that follows (3:10-11). A single command to Timothy interrupts the description of evil persons to come: "Avoid them!" This links the current passage to the preceding one (2:14-26), which was structured around variants of that exhortation. It also marks a shift from the prediction of future distress to the concern for present dangers that dominates the rest of the passage (vv. 5-9).

◊ ◊ ◊ ◊

A conjunction in the Greek text (*de*, "but"), left untranslated by the NRSV (cf. NAB: "But understand this . . . "), explicitly connects and contrasts the exhortations for the ideal church leader in 2:22-26 with the prediction of rampant immorality in 3:1-9. This immorality is not, however, directly attributed to the opponents described in chapter 2. Rather, it defines the context within which the appearance of these people must be understood—the chaos of the "last days." In apocalyptic literature this chaos is often defined in both cosmic and ethical terms: the sun and the moon will be destroyed and all righteousness will be forsaken (2 Esdr 5:1-12; *2 Apoc. Bar.* 70:2-6; Mark 13:5-27). The focus here is exclusively on the prediction of moral decay, and in this regard the passage also resembles the testamentary literature of hellenistic Judaism.

In testamentary literature, which is thoroughly pseudonymous, a dying patriarch exhorts his offspring, usually in conjunction with a prediction of the spread of immorality and the appearance of dangerous enemies (*T. Moses* 5-9; *T. Gad* 8:2-4; *T. Dan* 5:1-6; see also Acts 20:18-35; 2 Pet 2:1-3; 3:3-10). In like manner, "Paul" here exhorts Timothy and predicts rampant immorality in the last days. This prediction is not supported in these letters by a pervasive apocalyptic outlook. Indeed, the companion letters of 1 Timothy and Titus, with their concern for church leadership positions, social stability, and the quiet and peaceable life, show little trace of such an outlook. Second Timothy contains more references to "that day" (1:12, 18; 4:8), but the real focus is on the end of Paul's suffering, not the end of the world. The message of the last days serves primarily as an interpretive device, locating the explanation of the opponents' success in the inevitability of apocalyptic decay. The primary concern, however, is to bolster the letter's warnings and exhortations, not to orient the church to the imminent end of the age.

The extensive but stereotypical list of vices shows some attention to alliterative arrangement. It opens and closes with similar items ("lovers of . . . ") and groups together the large number of words that begin with the Greek letter *alpha* (the equivalent of the negative English prefix "un-"). Six of the eighteen items on the list are found only here in the NT. Four are also found in Rom 1:29-31, a passage that may have served as a model for this one. There are, however, similar lists in the writings of Greco-Roman moral philosophers, especially those of Philo, who also contrasts love of self and love of God (*On Flight and Finding* 81).

Certain items in the list echo themes developed elsewhere in these letters. The opponents, for example, have been accused in several places of greed (1 Tim 6:5-10; Titus 1:11), and, contrariwise, absence of greed is a trait to be sought in those holding positions of leadership (1 Tim 3:3, 8; Titus 1:7). The aggressive and abusive behavior suggested by a number of these items is consistent with the battle imagery often used to describe the opponents' actions (see comments on 2:14, 23; 1 Tim 6:5; Titus 1:10). The charge of disobedience to parents (also found in Rom 1:30) implies an utter lack of the respect for social order that lies at the heart of many of the exhortations of 1 Timothy and Titus (1 Tim 3:4, 12; 5:1-2; 6:1; Titus 1:6; 2:5, 9; 3:1). It also stands in sharp contrast to the behavior exhibited by—and further encouraged of—Timothy, who is Paul's "beloved child" (1:2). The word translated "swollen with conceit" should probably be translated "deluded" instead (see comments on 1 Tim 3:6; 6:4; Lucian *Nigrinus* 1), for that meaning fits well the picture that emerges of opponents who are both deceivers and deceived (3:13), bereft of understanding (1 Tim 1:7; 6:4; Titus 1:15), and without knowledge of the truth (2:18, 25; 1 Tim 6:5).

It is difficult to see how people described with the terms listed here could be granted to have even the "outward form of godliness" (v. 5). Godliness (Gk. *eusebeia*) implies both a reverence for God and a reverent manner of life (see comments on 1 Tim 2:2), but the vices mentioned here leave no room for even a semblance of this piety. It is likely, then, that with this charge the author has begun thinking of his concrete opponents. These opponents' asceticism (1 Tim 4:3) provides a veneer of godliness, but their rebellious and divisive activities and their rejection of the truth belie the real presence of godliness in their lives (see also Titus 1:16). The rest of the passage (vv. 6-9) quite unambiguously addresses the problem of the author's contemporary opponents, who are depicted as having their origins in, and thus as partaking in the nature of, the apocalyptic manifestation of evil.

The central problem for this author is the teaching activity of his opponents. He addresses this problem here in several ways: with an injunction to avoid these teachers, with a description of their activities that is intended to belittle them, and with a comparison to two Old Testament figures that suggests their ultimate defeat. He describes these teachers in a way that suggests the activities of clandestine warfare: They slip or insinuate themselves into (Gk. *endynein*) houses where they take prisoners (Gk. *aichmalōtizein;* NRSV: "captivate") with their deceptive words (3:13) and false doctrines (4:3-4).

His description of the "captives" draws on cultural stereotypes of women and is intended to denigrate the teachers by denigrating the audience to whom their teaching appeals. (Origen employs a similar tactic in *Against Celsus* 3.55.) He describes them as "little women" (*gynaikaria,* the diminutive of the Greek word *gynē*). Taken by itself this term is not as pejorative as the NRSV translation, "silly women," suggests. It can be used in a relatively neutral way (Epictetus *Enchiridion* 7; Marcus Aurelius *To Himself* 5.11), though the other phrases used in this passage to describe the women create a negative context for evaluating it. The women are "heaped up" (NRSV: "overwhelmed") with sins and led by "all kinds of desires." The author does not specify the nature or object of these desires. A few manuscripts refer to "desires *and pleasures,*" which suggests sensual appetites (Jas 4:3-4; 2 Pet 2:13-14), but that is not necessarily connoted by the original text. To be "swayed by . . . desires" simply represents the opposite of the temperate, godly, dignified, and contented life that the author holds up as the Christian ideal (1 Tim 2:2; 6:6).

It has been argued that the women who were victims of the opponents' guile were not Christians, since they could "never arrive at a knowledge of (saving) truth"; but that rests on too narrow and too literal a reading of the text. The concern found elsewhere in these letters to protect women of the church from the ascetic message of the opponents (1 Tim 2:11-15; 5:13-15; Titus 2:3-5) shows that the author clearly perceived them to be a sympathetic audience for the opponents' views. Moreover, complaints about students'—or opponents'—failure to attain real knowledge or to use it properly were familiar in philosophical circles (Epictetus *Discourses* 2.1.30; 2.9.13; Lucian *Runaways* 10) and often acquired a tone of mockery, especially when leveled against women. Horace, for example, mocks women who lie with philosophical works between their pillows (*Epodes* 8.15-16), and Epictetus complains that women pay attention only to the words of Plato, not to his meaning (*Discourses* frg. 15; cf. Musonius Rufus *Orations* 3). Juvenal bitterly denounces the woman who, in her desire to be deemed wise, "discourses . . . like a philosopher" and parades her knowledge before all (*Satires* 6.434-56). The description of the women in verse 6 thus draws on a cultural stereotype and was intended to defame the opponents as teachers who could only persuade people who were incapable of recognizing the truth.

Jannes and Jambres are the names given in some extracanonical writings, including the Dead Sea Scrolls, to the magicians who opposed Moses and Aaron—and God—at the time of the Exodus (Exod 7:11, 22; CD 5.18-19; Midrash *Tanḥuma* on Exod 32:1). By linking the opponents to these figures, the author provides a second interpretive perspective on the opponents, one that avoids the implication that they portend the end of the present age. They are instead viewed as the current example of a recurring pattern of opposition that has roots deep in Israel's history (see also v. 12).

The reference to Jannes and Jambres also provides reassurance about the fate of the opposition. Just as the two magicians were bested in their confrontation with Moses (Exod 8:18-19; 19:11), so too the opposing teachers will be bested in the current conflict. The author uses, however, the language of "progress" (Gk. *prokopē*, a technical term in Stoicism for moral development), to describe their fate (see comments on 1 Tim 4:15). While Timothy is instructed in how to progress to greater spiritual strength (1:6-14; 2:15, 22; 3:14-15), the opponents have been presented, with heavy irony, as those who "progress" only to worse conditions. (The final clause in 2:16 reads literally, "they will progress into more and more impiety"; see also 3:13.) The same point is made here, but now with the irony of understatement: "They will not progress much."

◊ ◊ ◊ ◊

Though the passage communicates the straightforward ethical advice to avoid evil people, its more basic message arises out of the connection with the passages that precede and follow. The message of this larger section is less about avoiding evil than it is about promoting apt teaching. This is communicated through the starkly contrasting portraits of "the Lord's servant" (2:24-26) and Paul (3:10-16) on the one hand, and the heirs of Jannes and Jambres on the other. The ideal Christian teacher is to avoid arguing with opponents, but he is not to avoid the opponents themselves. With them he is to be gentle, patient, and kind, and to act always out of hope for their salvation. The teachers described in 3:1-9 are associated—though not directly charged—with abuse, arrogance, and self-love. They employ deceitful tactics and capture, rather than effectively instruct, their students. Thus they reinforce the author's portrait of good teaching by depicting its opposite. At the same time, though, the author's tactics in 3:1-9 undercut his message in the previous passage. His rhetorical treatment of the opponents in 3:1-9 is far from gentle, and his instructions to avoid such people leaves no opportunity to instruct them. The author's rhetorical device of presenting the opponents as a negative foil for the description of apt teaching precludes the possibility of using them also to illustrate the gentle treatment that he advocates. One has to distinguish carefully between the ethical message proclaimed by the passage and the one implied by its rhetorical style. The latter derives from the hortatory techniques of hellenistic rhetoric; the former from the author's vision of universal grace.

Charge to Timothy (3:10–4:8)

This passage illustrates well the difficulty of dividing this particular letter into discrete sections. The first portion (3:10-13) is clearly meant to be read in conjunction with the preceding description of the opposing teachers, for the opening words of verse 10 (Gk. *sy de*; NRSV: "Now you") define what follows as a contrasting pattern of behavior. Indeed, the virtues listed in verse 10 stand in stark contrast to the conduct imputed to the opponents in 3:1-9. On the other hand, the Pauline model in 3:10-13 also forms the basis for the exhortations that follow in 3:14–4:5. Likewise, the description of Paul's imminent departure (4:6-8) is clearly intended to complement the exhortation of verse 5: "As for you . . . carry out your ministry fully. As for me . . . I have kept the faith." At the same time, though, this word of departure motivates the personal request to Timothy that follows in verse 9: "Do your best to come to me soon." Nevertheless, it is possible to consider 3:10–4:8 as a coherent unit. Exhortations to Timothy (3:14; 4:2, 5), which repeat those made earlier in the letter (1:6, 8, 13), constitute the core of these verses. References to the opponents described in 2:14–3:9 motivate these exhortations (3:13; 4:3-4) and, as in 1:6–2:13, Paul is presented as a model for Timothy to follow (3:10-11; 4:6-8). In fact, statements about Paul form a frame around the exhortations to Timothy, with 3:10-11 presenting the model of the suffering apostle (see also 1:15-16; 2:9-10), and 4:6-8 affirming the promise of eschatological reward (see also 2:11-12).

The passage is thus a reprise of themes introduced earlier in the letter. As such it contains various sorts of material: In addition to the exhortations there are reminders of Paul's career (which include a fairly traditional virtue list), a doctrinal statement about scripture, and several predictions of problems to come. The basic pattern of the argument is a series of contrasts and comparisons involving the opposing teachers, Timothy, and Paul and demarcated in the text by the phrases, "as for you" or "now you" (3:10, 14; 4:5) and "as for me" (4:6).

Example of Paul's Life (3:10-13)

The pattern of example and counterexample that is developed in this portion of the letter is very complex, with sometimes Paul and sometimes Timothy functioning as the positive role model. The opening words, "Now *you* have observed my teaching . . . ," create a clear distinction between Timothy, who has closely followed and patterned his life on that of Paul, and those who, like Jannes and Jambres, have opposed God's appointed leaders (1:11) and the gospel that has been entrusted to them. The NRSV's translation is somewhat misleading here, for the Greek verb *(parakolouthein)* suggests more than merely observing and points instead to properly understanding and actively following a teaching (1 Tim 4:6; 2 Macc 9:27). For Epictetus this word defined the difference between those who were capable of pursuing the philosophical life, with its emphasis on rational arguments and moral behavior, and those who were not (*Discourses* 1.7.33; 2.24.19). The same contrast is intended here. Timothy has grasped and followed the truth as it was embodied in Paul's life; the opposing teachers, with their corrupt and depraved minds (3:8; 1 Tim 6:5), oppose it.

If the initial contrast is between Timothy's observant following and the others' foolish opposition, it is Paul's life of steadfast virtue that is set against the moral vices of these opponents. The first aspect of Paul's life that is mentioned for emulation is his teaching. The word can, and here probably does, refer to both the activity and the content of Paul's teaching, for both the manner and the content of the opponents' teaching have been sharply criticized (2:18; 3:6-7). Throughout these letters, but especially in this section, teaching has emerged at the center of the author's concerns (3:14, 16; 4:2, 3), but doctrine and conduct go hand in hand (see comments on 1 Tim 1:10). Thus the second item on the list is Paul's conduct or manner of life. This conduct is not described here, nor is his "aim in life" (but see 2:10), but the four virtues that follow indicate its characteristic traits. Faith and love are the basic Christian virtues (1 Tim 1:5, 14; 2:15; 1 Cor 13:13); here they are supplemented with patience (2:24; 4:2) and endurance (NRSV: "steadfastness"; Gk. *hypomonē*), virtues that are promoted in the surrounding exhortations (see also 2:10, 12; Titus 2:2).

As in the opening chapters, the focus is on Paul's suffering (see 1:8, 12, 16; 2:9), which is linked for the first time in this letter directly with persecutions. This is in harmony with Paul's own statements (2 Cor 4:9; 12:10; Gal 5:11; 6:12) and with traditions about him preserved in the book of Acts (13:50). The latter seems to be the author's immediate source, for the reference to persecution in the three cities in south central Asia Minor follows closely the narrative in Acts 13–14. Though it is suffering and persecution—and the apostle's steadfastness in enduring it—that is emphasized here, the author introduces the message of rescue in verse 11, perhaps drawing directly on Psalm 34 (see Ps 34:7, 17, 19; LXX: 33:8, 18, 20). This message recalls the opening exhortation to rely on the power of God (1:8) and reappears with greater emphasis later in the letter (4:17, 18). Here the author is concerned to identify the persecution of the faithful and the prosperity of the wicked as part of a general pattern (vv. 12-13). He does not say who will persecute the Christians. The words are written against the backdrop of Paul's Roman imprisonment, but according to Acts the persecutions in Antioch, Iconium, and Lystra came at the hands of the Jews. Here, though, the author links persecution with neither of these but suggests a connection with the appearance and spread of opposition *within* the church.

The statement that "wicked people" will go (literally, "make progress") "from bad to worse" alludes to the traditional expectation that evil will proliferate in the "last days" (see comments on 3:1). More concretely, it anticipates the success of the author's opponents (in contrast to the suffering of the righteous), but as with other "predictions" in these letters, this one is probably a fairly accurate depiction of the situation faced by the author and his church. The author is not, however, pessimistic about the future. The change from bad to worse also signals the ultimate demise of his opponents (in contrast to the rescue of the righteous).

These "wicked people" are also called by a Greek word (*goēs*) that means both impostor and sorcerer. Though a common label employed in debates between philosophers and their opponents, the sophists (Plato *Symposium* 203d; Lucian *Fisherman* 42), it suits this author's polemic well, underscoring the connection with the magicians Jannes and Jambres and hinting at methods of trickery and deceit (3:6-8). The author also draws on a cliché of these debates when he charges opponents with being not simply deceivers, but *deceived* deceivers (Dio Chrysostom *Orations* 4.33; Philo *Migration of Abraham* 83; see also 1 Tim 2:14; 4:1; Titus 1:10). With this phrase he alludes to earlier accusations concerning their methods (3:6), their corrupted understanding (3:8; 1 Tim 1:7; 6:5), and their entrapment by the devil (2:26). Immediately following this sweeping accusation, the author exhorts Timothy to the opposite way of life.

The Charge Proper (3:14–4:5)

The basic pattern of contrast continues with the second occurrence of the Greek phrase, *sy de* (NRSV: "But as for you . . . "), in this section (see 3:10; 4:5). In an ironic parody of the Stoic ideal of progress in virtue (see comments on 3:9; 1 Tim 4:15), the author contrasts the "progress" of wicked people from bad to worse with the image of steady constancy: "Continue (or remain; Gk. *mene*) in what you have learned and firmly believed."

"What you have learned" clearly refers to the sound teaching (1:13; 4:3), the gospel preserved and protected by the church as its tradition or "deposit" (1:14; 1 Tim 6:20). Since this is so, the one from whom Timothy learned it must be Paul, who is presented throughout these letters as Timothy's instructor in the faith (1:13; 2:2; 1 Tim 1:18). Yet the relative pronoun ("whom") is plural in most of the Greek manuscripts *(tinōn)*, giving rise to the suggestion that Eunice and Lois, Timothy's mother and grandmother, are included in it (1:5). While the reference to his childhood (v. 15) would seem to support this hypothesis, it goes against the insistence of these letters that Paul and the ordained clergy are the only transmitters of official church teachings. Indeed, a small number of manuscripts have the masculine singular pronoun (Gk. *tinos*), clearly a reference to Paul as Timothy's sole instructor. While these manuscripts are not early enough or reliable enough to represent the original reading, they do show how some scribes interpreted the text. The plural pronoun is thus best understood as referring primarily to Paul but also including those through whom, or with whom, Paul transmitted the deposit of faith (2:2).

Knowledge of the source or mediator of the tradition provides one basis for Timothy's confidence in it. His firm grounding in scripture, which confirms the tradition, provides another (v. 16). The "sacred writings" (Gk. *ta hiera grammata*) are the Jewish

Scriptures. (The article, *ta*, is absent in some significant Greek manuscripts, but that does not alter the meaning.) This is a common way of referring to them in hellenistic Judaism (Philo *Life of Moses* 2.292; Josephus *Ant.* 10 §210), though the phrase was also used of pagan writings (Strabo *Geography* 17.1.5) and, somewhat later, of Christian ones (Methodius *Symposium* 5.1). Though by the author's time, children were being born into Christian homes where writings such as Paul's letters were highly revered (1 Tim 5:14; Titus 1:6), the pseudonymous recipient of this letter (i.e., Timothy) can only have been instructed in Jewish Scriptures, not Christian ones, from his babyhood (Gk. *apo brephous*). These Scriptures, however, when interpreted christologically, are able to provide instruction (Gk. *sophisai*; literally, "make one wise") concerning the Christian faith (see, e.g., Rom 1:2; 15:4; Gal 4:21-31).

The author digresses briefly to discuss the usefulness of scripture. The Greek word translated "scripture" in verse 16 is different from the word in verse 15 (the singular noun, *graphē*, rather than the plural one, *grammata*). It can mean simply "a writing," but in Jewish and Christian contexts it was almost a technical term for scripture (Rom 4:3; Gal 4:30) and probably means that here. It is the author's somewhat enigmatic reference to scripture's inspiration, however, that has spawned the most vigorous debate. This debate centers on the fact that the phrase "inspired by God" can be either attributive, identifying which scripture is meant ("All/every scripture inspired by God is also . . . "; so REB, NEB; see also NRSV, NJB, and NAB textual notes), or predicative, making an assertion about scripture ("All/every scripture is inspired by God and . . . "; so NRSV, RSV, NJB, NIV, NAB). The first reading suggests that there are writings or scripture or scripture texts that are not inspired; only the inspired ones are useful. The second affirms the opposite: *All* scripture or *every* scripture text is inspired and therefore useful. Grammatically it is impossible to adjudicate between these two readings. In either case, the author is not developing here a theory of inspiration (cf. 2 Pet 1:19-21; Philo *Special Laws* 1.65; 4.49; Josephus *Ag. Ap.* 1 §37; Plutarch *Oracles at Delphi* 7). He takes the inspiration of scripture for granted, and mentions it here only to underscore scripture's divine origin and thus its inherent authority, which complements its proven usefulness for ministry.

It is clear from the development of the sentence that the author's emphasis is on the usefulness (Gk. *ōphelimos*) of scripture (see also 1 Tim 4:8; Titus 3:8), which stands in sharp contrast to the opponents' myths that merely "tickle the ears" (see 4:3-4). It is harder to say whether the phrase "*all* scripture" is also intended as a polemic against the opponents' preference for only certain parts of scripture that could be interpreted as "myths" (see comments on 1 Tim 1:4).

The Greek word used here *(theopneustos)* is not the usual one for inspiration. (*Enthousia* and related words are found most frequently in discussions of the topic.) *Theopneustos* means literally "God-breathed," a word that recalls the Greek Delphic oracles. (These oracles were spoken by persons—usually women—thought to be filled with Apollo's breath [Plutarch *Obsolescence of Oracles* 40-42, 50-51; *Sibylline Oracles* 5.308].) The word also recalls, however, the account of creation in Genesis 2, which describes the creative, life-giving power of Yahweh's breath (Gen 2:7; see also Job 33:4; Ps 33[32]:6). These, however, are merely echoes. The thrust of the sentence is in a more practical direction.

The list of practical uses for scripture begins with teaching, thus giving that activity particular emphasis (see also 3:10; 4:2-3). It continues with other activities—reproof, correction, training—highlighted throughout these letters, especially, but not exclusively, in discussions of refractory opponents (2:25; 4:2; 1 Tim 5:20; 6:11; Titus 1:9, 13; 2:12, 15). The connection between verse 17 and the preceding statement about scripture's usefulness is not altogether clear. In the NRSV's translation the verse seems to present the purpose of the various teaching and correcting activities, to wit, to encourage good works among the people of God (1 Tim 6:18-19; Titus 2:11-14; 3:1). The Greek text, however, does not refer to "everyone who belongs to God" (i.e., every Christian) but to "the man of God" (Gk. *ho tou theou anthrōpos*). The same phrase appears in 1 Tim 6:11, where it refers to Timothy in his role as church leader. In light of this, and in light of the whole thrust of 2 Timothy, which addresses Timothy's role as church leader, it is likely that here, too, the author has the church leader and his ministry in mind (see also 2:21). Scripture, says the author, is an inspired and useful resource to the church leader, especially as he corrects and instructs opponents.

After the digression that began in verse 14*b*, the author returns in 4:1 to direct exhortation, which forms the climax of the body of the letter. Indeed, the exhortations in these verses summarize the main thrust of the letter and are introduced and emphasized by a solemn oath (see also 1 Tim 5:21; 6:13). Though God and Christ are mentioned together in the oath formula, the emphasis is on the eschatological role of Christ. The apocalyptic images of the final judgment of *all* people (implied by the phrase, "the living and the dead"; see also Acts 10:42; 1 Pet 4:5; 2 *Clem.* 1.1), of Christ's appearing (Gk. *epiphaneia*, here a reference to the parousia; see also Titus 2:13; cf. 2 Tim 1:10) to render that judgment, and of his kingdom, promised for the righteous after that judgment (4:8, 18) give the exhortations that follow a particular urgency. Timothy is motivated to zealous ministry not only out of consideration for the judgment he himself will face (cf. 1 Cor 3:10-15) but also for the judgment his flock will face.

The oath also gives to the final set of exhortations the quality of a formal charge. These exhortations repeat the substance and even the wording of those that fill earlier portions of this letter, but in a way and context that make it clear that Timothy is to take up the banner from Paul. The verses that follow refer to Paul's imminent departure (vv. 6-8) and the exhortations urge behavior that imitates Paul's. Paul, for example, has preached the gospel (1:11), been steady in unfavorable times (3:10-11), urged and exhorted (a better translation of the Greek verb *parakalein* than the NRSV's "encourage," given the context of opposition established by vv. 3-4), and taught with great patience (3:10). Teaching appears last, not first, on this list (cf. 3:10, 16), but this is still an emphatic position. Moreover, in that position it provides a smooth transition to another warning about the opposing teachers.

Though presented as a prediction of a time that is coming (see also 3:1; 1 Tim 4:1), verses 3-4 actually describe the situation in the author's own day, an unfavorable time in the church for sound teaching (v. 2). Here, as in 3:6-7, the author places responsibility for that situation in large part on the hearers rather than the teachers of the opposing doctrines. The common metaphor of "itching ears" (Gk. *knēthomenoi tēn akoēn;* see Plutarch *Superstition* 5; *Advice About Keeping Well* 7; Lucian *The Double Indictment* 1) alludes to an eagerness for novelty that is accommodated by the opponents' speculations, myths, and debates (2:16; 3:7; 1 Tim 1:4; 6:4-5; Titus 1:14; 3:9). The picture these verses evoke is one of large-scale defections to the opposing teachers (see also 1:15; 2:17; 3:13): People will not tolerate or put up with sound but familiar doctrine; they will "heap up" or accumulate (see 3:6) exciting teachers; and they will turn away from the truth (see 2:18; Titus 1:14) and follow after pleasing myths (see comments on 1 Tim 1:4). This sense of abandonment is reinforced on a more personal level in the final section of the letter when "Paul" mentions by name some of those who have left him.

This portrait of negative behavior leads to another contrasting exhortation ("As for you," Gk. *sy de*), summarizing again, but in a more general way, earlier portions of the letter (see, e.g., 2:14-26). The call to soberness (1 Tim 3:2, 11) is a call to clear-sightedness and prudence in the face of the challenge posed by fickle congregations and competing claims (see Philo *On Sobriety* 2-5). "Endure suffering" clearly refers to enduring the opposition presented by the new teachers. In this context it goes hand in hand with doing "the work of an evangelist." This does not refer to a special office within the church (see also Acts 21:8) but to the basic task of proclaiming and teaching the gospel, the "evangel" (4:2). The final exhortation then sums up the whole.

Completion of Paul's Ministry (4:6-8)

The author returns to the example of Paul's life (see 3:10-13), which forms a frame in this final section around the exhortations to Timothy. These particular verses do more, however, than provide an apostolic model of the behavior demanded of Timothy. They hint strongly at Paul's imminent death and thus bestow on the entire letter the quality of a final testament. The exhortations thus acquire added weight, not only because of the pathos of the situation (see also 1:3-4), but also because of its finality. Timothy must carry out his ministry not only in imitation of Paul, but in place of Paul. The allusions to Paul's impending death raise starkly the question of the continuity of the Pauline traditions, especially in the face of the competing messages of other teachers.

The preceding exhortations to Timothy (4:1-5) are explicitly grounded (Gk. *gar;* literally, "for") in the biographical statements in this passage, and the emphatic "as for me" of verse 6 (Gk. *egō*) corresponds to the equally emphatic "as for you" of verse 5 (Gk. *sy de*). With these words the author draws a contrast between Timothy's struggle, which continues, and Paul's, which is completed (cf. Prior 1989). The use of the drink offering as a metaphor for death probably derives from Phil 2:17, where the same Greek word appears *(spendomai).* The drink offering was a libation poured out, often on or around an altar, in honor of a god (Homer *Odyssey* 12.363; Plutarch *Obsolescence of Oracles* 49; Exod 29:38-42; Num 28:7; 2 Sam 23:16; Hos 9:4). As a metaphor for Paul's death, it gives to the apostle's final suffering a sacramental quality, a sign of his total dedication to God (see also Philo *On Drunkenness* 152). The reference to his departure (Gk. *analysis*) also echoes Philippians (1:23) where, as here, it refers to Paul's death (see also Philo *Flaccus* 187; Malherbe 1977a, 285).

The author draws on familiar images to summarize Paul's life (see 1 Cor 9:24-27). The first phrase refers to the athletic contest (Gk. *agōn*), not the battlefield (see also 2:5; 1 Tim 4:7-10; 6:11-12; cf. 1 Tim 1:18), and the emphasis is on untiring struggle (see also Phil 1:30; Col 2:1; 1 Thess 2:2). The footrace as a metaphor for life, especially the philosophical life, was commonplace (Marcus Aurelius *To Himself* 4.18, 51; Seneca *Epistles* 34.1-2; 109.6). Paul also used the image often (1 Cor 9:24; Gal 2:2; Phil 2:16; 3:13-14), and the same words found here are ascribed to him in Acts 20:24, though there the completion of the race is a future hope, not an accomplished event.

The final clause (NRSV: "I have kept the faith") abandons metaphor to speak straightforwardly of Paul's fidelity. The passage either picks up the distinctive use of the words "the faith" in these letters to refer to the content of Christian teaching (see comment on 1 Tim 4:1) and indicates Paul's faithful preservation of that teaching (1:14), or simply reflects a fairly fixed formula for having "kept faith" (see Josephus *J. W.* 6 §345). All three clauses show Paul having successfully completed what the letter asks of Timothy and other church leaders (1:13-14; 2:3-5, 15; 4:5). Paul has, in fact, summed up in his life and death the ideal of church leadership. What awaits is the eschatological reward, here described as the "crown of righteousness." The phrase is somewhat ambiguous, but just as the imperishable crown or wreath (Gk. *stephanos*) in 1 Cor 9:25 refers to the reward of imperishability itself (see 1 Cor 15:50-54), this crown probably refers to the gift of righteousness (Phil 3:9), which will be bestowed by the Lord on "that day," that is, on the day of judgment (1:12, 18). This is also the day of the Lord's appearing or epiphany (4:1; 1 Tim 6:14; Titus 2:13), and those who long for that day (literally, "love" it) are those who wait for it in hope and confidence (2:11-12; see also Titus 1:2; 2:13).

◊ ◊ ◊ ◊

The similarities between the message about suffering in 3:10–4:8 and Paul's words to the Philippians are striking enough to suggest that the author of 2 Timothy relied on that letter for his language and, to some extent, for his thought. At the same time, there are significant differences between the two. In Philippians, Paul views his "being poured out as a libation," that is, his death, as a possibility (Phil 2:17), but it is by no means a certainty (Phil 1:19-26). In 2 Timothy the libation is "already" happening. In Philippians, Paul's self-offering is joined to that of the Philippians (Phil 2:14-18) so that they rejoice in each other and in God's work in them. In 2 Timothy the focus is almost exclusively on the faithfulness of Paul and the corresponding exhortation of Timothy, with bare glimpses of a wider community in 3:12 and 4:8. In Philippians, Paul rejoices in what God is accomplishing through him and through the church (Phil 1:28-29; 2:13; 3:9). In 2 Timothy, especially in 4:6-8, Paul proudly presents what he himself has accomplished. And in Philippians, both Paul's suffering and the Philippians' are defined through the Cross (2:3-11), while the discussion of suffering in this passage has little christological content or context. The passage thus draws on the language of Paul, but it does not reproduce the apostle's ethical or theological emphases. This author's concerns are slightly different.

This passage reflects a view of the world, common in prophetic and apocalyptic literature, in which the righteous suffer and the wicked prosper (3:12-13; see also 2 Esdr 6:55-59; *2 Apoc. Bar.* 15:1-8). Within the specific situation envisioned in this letter, this means that the loyal church leader will suffer, while the opposing teachers will meet with success. In earlier portions of the letter, suffering derived primarily from the struggle to proclaim the gospel. That view is present here as well (4:5), but there is also a new emphasis on suffering as a consequence of persecution. Thus the earlier insistence that Timothy endure suffering (i.e., the suffering that defines the "work of the evangelist") is now complemented by the message of rescue from suffering (i.e., from suffering inflicted by enemies).

The theological grounding for both of these messages is provided in the sure saying of 2:11-13, especially in the promise that "if we endure, we will also reign," and that in all circumstances God remains faithful. The response to suffering—both kinds—that emerges from this is rooted in confidence in God's power and in God's faithfulness. Paul is thus presented as one who has experienced God's power and faithfulness when he was rescued from persecution (3:11; see also 4:17-18), who has completed the struggle that defined his ministry, and who thus faces the end of his life with equanimity, confident of his final reward. There is thus direct correspondence between the way Paul faces death, his experience of God's faithfulness during his ministry, and the message he proclaims. "If we endure, we shall reign." Paul's life and the confident way he faces death thus confirm the promises of God.

Throughout this letter, but especially in this passage, Paul's life is a model for Timothy's behavior and thus for the behavior of church leaders. Along with this model, however, goes a warning, for the promises of God are conditional. The sure saying makes that point very clear: "*IF* we endure, we shall reign." The author reinforces the point by placing the exhortations to Timothy directly under the shadow—or in the light—of the final judgment (4:1). Paul's faithful execution of his ministry allows him to face his judge with utter confidence (4:8). Timothy's response to the exhortation should also be made "in view of his appearing and his kingdom," that is, in awareness of the eschatological consequences of faithful obedience and of faithless ministry.

Theological interest in this passage has been focused almost exclusively on the question of the inspiration of scripture. For the author, however, that was not an issue at all. What he was concerned about was inspiring effective church leadership in a crisis situation. Paul provides a model for it; scripture provides a resource for it; and the final judgment provides motivation for it.

PERSONAL INSTRUCTIONS AND GREETINGS (4:9-22)

The final section of the letter comprises personal tidings, information about various coworkers, greetings, and a final benediction. Woven throughout is the request, repeated in several forms, for Timothy to come to Paul (vv. 9, 11, 13, 21).

Paul, following hellenistic conventions, closed most of his letters with personal greetings and travel plans (Rom 15:22–16:23; 1 Cor 16:5-24; Phlm 22-25; see also Titus 3:12-15), and a pseudonymous author, writing in Paul's name and emulating Paul's style, would be inclined to include similar details. Yet the greetings and instructions found here are so detailed and ordinary, and so realistic in their ordinariness, that they raise anew questions of authorship and motive.

Advocates of the authenticity of the Pastoral Letters find in these verses some of their strongest supporting evidence. Even proponents of pseudonymity are tempted to invoke here the hypothesis of fragments of authentic letters or authentic oral traditions to account for the striking details. Proponents of pseudonymity are also forced to confront here the specter of intentional deceit, for the inclusion of details such as the cloak and parchments seems to go beyond the formal demands of epistolary conventions and to arise instead from the author's intent to gain credibility for his pseudonymous creation, that is, from the author's conscious effort to deceive (see Introduction). Many of the personal details, however, complement or illustrate the message presented earlier in the letter (see also comments on 1:15-18). The section can thus be seen as a typical feature of hellenistic letters that has been creatively employed by the author to give concrete shape and a Pauline stamp to his theological message.

Though unified by the intimate tone and personal names, the material contained here falls into four parts: instructions to Timothy, which are interspersed with, and reinforced by, information about the doings of other coworkers (vv. 9-15); a reminiscence of Paul's experience earlier in his trial, which culminates in a formal word of praise to God (vv. 16-18); greetings to and from various persons, some unknown and some known from other New Testament writings (vv. 19-21); and a final benediction composed of elements found in other letters (v. 22; see also Gal 6:18; Phil 4:23; 1 Tim 6:21; Titus 3:15).

Travel Arrangements (4:9-15)

The theme of reunion with which the letter opens (see comments on 1:4) returns in these final verses, underscoring the bond between Paul and Timothy. The preceding reference to Paul's imminent death (vv. 6-8) adds a new note of urgency, though as the passage unfolds the sense of urgency fades. In fact, the explicit reason given for the request is Paul's loss of companions and coworkers, not his impending death. This message of abandonment is strong through most of the passage (vv. 10, 11, 16) and it picks up a motif introduced earlier in connection with Onesiphorus (1:15-18). In both places Paul is presented in circumstances that Timothy himself will face when the prediction of 4:3-4 is fulfilled—circumstances that the author's church already faced (see comments on 4:3-4)—and thus Paul's response to these circumstances serves as a model for later church leaders.

Demas is mentioned in other Pauline letters (Col 4:14; Phlm 24) without a trace of criticism. The reason given here for his departure (love for the present world) stands in contrast to the attitude praised in verse 8 (love for the Lord's epiphany). Love for the world probably connotes, not a purely hedonistic attitude, but a reluctance to embrace the tribulations and possible martyrdom that accompany the proclamation of the gospel (see, e.g., Pol. *Phil.* 9.2). Though mentioned in the same breath, the departures of Crescens (mentioned only here in the NT) and Titus (presumably the same Titus addressed in another letter) are not negatively motivated. In fact, they are not given any motivation; they are mentioned to enhance the portrait of the lonely apostle. Luke (see Col 4:14; Phlm 24), like Onesiphorus (1:16), is presented as an exception to the pattern of "desertion."

Tychicus is closely associated with the Pauline mission (Acts 20:4; Eph 6:21; Col 4:7; Titus 3:12), though no details of his work are given. It is possible that the author intends to imply that Tychicus will take over Timothy's work in Ephesus, though that is far from clear. Such an understanding would reduce somewhat the tension between the request for Timothy to leave Ephesus and come to Paul and earlier exhortations to him to continue diligently in his work, for his work would continue through Tychicus (2:15, 23-25; 3:14; 4:2-5).

The request for the cloak, books, and parchments is one of the most puzzling features of these letters. The desire for such "luxuries," which would take several weeks to arrive, seems to contradict the expectation of a really imminent martyrdom. Attempts to find special or symbolic value in the items find little support in the text. Nothing indicates that the mantle represents authority (cf. 2 Kgs 2:13), and even the rather widespread view that the parchments were the sacred scriptures (see 3:15) or copies of Paul's own letters is seriously undermined by evidence that the Greek word (*membranai*) is actually a common term for notebooks (see REB, NEB). The second item on the list (Gk. *ta biblia,* "the books") seems also to be void of special significance. According to one study, the word translated "above all" in the NRSV actually identifies the books with the notebooks: "bring . . . the books, that is, the notebooks" (Skeat 1979).

Alexander is certainly the same figure mentioned in 1 Tim 1:20, but it is not possible to determine if he is also identical to the enigmatic person referred to in Acts 19:33, or if he was an actual opponent of Paul or of the later church. His opposition mimics that of Jannes and Jambres (3:8), and implicit in the warning to Timothy is the assumption expressed earlier that those who follow Paul in ministry can expect to follow him in persecution as well (3:12).

The note of eschatological triumph reappears, however, in the reference (probably drawn from the Psalms [Ps 62:12; 28:4; cf. Rom 2:6]) to God's retribution (v. 14; see also comments on 3:9, 13; 4:1, 8). The conviction that God punishes the faithless (2:12*b*) finds its corollary in the conviction that God rewards the faithful (2:11-12*a*), and this second theme dominates the next section.

Results of the "First Defense" (4:16-18)

The author returns in these closing verses to his central theme of reliance on God (1:8, 12; 2:11-13, 19; 3:11; 4:8). He repeats and universalizes the charge of 1:15 and 4:10: "All" have deserted Paul. The situation in which this occurred is presented as Paul's "first defense" (Gk. *prōtē apologia*) in the NRSV. Many supporters of the letter's authenticity understand this to be a reference to Paul's first Roman trial and imprisonment (Acts 28), which resulted in the apostle's release (2 Tim 4:17), subsequent mission work including his work in Crete and new work in Ephesus, and then his second arrest and imprisonment in Rome. Yet the author does not refer anywhere else to an earlier Roman imprisonment, even when the context would encourage it (3:10-11). It is therefore likely that the verse actually refers to an earlier phase of the same trial (REB and NEB: "at the first hearing of my case"), similar to the hearings described in Acts 23:1-11; 24:1-21; 26:1-23.

The emphasis, however, is on the strength, support, and rescue that the Lord provides. Paul's experience thus offers an object lesson for Timothy, who was earlier urged to rely on the power and strength of God (1:8; 2:1). The proclamation of the message to the Gentiles does not necessarily imply Paul's release. As Phil 1:12-14 and Acts 28:16-31 indicate, the Christian message could be effectively proclaimed during, and even by means of, the apostle's imprisonment. Rescue "from the lion's mouth" is not to be taken literally. The phrase picks up the language of Ps 22:21*a* (see also Ps 7:2; 17:12; Dan 6:20-22, 27; 1 Macc 2:60) to refer to utter calamity.

Like the psalmist, "Paul" in this letter celebrates his rescue from the jaws of death (Ps 22:21*b*, 24) and expresses his confidence in future rescues as well.

This confident expectation of rescue seems directly to contradict the strong intimations of imminent martyrdom found in verses 6-8 (see Prior 1989). The rescue, however, is a rescue for the heavenly kingdom, not a rescue for life "in the flesh" (cf. Phil 1:22-26). Nevertheless, several comments in this section of the letter seem to presuppose an ongoing ministry of some sort: the request in verse 11 that Mark be brought to help (Gk. *eis diakonian;* possibly "for service [to me]" [see Phlm 11], but more likely a reference to the Christian ministry [see 4:5]) and the request for books (v. 13). It is also noteworthy that the author cites as a motive for haste (v. 21) the impending advent of a season when sea travel was difficult (winter) rather than Paul's impending death.

The language of verse 18 is strongly reminiscent of the final petition of the Lord's Prayer (Matt 6:13), but it also reflects the language of the psalms, especially their petitions for, and trust in, divine deliverance (see, e.g., Ps 31:2, 22; 71:2, 4, 23; 144:2, 7, 11; see also 2 Cor 1:10; 2 Thess 3:2-3). The passage, which is brimming with confidence and trust, concludes appropriately with words of praise that probably reflect the church's liturgy (see also 1 Tim 1:17; 6:15-16).

Final Greetings and Benediction (4:19-22)

Personal greetings were a common feature in Paul's letters. They extend and confirm the bonds of friendship and affection that link the widely spread churches. Many, but not all, of the persons mentioned here are known from other New Testament writings. Prisca and Aquila, for example, apparently resided for a time in Ephesus (Acts 18:18-19, 24-26; cf. Rom 16:3; 1 Cor 16:19). Onesiphorus was mentioned earlier in the letter (1:16), but the reference to his household instead of to himself suggests that he was known to have died. An Erastus is associated in Acts 19:22 with Timothy and, according to Rom 16:23, was a resident of Corinth. The same person may be intended here. Trophimus is briefly mentioned in Acts 20:4; 21:29. The persons who send greetings are unknown, but the large number of them softens the portrait of stark abandonment that dominates the passage.

◊ ◊ ◊ ◊

The concluding verses of the letter present a portrait of Paul that confirms the letter's fundamental theological messages about the need to suffer and the promise of eschatological reward. The apostle is in prison, alone, abandoned by some, opposed by others. In short, he is suffering for the gospel (1:8). There is, however, no sign of weakness or regret. Though awaiting death, Paul still energetically directs the work of proclaiming the gospel (4:11-12). Moreover, he professes his utter confidence in God's strengthening presence, faithful support, and promised heavenly reward. In all of this he models the behavior demanded of Timothy.

When Timothy is urged to come to Paul, this constitutes a request to demonstrate his loyalty to the apostle and also his lack of shame at both Paul's circumstances and Paul's gospel. He is asked, in effect, to imitate the much-praised Onesiphorus (1:16-18). Subsequent generations—the author's contemporaries—demonstrate their loyalty and lack of shame by not abandoning the standard of sound teaching that originated with Paul, even when they are abandoned and reviled by others.

The example of Demas suggests that failure to accept the hardships associated with ministry is equivalent to deserting Paul and betrays as well a dangerous preference for the present world over the future epiphany and the kingdom that it brings. The example of Alexander suggests that opposing the Pauline message is tantamount to betraying Paul himself (4:11-12), thus equating those who opposed Paul—whether in Paul's own time or the author's time—with those who persecuted him (3:11).

At the same time, the overwhelming number of persons mentioned in connection with Paul—Crescens, Titus, Luke, Mark, Tychicus, Carpus, Prisca, Aquila, Erastus and the rest—indicates that the Pauline churches, the Pauline tradition, and the Pauline gospel can survive the death of the apostle. The struggle will continue (3:1, 12; 4:3), but the Lord remains faithful (2:13).

COMMENTARY: TITUS

SALUTATION (1:1-4)

The salutation of Titus resembles most closely that of 1 Timothy. Both refer to God's command, to hope, to God as Savior, and to a loyal child. The salutation in Titus is, however, considerably longer. In fact, it is longer than most of the other Pauline salutations. Only the one to Rome, with its lengthy description of the gospel, and the one to Galatia, which includes a doxology, exceed it in length and complexity. In Titus the added length arises from an elaborate presentation of the goal and foundation of Paul's apostleship, an odd feature for a letter ostensibly written to a trusted coworker (cf. Phlm 1-3). Some see it as an indication that Titus originally stood at the head of the Pastoral Letters, where its salutation functioned as an introduction to all three. Its compressed phrases, however, make precise analysis of its contents difficult.

◊ ◊ ◊ ◊

Paul is introduced in this letter with two titles: the familiar "apostle of Jesus Christ" and a new one, "servant (or slave) of God." In the undisputed letters, Paul refers to himself as servant or slave (Gk. *doulos*) of Jesus Christ (Rom 1:1; Gal 1:10; Phil 1:1), indicating the one he serves as Lord. He knows, however, that all believers are enslaved to God (Rom 6:22), which is for him another way of saying that they are enslaved to righteousness (Rom 6:18), that is, compelled to a life of righteous obedience. He does not, though, apply the title "servant of God" to himself or to any other person. The title is, however, found in the Old Testament, where it was frequently used of those who served God's purposes through their leadership roles in Israel. Thus Paul is here identified by this ancient title of honor as one who, like David (2 Sam 7:5), Abraham (Ps 105:42), and especially Moses (Josh 1:1-2) and the prophets (Jer 25:4; Amos 3:7), speaks and acts in God's name and at God's command (1:3; see also 2 Tim 2:24).

The author clarifies the nature of Paul's apostleship by indicating its goal (NRSV: "for the sake of"): faith and knowledge of truth. Here, as elsewhere in the Pastoral Letters, these terms are linked so closely together that they appear to be almost synonymous, though "knowledge" emphasizes the rational side of belief (see 1 Tim 4:3*b*; also 2:4; 2 Tim 2:25). The precise content of this "truth" is nowhere clearly indicated, though it certainly includes the basic elements of Christian proclamation (1 Tim 3:15-16; 4:3-4; 2 Tim 2:18). As used in these letters, however, the word has a distinctly polemical thrust, for this author constantly warns against teachers who present a message that stands opposed to the truth (1:14; 2 Tim 3:8) and is no more reliable than a myth (1:14; see comments on 1 Tim 1:4). As he does frequently in these letters, the author further describes this truth as being in accordance with godliness (Gk. *eusebeia*), that is, as fostering a life of piety and obedience (see comments on 1 Tim 2:2; 6:3-10).

It is not clear whether "the hope of eternal life" further defines the goal of Paul's apostleship, the nature of godliness or truth, or the basis or goal of faith and knowledge (Spicq 1969, 2:593). In this passage the phrase serves primarily to provide a reasonably smooth transition to the next point, which concerns the revelation of God's long-hidden plan. This pattern is familiar from the Pauline letters (Rom 16:25-26; 1 Cor 2:7-10; Col 1:25-26), though the language here is distinctive and the syntax is awkward. The basic contrast is between a promise given "before the ages began" (Gk. *pro chronōn aiōniōn;* literally "before eternal times"), probably in God's preexistent will (see 2 Tim 1:9-10), and its revelation through the proclamation of the gospel. The text literally speaks of a revelation of God's word (Gk. *logos*) "in its own appointed times" (author's translation). The plural "times" (Gk. *kairoi;* see also 1 Tim 2:6; 6:15) can have a singular sense, referring to time in general (so NRSV: "in due time"), but the intended meaning here is probably plural, for the apostolic proclamation reveals the existence and nature of God's promise of salvation on repeated occasions, each one part of God's predetermined plan. The "word" is thus the gospel message (see 2 Tim 2:9), which reveals and actualizes the eternal promise when it is proclaimed by Paul, by Titus (3:8), or by appointed church leaders (1:9).

God is appropriately called Savior here (see also 3:4; 1 Tim 1:1; 2:3) because it is God's unwavering promise of salvation that lies behind the proclamation. Yet in the next verse Christ is also called Savior because, as 2:13-14 and 3:6-7 make clear, it is only through Christ that the promised salvation can be realized.

Titus, like Timothy, is greeted as Paul's loyal or "legitimate" child, with an added reference to "the faith we share" (Gk. *kata koinēn pistin*). The Greek is not entirely clear (literally, "according to [the] common faith"), but this is probably a reference to the faith or religion (see comments on 1 Tim 4:1) shared by all sound Christians (1:1; see also 2 Tim 1:3-5). In the context of this salutation, though, the phrase highlights the commonality of Paul's and Titus's faith in particular. Thus when the opponents are mentioned later in the letter, the contrast with Titus becomes clear, for they are presented as those who do not share the apostle's faith (1:13, 16; 3:11) and are therefore not his legitimate heirs (see comments on 1 Tim 1:2).

◊ ◊ ◊ ◊

The distinctive feature of the Christology of the Pastoral Letters lies in the interpretation of the coming of Jesus as an epiphany, a revelation of God's saving intent. Indeed, the author often views the Christ-event as a whole, compressing it into a single revelatory moment (2 Tim 1:8-10; Titus 3:4; also 1 Tim 2:3-6). He makes no attempt, however, to connect this moment with earlier revelations of God's saving nature: the Exodus from Egypt, the covenant on Mt. Sinai; the promises to David. Seen from the perspective of what is often called "salvation history," then, the picture that emerges in these letters seems static and isolated, a sudden illumination of God's plan of salvation.

The salutation of this letter reveals, however, the rather different view of its author. He has a dynamic view of revelation, but the dynamism is to be seen not in terms of earlier revelations to Israel, but in terms of subsequent revelations through the proclamation of Paul and his legitimate heirs (2 Tim 1:10*b*). Indeed, the letters hint at a number of revelatory moments. The Christ-event is the primary revelatory event, but the apostolic proclamation also reveals God's salvation. Likewise, Paul's life reveals God's saving grace (1 Tim 1:13-16) and the exemplary lives of local church leaders reveal the transforming power of this grace (1 Tim 4:11-16). Even the letters themselves, perhaps *especially* the letters themselves, with their emphasis on God's kindly nature and desire that everyone be saved (1 Tim 2:4), contribute to the ongoing revelation of God's saving intent.

BODY OF THE LETTER (1:5–3:11)

After the salutation, the author moves directly into the body of the letter. There is no trace of the thanksgiving that opens most of the Pauline letters, not even a prologue like that found in 1 Tim 1:3-20.

The letter is presented as a reminder or clarification of why Titus was left in Crete: to "put in order what remained to be done," which specifically includes the appointment of elders. The opening section addresses the task of appointing these elders and includes a warning about some "rebellious people" the elders are charged to refute. The heart of the letter comprises instructions concerning the behavior of various groups in the church (2:1-10) and of the church at large (3:1-2). Lengthy theological passages buttress these instructions (2:11-14; 3:3-8*a*). The letter closes with additional instructions concerning the rebellious people, various travel arrangements, and final greetings (3:8*b*-15). All the exhortations are given directly to Titus, who is instructed at several points to pass them on to the members of the church (2:15; 3:8).

The theological passages thus elaborate the content of the faith of God's elect (including the hope of eternal life) and the instructions promote the godly behavior that confirms the truth of the gospel—issues highlighted in the salutation. All is set within a framework that underscores the urgency of the situation by identifying opposing forces within the community.

The instructions concerning the appointment of elders consist of a straightforward listing of the qualities to be sought or avoided in these elders (see comments on 1 Tim 3:1b-13). The shift in terminology from elders to bishop in verse 7 may indicate that two earlier lists have been combined here. It also raises questions, however, about the relationship between elders and bishops, especially if one assumes, as many do, that 1 Timothy and Titus reflect the same forms of church leadership. As in 1 Tim 3:1-13, most of the virtues listed in the passage promote a general ideal and are not traits directly related to the duties of an elder or bishop. Only in verses 6b and 9 do specifically Christian requirements emerge, and they do so in response to the problem of "rebellious people" within the church community.

These "rebellious people" are described with a list of primarily stereotypical vices. Some elements of the passage provide, however, concrete information about the origin and nature of these opponents, which agrees with information found in 1 and 2 Timothy.

Appointment of Elders (1:5-9)

As he did in 1 Tim 1:3, the author uses the first words of the body of the letter to suggest a historical context, but there is no supporting evidence in Paul's letters or in the book of Acts for a Pauline mission to Crete. Proponents of Pauline authorship must therefore assume that the visit to Crete occurred after Paul's presumed release from the Roman imprisonment described in Acts 28:16-31. If the letter is pseudonymous, though, the author's reasons for choosing a Cretan setting are unrecoverable. The island had a sizable Jewish population (Philo *Embassy to Gaius* 282), so the Jewish cast of the opposition is plausible (v. 10). Its ports were infamous for harboring pirates, and its inhabitants were widely regarded as incurable liars (Lucian *Lover of Lies* 3).

The initial instruction to Titus is exceedingly vague: Beyond appointing elders it is not clear what else "remained to be done."

The rest of the letter (chaps. 2–3) contains rather basic ethical exhortations that do not seem to fit the category of remaining things.

The list of qualifications for church leaders can be divided into two parts, one associated with elders (v. 6), the other with the bishop (vv. 7-9). Both parts begin with the same qualification: blamelessness. Though some assume that the two terms, elder and bishop, are interchangeable and refer to the same leadership position, the information provided in 1 Timothy, if it reflects the same church structure, suggests instead separate roles and positions. The bishop, for example, is expected to exercise a teaching role (v. 9; 1 Tim 3:2), while only some of the elders perform that function (1 Tim 5:17). Since the qualifications for a bishop in verses 7-9 are presented as a rationale for the instructions concerning the appointment of elders ("for a bishop . . . "), it is likely that the bishop was chosen from the ranks of the elders as leader over them and over the church of a particular locale (see comments on 1 Tim 3:1-7). The qualifications for bishop and elder would thus overlap, though the positions were distinct. The author's interest, however, is not in the positions *per se,* but in the qualifications for them. These qualifications provide an edifying list of virtues that stand in deliberate contrast to the behavior of the "rebellious people" whom the bishop is charged to refute.

The arrangement and significance of the contents of the two-part list in verses 6-9 correspond closely with those of the very similar list in 1 Tim 3:1-7 (see above, pp. 66-69). Only a few items require further comment here. The requirements concerning the elders' children are framed with the presence of the "rebellious people" in mind. These children, for example, are not to be rebellious. They are to be faithful (Gk. *pista*). While this word surely constitutes a requirement that the children be "believers" (see also 1 Tim 6:2), that is, Christians, it also suggests a pattern of loyalty that is the opposite of rebellion. "Debauchery" (Gk. *asōtia*) describes the behavior of adult children, not young ones (see Luke 15:13; Eph 5:18), and this also encourages a connection with the opponents, whose behavior is described elsewhere in similar terms (3:11). The author's point is that an elder's ability to prevent rebellion and debauchery in his household held promise for success in dealing with instances of it in the church. This connection between family management and church leadership is not emphasized, as it is in 1 Timothy, by the identification of the church as God's household (1 Tim 3:15), but the definition of the bishop as God's steward—that is, as the servant who oversees the management of a household—conveys the same point. The final item in the list of qualifications is defined most expansively, marking it as particularly important (cf. 1 Tim 3:2, where it appears more tersely as "an apt teacher"). It concerns the actual activities of the bishop and reflects the author's pervasive concern for sound or healthy teaching that does not deviate from the received tradition (see also 2:1; 1 Tim 1:10-11; 4:6; 2 Tim 1:13; 2:24-25). In 1 Tim 3:2, the issue was the bishop's teaching ability; here, though, it is his knowledge of the content of the church's sound teaching. This knowledge is to ground both the bishop's exhortation (Gk. *parakalein;* NRSV: "preaching") of the faithful and his correction (Gk. *elegchein*) of opponents. A description of these opponents and their activities follows immediately.

Warnings About Rebellious People (1:10-16)

The initial denunciation of the "rebellious people" contains a number of elements that were common features of contemporary polemical rhetoric: accusations of greed and deception (see also 1 Tim 4:1; 6:5; 2 Tim 3:2); dismissal of opponents' views as myths and their speech as idle talk (1 Tim 1:4; 4:7; 6:20); the charge that their deeds belie their words (2 Tim 3:5); and a catalogue of their vices (1 Tim 6:4-5; 2 Tim 3:2-7) (Karris 1973). The passage is not, however, merely a sampler of traditional name-calling. It contains some concrete information about the opponents and it has been carefully composed for its role in this letter. That role is to sharpen the letter's exhortations in two ways: first, by defining the urgency of the situation and, second, by providing an edifying description of those who choose to reject "the truth that is in accordance with godliness" (1:1).

The passage opens with a description of the troublemakers as "rebellious" or disruptive of order (Gk. *anhypotaktoi*), a charge that stands out from the more stereotypical items that follow. This charge is anticipated in verse 6, where one of the requirements for elders is that they show some evidence within their households of being able to quash this sort of behavior. The Greek word is formed by adding a negative prefix ("an-") to a word meaning "subordinate" and it describes an unruly independence of spirit that refuses to show due respect and submission to proper authorities. The issue is thus initially framed in social rather than moral or theological categories, though, as the argument shows, a rebellion against the "truth" is also involved.

This condemnation of certain "insubordinate" people indicates that the threat to this church arose from within, from persons or groups that rejected the established leaders of the church and the message they proclaimed. It also seems to point to a wider problem within the church, for many of the letter's exhortations show a concern for maintaining social order: Wives are to be submissive to husbands (2:5); slaves to masters (2:9); and the whole church is to be subject to rulers and authorities (3:1).

The passage closes with another string of charges. These reveal less about the social situation of the church than they do about the rhetorical structure of the letter. The rebellious faction is first defined as "detestable" or loathsome or abominable (Gk. *bdelyktoi*), an extremely harsh epithet used elsewhere in the New Testament of the desecration of the temple that would serve as a sign of the final days of this age (Matt 24:15; Mark 13:14). Though indicating there some mysterious sacrilege, the word elsewhere has clear ethical overtones, which can be seen in its application to the "whore of Babylon" in the Apocalypse (Rev 17:5) and to proscribed behavior in the Greek version of Leviticus (Lev 18:26-30). This ethical nuance prevails in Titus as well, for the next two epithets in verse 16 clearly focus on the behavior of the rebellious people: They are "disobedient" and "unfit for any good work." The same ideas reappear in positive form in the letter's summary exhortations: "Remind them . . . to be obedient, to be ready for every good work" (3:1). In fact, insistence on "good works" is a recurrent theme in this letter (2:7, 14; 3:1, 8, 14).

In spite of the traditional and rhetorical character of its polemics, the passage also reveals or confirms some concrete facts about the rebellious faction. There were, for example, "many" of them (v. 10). This is one of several indications that the opposition had substantial numbers (see also 2 Tim 3:1-2; 4:3). They arose, as indicated above, from within the church, and though they had become corrupt in mind and conscience (see also 1 Tim 1:5-6, 19; 4:2; 6:5), the author holds out some hope that they "may become sound in the faith" (v. 13; see also 1 Tim 1:20; 2 Tim 2:25). There is some link between the opponents and Judaism (vv. 10, 14). This was hinted at in 1 Tim 1:7, though there, as here, the nature or significance of this connection is not spelled out. There is no indication, for example, that the issue is the Pauline one of the role of works of the law (see Rom 3:19-31; Gal 3:10-29). It seems to be linked instead to Jewish myths and genealogies—speculations, perhaps, of a Gnostic character rooted in the scriptures of Judaism. The author's refusal to engage his opponents in a substantive debate does not allow us to identify their theology with any precision.

The charge that the rebellious faction was "upsetting whole families" (v. 11) resembles stereotypical polemic, but there is also a ring of truth about the charge. (The use of stereotypical features in polemics does not automatically preclude their relevance; one simply cannot assume such relevance.) Throughout these letters the author shows a pervasive concern for an ordered and stable family structure (2:4-5, 9-10; 1 Tim 3:4, 12; 6:1-2); he decries everything that, in his view, undermines this (1 Tim 2:11-12; 5:13-15); and at several points he charges his opponents with beliefs or actions antithetical to the orderly (i.e., patriarchal) family (1 Tim 4:3; 2 Tim 3:6-7).

How the families were being upset is not mentioned. It could have been through the quarrels and divisions the opponents fomented (3:9; 1 Tim 6:4-5), through moral corruption (3:11), or through the destruction of sound faith (2 Tim 2:18). There is certainly a connection between the opponents' rejection of marriage (1 Tim 4:3) and the charge that they upset families, for a refusal to marry undermines the very foundation of the family. The belief that "nothing is pure" (v. 15) was the basis for the opponents' ascetic withdrawal from the material world (1 Tim 4:4).

The counterargument ("to the pure all things are pure") represents a view found in a number of New Testament texts (Mark 7:14-23; Luke 11:41; Acts 11:9; Rom 14:14, 20; see also 1 Cor 10:23-30) and is based on a positive view of creation. Those who are "pure" (Gk. *katharoi*) are those with pure or clean hearts (1 Tim 1:5; 2 Tim 2:22) and consciences (1 Tim 3:9; 2 Tim 1:3), not those who follow an ascetic regimen (see comments on 2 Tim 3:5). Indeed, the latter are accused of having corrupt or "stained" consciences and the author condemns them soundly, citing the words of "their very own prophet" against them. The prophet is not mentioned by name, but later church writers (e.g., Clement of Alexandria) identified him as Epimenides, a sixth-century BCE seer and writer, only fragments of whose work have survived.

◊ ◊ ◊ ◊

The basic problem that emerges in this opening chapter is that some people within the church were teaching "what it is not right to teach" (v. 11), an act of flagrant insubordination. The content of this teaching is not clearly indicated, but it certainly included some theological speculations to ground their ascetic way of life. By challenging basic authority patterns and by forbidding marriage, these people were upsetting the family structure that served as the basic unit of, and model for, the church.

Throughout these three letters the author addresses the problem of these opponents, but nowhere is his condemnation as harsh as in this passage. This is due in large part to the tone of the quotation he cites, which repeats a familiar racial slur in a particularly virulent form. Through it the opponents are dehumanized (Gk. *kaka thēria*; NRSV: "vicious brutes"), and the accompanying instructions are to muzzle or gag them (Gk. *epistomizein*; NRSV: "silence"). Moreover, all Cretans are included in this brutal condemnation. Since the letter is pseudonymous and the Cretan setting is probably artificial, one does not need to speculate on the impact of such an attitude on Titus's missionary activity in Crete. Yet the passage still sends a mixed pair of messages, one theological and one ethical.

On the one hand, it is possible, perhaps even likely, that the Cretan setting was chosen precisely because the island was both within the area covered by Paul's mission and notorious for its wickedness. Thus it provided an ideal setting for the gospel of God's goodness and loving-kindness (3:4). There is, for example, a striking similarity between the author's description of the Cretans here and his presentation of Paul's own pre-Christian life as one enslaved to various passions and pleasures, filled with malice and envy, and generally despicable (3:3). Since the goodness of God resulted in Paul's salvation in spite of his former life, one can infer that the salvation of the Cretans, even the rebellious ones, is also possible. Indeed, the author holds out strong hope for their salvation (1:13) and insists again that the grace of God brings salvation to all (2:11; 1 Tim 2:4-6). Thus while the exceedingly negative portrait of the Cretans provides an illustration of the perils of disobedience and rebellion, it also provides an effective foil for the message of God's grace. Even such as they are capable of being saved, though the author does not display enthusiasm for the endeavor (3:10-11).

On the other hand, the passage provides a questionable model for church leaders. Both Titus and the bishop are charged to refute or rebuke (Gk. *elegchein*) opponents sharply (vv. 9, 13), and verses 10-16 are surely intended to set the tone for this activity. This tone, however, is exceedingly harsh. Paul himself was certainly capable of strident rhetoric (2 Cor 11:13-15; Phil 3:2). Indeed, caustic words were commonplace in polemical writings of his age (Johnson 1978/79). In 2 Tim 2:25, though, the author provides a more positive paradigm for dealing with opponents, one that advocates gentleness instead of invective. Certainly the second model mirrors more closely the actions of God and Christ that this author describes (3:4; 1 Tim 1:16).

Instructions for Various Groups (2:1-15)

The instructions of 2:1–3:8 together with their theological warrants constitute the heart of this hortatory letter. In contrast, the preceding chapter has an essentially preparatory function. The discussion of church leaders in 1:5-9 serves in large part to introduce the problem of the rebellious people these leaders are charged to refute. The description of the vices of these people provides, in turn, a backdrop for the instructions concerning proper, orderly behavior in chapters 2–3 (see also 3:9-11).

Within this section, a minor break occurs at 2:14, where the contrast between the actions of the rebellious people, who are unfit for any good deed (1:16), and the goal of the exhortations to produce people who are "zealous for good deeds" (2:14) reaches its rhetorical climax. Verse 15, with its general reference to "these things," then provides a transition to the next subsection (3:1-8). Each subsection has the same three components: exhortations (2:1-10; 3:1-2), a doctrinal foundation for the exhortations (2:11-14; 3:3-7), and a concluding transitional statement (2:15; 3:8).

The lists of desired and proscribed behavior in chapter 2 resemble in many ways the material in 1:5-9 (also in 1 Tim 3:1-13), but here they are presented under the rubric of general ethical instructions (to be passed on to the appropriate groups) rather than qualifications for church leadership positions. The basic categories for the instructions are age groups within the church (mentioned also in 1 Tim 5:1-2), but elements of another framework, derived from the household management tradition, can also be discerned (Balch 1981). Jewish, Christian, and Greco-Roman exhortations borrowed from this tradition, which defined the proper relationships among various members of the household. These relationships were often presented in paired groupings (husbands and wives, fathers [or parents] and children, masters and slaves), highlighting the patterns of authority and subordination that defined the patriarchal family. Aristotle may have been the first to define the basic three-part structure of domestic relationships with his terse comment that "the free (master) rules the slave, the husband the wife, and the man (parent) the child" (*Politics* 1.5.6), but later formulations were more expansive (Seneca *Epistles* 94.1-2).

The influence of this model can be seen in the instructions to younger women (who are to be submissive to their husbands) and to slaves (who are to be submissive to their masters). Whether addressed to age or family groups, though, the exhortations in this passage mirror the ethical ideals promoted by Greco-Roman and Jewish society (see comments on 1 Tim 6:1-2). The particularly Christian elements are found in the purpose clauses (Gk. *hina*) in verses 5, 8, and 10, and, of course, in the traditional material cited in verses 11-14 as the theological warrant for the exhortations.

The Exhortations Proper (2:1-10)

The passage opens with words that highlight the contrast between Titus and the rebellious opponents described in the preceding paragraph ("But as for you . . . " [Gk. *sy de*; see also 1 Tim 6:11; 2 Tim 3:14; 4:5]). The author thus wedges the description of the rebellious people between two counterexamples of loyal behavior: the bishop, who is faithful to the church's teaching (1:9), and Titus, who declares (Gk. *lalei*; NRSV: "teach") what is consistent with sound doctrine (2:1). Concern for sound (literally "healthy") doctrine permeates these letters (1:9; 1 Tim 1:10; 6:3; 2 Tim 1:13; 4:3), but the passage that follows defines, not the content of this doctrine, but the moral behavior consistent with it. Fundamental to the logic of these letters is the conviction that good behavior flows from sound doctrine, while deviation from this doctrine can only produce moral disaster and social disorder. The author chooses to engage the issue first at the level of behavior.

The instructions to older men open with a triad of virtues that reflect the ideal of moderation shared by this author and his culture. In 1 Timothy the same virtues are presented as qualifications of both men and women for various church leadership roles (3:2, 8, 11); here they define the ideal behavior of all older men, probably understood as those over the age of fifty (Philo *On the Creation* 105). Faith and love, the nucleus of the next triad, are more identifiably Christian virtues. "Endurance" completes the triad instead of the similar, but more familiar item, "hope" (see also 1 Tim 6:11; 2 Tim 3:10; cf. 1 Cor 13:13; Gal 5:5-6; Col 1:4-5; 1 Thess 1:3; 5:8). The endurance (Gk. *hypomonē*) that the author has in mind here is not patience in the face of affliction, for no affliction is mentioned in this letter (cf. Rom 5:3; 2 Cor 1:6). The context suggests instead patient waiting for the fulfillment of the hope of eternal life (1:2; 2:13; 3:7; cf. Rom 8:25), or steadfastness in doing good works (2:14; 3:1, 8, 14; cf. Rom 2:7) or in adhering to the truth (1:1; cf. 1:14). The emphasis falls, however, on the issue of soundness, which highlights the contrast with the opponents (1:13).

The first three instructions to older women repeat points made in earlier exhortations to women, but the language is different. They are exhorted, for example, not simply to the modest and decent behavior expected of all Greco-Roman women (see comments on 1 Tim 2:9), but to the reverent behavior (Gk. *hieroprepeis*) appropriate to holy persons. This word does not imply that the women had a priestly function in the church; indeed, it connotes no more than the holy behavior expected of all believers (1 Tim 2:15; 2 Tim 2:21). The author's primary purpose in using this striking word in this context was to draw as sharp a distinction as possible between the behavior of Christian women and the defiled (1:15) and loathsome (1:16) lives of the rebellious teachers.

As in 1 Tim 3:11, the women are warned against slanderous talk. Warnings about excessive or inappropriate speech abound in Greek and Roman ethical discourse, where silence was the ideal for women (Aristotle *Politics* 1.5.8; Plutarch *Advice to Bride and Groom* 32) and where the talkative woman or the complaining wife was a stock figure for ridicule or reproach (Juvenal *Satires* 6.398-402; Plutarch *How to Profit by One's Enemies* 8). The particular wording here (Gk. *diabolous;* NRSV: "slanderers") evokes, however, the moral decay of the last days (2 Tim 3:3) and the defining trait of Satan, who is called the "Slanderer" (Gk. *ho diabolos;* NRSV: "the devil") in 1 Tim 3:6-7 and 2 Tim 2:26. Warnings against drunkenness were also quite traditional in Greek and Roman literature and occur frequently in these letters as well (1:7; 1 Tim 3:3, 8, 11). Only here, though, does this author speak of *enslavement* to drink. (See, however, 3:3; a contrast with enslavement to God [1:1] may be implied in both places.)

A new note is struck when the author insists that the older women be *kalodidaskalous*, a Greek word found only here, perhaps coined by this author, and meaning either "good teachers" or, more likely, those who "teach what is good" (NRSV). This teaching is distinct from that prohibited in 1 Tim 2:12 in a number of ways. It was done in the context of the home, not the worship service; it concerned only domestic issues, not doctrinal ones; and the students were young women, not the church at large.

It has been suggested that the older women mentioned here are the women deacons of 1 Tim 3:11 and that this teaching constitutes their assigned responsibility. There are some similarities between the virtues expected of older women and those required of women deacons (if such they were), but neither list of virtues is specific to an office. Moreover, nothing in this passage suggests that the older women held a leadership position in the church, even though the behavior they taught was encouraged on behalf of the church (v. 5b). In fact, training in the domestic skills mentioned here was the traditional provenance of older women (Lefkowitz and Fant 1982). This was such an established procedure that some Neopythagorean treatises on the proper behavior of women—including instructions for a wife to "be full of love for her husband and children" and to "live for her husband according to law and in actuality, thinking no private thoughts of her own"—though probably written by men, were published pseudonymously under the names of women (Pomeroy 1975, 133-39).

Since the proper behavior of the younger women is presented as a subordinate clause of the instructions to older women—that is, as the desired result of *their* teaching—the pattern of parallel instructions to different age groups is broken, focusing attention somewhat on the interruption. Unlike the instructions for the other age groups, the ones to young women are specific to their situation and this, together with the substantial length of these instructions, suggests a particular interest in this group. Indeed, it seems likely that the disruption the opponents were causing (1:11) was particularly acute in families of young matrons, leading the author to focus his comments concerning these women on issues that strengthen the family structure.

The instructions for the young women all promote the Greco-Roman and Jewish ideal for domestic behavior, opening and closing with comments on the proper relationship of wives to their husbands. This is a standard feature of the household management tradition, but there is in this letter no corresponding set of instructions to the husbands. Love of husbands (and of children) was a widely praised virtue of women, and submission to their husbands was the attitude society desired and expected of them (Treggiari 1991, 202-3). The early Christian adoption and adaptation of the household management tradition emphasizing this relationship (see Eph 5:22–6:9; Col 3:18–4:1; 1 Pet 2:18–3:7) may have been intended to counter the perception (or the reality) that the Christian message undermined the traditional patriarchal structure of the family (Matt 23:8-12; Gal 3:28; 1 Cor 7:1-7). For the author of these letters, that problem was compounded by the ascetic message of the opposing teachers, which threatened the family unit itself (1 Tim 4:3). The author thus urges behavior that reinforces the traditional family structure to counter both the impact of the opponents' teaching and the destabilizing legacy of Paul's own message.

The NRSV's translation of the fifth item in the section on young women ("good managers of the household") is somewhat misleading. The Greek term *(oikourgous)* simply describes one who works at home and does not highlight a managerial role there. An alternative reading found in some Greek manuscripts *(oikourous)* speaks only of staying at home. This was a widely praised trait in women of that time (see Plutarch *Advice to Bride and Groom* 30, 32) and corresponds closely to views the author has expressed elsewhere (1 Tim 5:13). Nevertheless, the rarer word *oikourgous* is found in the earlier and better manuscripts and is probably the original reading. It defines the household as the appropriate sphere for women's activities without implying the considerable authority the matron of a house could have within that sphere (cf. 1 Tim 5:14).

The adjective "good" (Gk. *agathas*) either describes the quality of the domestic work or, more probably, stands as a separate item encouraging the trait of gentleness or amiability that was valued in spouses (Treggiari 1991, 241-43). (Oddly, it appears in both roles in the NRSV's translation, where young women are urged to be *good* managers and *kind*.) Like the older and younger men, the young women are also urged to be self-controlled or prudent (Gk. *sōphronas*). This was one of the cardinal virtues of Stoic philosophy and a favorite of this author as well (see comments on 1 Tim 2:9). When applied to women it usually acquired the sense of sexual restraint, a point reinforced in this list by the adjacent term "chaste" (Gk. *hagnas*). In the context of this letter, the words do not refer to sexual abstinence (a position firmly opposed by the author) but to a wife's sexual fidelity to her spouse.

Attached to the passage concerning young women, and linked most closely to the issue of their submission to their husbands, is the first of three clauses giving the purpose of the various sets of instructions. The young women are to behave in the prescribed manner "so that the word of God (i.e., the gospel) may not be discredited" (v. 5). The author's concern was that public disapproval of Christian women who did not behave according to the norms of Greco-Roman society would undermine the church's fundamental work of proclaiming the gospel to that society (see also 2:10; 1 Tim 5:14; 6:1). This possibility was exacerbated by the widespread expectation in the Roman world that foreign cults (such as Christianity) would upset family relationships and thus undermine the political as well as domestic order (Balch 1981). The author seeks to allay that suspicion by encouraging model domestic behavior of the young women and slaves (see below), while at the same time deflecting the charge of disruption onto his opponents (1:11). The instructions have the added benefit of strengthening the social fabric of the church at a time when "many" were undermining it with their message promoting a celibate life.

In contrast to the detailed instructions concerning young women, those concerning the young men are exceedingly brief. This group is simply urged (the only true imperative verb form in vv. 2-10) to exercise the self-control promoted so strongly in these letters. ("In all respects" may reinforce the instructions concerning young men in verse 6 instead of those concerning Titus's behavior in verse 7 [so REB]. The Greek in this portion of the passage is particularly dense, and it is difficult to determine the meaning with exact precision.) While this completes the instructions for various age groups, the words directed to Titus supplement the preceding material. He is instructed to be a model, certainly for the young men but probably for the rest of the church as well (cf. 1 Tim 4:12).

The remaining instructions to Titus concern his leadership role within the church. It is not clear if the first point is for him to show integrity in the way his teaching is conducted (cf. 1:11; 2 Tim 3:6-7) or in its content (cf. 1:9). In either case the contrast with the opponents is strong. Attached to these instructions is the second clause indicating purpose. Unlike the other two purpose clauses, which focus on the reaction of the wider society to the behavior of Christian women and slaves (vv. 5*b*, 10*b*), this one seems to address the impact of the behavior of the leaders of the church. The opponent (Gk. *ho ex enantias*) could be anyone hostile to the Christian message or, specifically, the adversaries mentioned earlier in the letter ("those who contradict," 1:9). These adversaries should be given no opportunity to respond to criticism of their behavior (1:10-16) with attacks of their own.

The final group (slaves) derives from a different set of categories, one based on family role rather than age. It shows most clearly the influence of the household management tradition (see comments on 1 Tim 6:1-2), which included as a standard feature the insistence that slaves be submissive and obedient (see Eph 6:5-9; Col 3:22–4:1; 1 Tim 6:1-2; 1 Pet 2:18-25), but, as in 1 Tim 6:1-2, it lacks parallel instructions to masters. Whereas the similar passage in 1 Timothy addresses the distinctive problem of the relationship of Christian slaves to Christian masters, the focus here is on the basic issue of subordination. This concern, which is emphasized at several points in the letter (2:5, 9; 3:1), was probably an antidote to the rebellious behavior endangering the church (1:10). While pilfering was part of the stereotypical Greco-Roman view of slaves' behavior (Xenophon *Memorabilia* 2.1.16; Pliny *Natural History* 33.6.26-27), back talking (Gk. *antilegontas*) was characteristic of the opponents (1:9). Even the insistence that slaves "show complete and perfect fidelity," though a straightforward enough expectation of a servant group, advocates behavior that is the opposite of rebellion.

Though the words concerning slaves are clearly shaped by the portrait of the rebellious teachers, the instructions close with a clause that defines their purpose as one of enhancing the Christian witness (see also v. 5). By their submissive, satisfactory, and honest service, Christian slaves will commend their religion to outsiders as one that produces members of society whose behavior is utterly appropriate to their rank and station.

Doctrinal Foundation for the Exhortations (2:11-15)

With the word "for" (v. 11) the author introduces the theological basis for the instructions given in verses 1-10. The lofty tone of this passage and the concentration in it of theological terms found nowhere else in the Pastoral Letters suggest that it derives in large part from the church's liturgy. Within the present context, however, the passage makes three important points about the behavior urged in the preceding verses. First, this behavior serves God's plan for bringing salvation to all; second, it derives from (and thus is a sign of) the transforming presence of God's grace within the community; and, third, it rests on the redemptive death of Jesus Christ. Many of the points made here are well attested in the undisputed Pauline letters, though the language in which they are presented has few exact parallels.

The first point connects the behavior urged in verses 2-10 with God's desire to save all people (see also 1 Tim 2:4; 4:10). This behavior is thus commended because, insofar as it makes the Christian message attractive to outsiders, it promotes God's plan to save them. The author thus reinforces the point made in verses 5 and 10, that Christian behavior, when it conforms to the highest standards of society, enhances the witness of the church to the world.

The second point links the behavior urged in verses 2-10, not with the inclusive goal of God's grace, but with its transforming power within the community of believers. This is expressed in terms of education or training (Gk. *paideuein*), a process that often involved discipline and punishment (Plutarch *The Education of Children* 12, 16; see also 1 Tim 1:20; 1 Cor 11:32; 2 Cor 6:9; Heb 12:3-11) but here is viewed exclusively in terms of moral improvement. This progress is described in the language of Greco-Roman philosophy but within an eschatological framework provided by Paul's theology. That is, as in Paul's letters (Rom 6:1-5; 1 Cor 7:29-31), God's grace is understood here as a power that brings about a real moral transformation in the present. As a consequence, it also enables believers to look forward with hope to the parousia (second coming) of Christ, described here as elsewhere in these letters as a second epiphany or "manifestation" (see also 1 Tim 6:14; 2 Tim 4:8), and to eternal life (1:2; 3:7) (Bultmann 1955, 2:183-86).

The nature of this morally transformed life is described in terms of three cardinal virtues that are emphasized throughout these letters: self-control, uprightness, and godliness. The first (Gk. *sōphronōs*) repeats a virtue highlighted in the preceding exhortations (2:2, 5, 6). Uprightness (Gk. *dikaiōs*) describes one who conforms to established norms (see 1 Tim 1:9); this virtue is confirmed elsewhere in these letters as the goal of Christian training (2 Tim 3:16). Godliness (Gk. *eusebōs*) is the opposite of the renounced impiety (Gk. *asebeia*). It implies a reverence for God and moral behavior appropriate to that reverence, including respect for the divinely ordained orders of life such as traditional family structure. Thus it aptly summarizes the specific exhortations of verses 2-10, especially those to young wives and slaves, as well as the temporal goal of all Christian existence (1 Tim 2:2).

Christian existence is also defined in this passage as a time of waiting, though waiting is not stressed elsewhere in these letters (cf. Rom 8:18-25; 1 Thess 1:10). What is awaited is the second coming, described as an epiphany of glory. Here as elsewhere in the NT, glory, the visible sign of God's presence, is ascribed to the risen, returning Christ (see also Mark 8:38; 13:26). And just as God was called Savior in 2:10, here Christ is given the same title (see also 1:3-4). The returning Christ even seems to be designated "God," one of very few places in the New Testament that explicitly does so (John 20:28; Heb 1:8). The interpretation of the phrase is, however, disputed.

Though the Greek permits a translation that maintains a distinction between "God" and "our Savior" ("the glory of the great God and [the glory] of our Savior Jesus Christ"; so NAB; see also NRSV and REB textual notes), it does not strongly support it. A single article and a single personal pronoun unite the two nouns, God and Savior, and the sentence continues in verse 14 with a description of Jesus' activity alone (Harris 1980). Moreover, inscriptions from the period show that the titles were often paired: Deified hellenistic rulers and Roman emperors as well as the gods and goddesses of the mystery religious were often honored as both god (or goddess) and savior (Bousset 1970, 310-17). The author does not adequately develop his thought here (which may have been influenced by liturgical formulations) to indicate his understanding of the christological implications of this phrase. He has, however, already called Christ's first coming an epiphany of God's grace (2:11; 2 Tim 1:9-10) and later in the letter he refers to it as an epiphany of "the goodness and loving kindness of God our Savior" (3:4). It would not be out of the question for him to refer to the second coming as an epiphany of the glory of God our Savior (a common OT epithet, see Ps 106:21; Isa 45:21; Luke 1:47), with "Jesus Christ" added loosely to the construction to indicate the vehicle of that epiphany. (Grammatical connections are imprecise throughout this passage.) Whatever the significance of the phrase here, it does not prevent the author from emphasizing elsewhere Jesus' earthly humanity (1 Tim 2:5) and Davidic descent (2 Tim 2:8), nor does he see this as a challenge to his monotheistic faith (1 Tim 1:17; 2:5).

In the final clause of this section (vv. 11-14 form a single sentence in the original Greek), the author shifts from the hellenistic epiphany language he has employed to describe Jesus' first and second comings to the traditional Christian interpretation of Jesus' death in terms of his self-giving (Isa 53:12; Mark 10:45; Gal 1:4; 2:20; Eph 5:2; also 1 Tim 2:6). The emphasis is on the goal or consequences of this act, which the author cites in order to define Christ's unique role in the workings of God's grace (v. 11).

The passage probably derives from Jewish-Christian liturgy, for its phrases reverberate with language from the Jewish Scriptures. Paul, for example, speaks often of Jesus' death as an act of redemption or buying-back (Rom 3:24; 1 Cor 1:30; 6:20), but the phrase found here ("redeem us from all iniquity") is a nearly direct quotation of Ps 130:8. The next phrase ("purify for himself a people of his own") is clearly influenced by passages like Ezek 37:23; Exod 19:5; and Deut 7:6, though the author of this letter had Christ, not God, in mind. Just as the book of Deuteronomy defines the goal of Israel's election in terms of obedience (Deut 6:20-25; 10:12-16; 26:18), here too the goal of Jesus' self-giving is to produce a people "who are zealous for good deeds." The contrast with the opposing teachers reaches its climax in this phrase. Whereas their teaching, described as speculations rooted in Jewish myths, produces people unfit for any good work (1:16), the author's sober exhortations conform to the moral purpose of Jesus' death. The author thus closes this subsection by emphasizing again the importance of his exhortations (v. 15, repeating *lalei* ["declare"] of 2:1).

Verse 15 is clearly transitional: "these things" refers to the contents of chapter 2 and also forward to the very similar contents of 3:1-8. Titus is also urged to "exhort and reprove," verbs that summarize earlier instructions to the church leaders as well as the two overarching and complementary goals of this letter (1:9, 13; 2:6). And he is to do this "with all authority." The Greek noun here *(epitagē)* derives from a verb *(epitassein)* that means "to impose commands." It thus reinforces the insistence on respect for order (Gk. *hypotassein*) found in the instructions concerning young wives (2:5), slaves (2:9), and, indeed, the whole church (3:1). The direct warning to Titus against letting people look down on him echoes the very similar warning to Timothy (1 Tim 4:12), but without reference to Titus's youth. This warning should thus be linked to the letter's general concern over rebellion against authority (1:6, 10) and not taken as an allusion to Titus's age or inexperience (cf. Ign. *Magn.* 3.1). The author continues this thought in the next subsection with a blanket admonition concerning obedience to authorities.

◊ ◊ ◊ ◊

Most of the ethical and theological issues raised by this passage are not new. They emerge throughout these letters and are, in fact, characteristic of them. The conservative social ethics (1 Tim 5:1–6:2), the conceptualization of the ethical goal of the Christian life in terms of the ideals of Greco-Roman moral philosophy (1 Tim 3:1*b*-13), the concern for the reaction of outsiders (1 Tim 3:7), the understanding of the ethical life of Christians as a consequence of God's act of grace (1 Tim 1:3-20), the use of liturgical material to buttress the argument (1 Tim 2:1-7), and the epiphany Christology (2 Tim 1:9-10)—all of these are familiar features of these letters. The only differences here are ones of emphasis, not content.

The emphasis in this passage and in those surrounding it is the submission of subordinate members of the community. In 1 Timothy, too, women and children are urged to be submissive (2:11; 3:4) and slaves are told not to be disrespectful (6:2), but here the issue receives striking emphasis. Within the same section of the letter, indeed, within the space of twelve verses, three different groups are instructed to be submissive and nearly identical purpose clauses reinforce the point at two places. These clauses define the author's hortatory goal as one of enhancing the church's message and facilitating its acceptance by outsiders. This, too, is not new, but there is here an implicit connection between the author's insistence on submission and the emergence of insubordinate (i.e., rebellious) people within the church.

Opponents appear throughout these letters with essentially the same traits: They are deceitful, quarrelsome, greedy. Only in Titus, though, is their opposition defined in terms of rebellion, that is, disrespect for order. This creates the perfect foil for the author's message of submission, or respect for order, but it is difficult to discern the primary goal of his rhetoric. If disorder posed a genuine threat to the community, the insistence on submission can be understood as the author's attempt to prevent the rebellious attitude from spreading, especially among susceptible groups. On the other hand, the use of examples, both negative and positive, was common in ethical writings, and the author of the Pastoral Letters may have emphasized the rebellious side of the opponents' actions in order to provide support for the submission that he wanted to promote for other reasons (to enhance mission or deflect hostility). This is not to say that a problem with opponents did not exist, only that the author may have chosen to define the problem in a way that also enhanced his other rhetorical purposes (Fiore 1986; Elliott 1981).

A central aspect of the theology of this passage is its broad ecumenical vision of God's redemptive plan. Here as elsewhere, though, this broad vision of salvation for all is directly connected with exhortations to social conformity that are presented as complementary to God's plan. The presupposition that such conformity will not only ensure the order and harmony of the community but will also promote the conversion of outsiders patently assumes that conversion will proceed from the top down, for this ethic is most reassuring for those with a stake in traditional patterns of authority and stability. The message of Gal 3:28, however, supports conversion from the bottom up, for only those on the bottom are rewarded by the eradication of social distinctions. Indeed, Paul's only explicit concern with the reaction of outsiders emerges over the practice of glossolalia (speaking in tongues), which is neutral with respect to the social status of those outsiders (1 Cor 14:6-25; the reference to outsiders in 1 Thess 4:12 does not seem to have their conversion in mind). The author of Titus, however, presents the Pauline message in a way that does not hinder, but positively encourages, the good will and even the conversion of the relatively well-to-do (see also 1 Pet 2:12; 3:1-2).

Though the author defines the Christian moral life in a way that is essentially indistinguishable from the moral life advocated by the moral philosophers of his age, and though he understands God's salvific will to embrace all people, there is still a clear boundary in these letters between "those who have come to believe in God" (3:8) and those who have not. God is "our" Savior, Christ gave himself "for us" to redeem "us" from iniquity. Indeed, the boundary is even more distinct when he defines the believers as "a people of his [Christ's] own" (2:14) or as "God's elect" (1:1). Though this exclusive language, which is drawn from Jewish Scriptures, defines the church as the new Israel, the author does not emphasize this contrast. The main contrast does not even seem to be with the pagan world, though that is clearly present, but, as the emphasis on good deeds suggests, with the opposing teachers and their followers. As presented in these letters, the real rift is not between the church and the outside world but between loyal and rebellious factions within the church.

For this author, however, the most important theological message of this passage may have been the pedagogical role of God's grace, for he clearly understands the exhortations of his letters to complement and reinforce this divine training. Such a thought is not foreign to Paul, though he tended to speak in terms of the Spirit as the divine power working both through him, and independently of him, to shape the communal and individual lives of believers (Rom 8:1-17; 1 Cor 7:40; 14:37).

Instructions for the Church (3:1-8)

The structure and content of these verses are nearly identical to those of 2:1-15, though the lengths of the respective parts vary considerably. Brief exhortations (vv. 1-2), apparently meant for the entire church, are followed by a lengthy theological passage (vv. 3-8*a*) that serves as their warrant. The concluding verse (v. 8*b*) is transitional, referring to the previous exhortations ("these things"), repeating the letter's emphasis on good works (1:16; 2:7, 14; 3:1), and anticipating both the counterexample of the sinful opponents (vv. 9-11) and the closing exhortation (v. 14).

The Exhortations Proper (3:1-2)

The author's pervasive concern for order is reflected in the letter's final exhortation to submissive behavior (Gk. *hypotassesthai*). This admonition concerns the relationship of the entire community to "rulers and authorities" (Gk. *archais [kai] exousiais*), presumably the civil authorities of the Roman Empire (Rom 13:1). This is not a dramatic shift from the previous discussion of behavior within the household (2:1-15), for the Greco-Roman world understood the household and the state to be intrinsically related. Order in one fostered order in the other, and disorder in one led to anarchy in the other (Cicero *Republic* 1.43).

The concern for civic behavior continues with the exhortation to obedience, for the infinitive has the specific meaning of obedience *to those in authority* (Gk. *peitharchein*). In the third phrase ("to be ready for every good work"), however, the author is clearly referring to Christian life in its fullness and not simply to political obedience. He is, in fact, drawing an implicit contrast to the opponents, who are "unfit for any good work" (1:16). The various arenas of behavior are thus linked by the concept of authority, especially in light of the instruction to Titus in 2:15 to reprove "with all authority." Obedience to political authorities, to church authorities, and to family authorities are all interconnected and such thoroughgoing obedience was regarded as essential to the maintenance of a wholesome order.

The list of instructions continues with items familiar from other vice and virtue lists in these letters. The bishop, for example, was also admonished to be gentle or reasonable (Gk. *epieikeis*) and not to quarrel (1 Tim 3:3), while the opponents' behavior includes evil speech (Gk. *blasphēmein*) (1 Tim 1:20; 6:4; 2 Tim 3:3), quarreling

(3:9; 2 Tim 2:23), and violence (2 Tim 3:2-4). Thus although the passage opens with instructions focused on relationships with external authorities, it quickly moves to terminology that reflects the internal schism. As in 1 Tim 2:2, the external situation seems to be free of tensions; it simply defines the parameters of behavior, while the internal situation shapes the argument.

Doctrinal Foundation for the Exhortations (3:3-8)

Just as the author cited traditional material in 2:11-14 to supply a warrant for the exhortations in 2:2-10, here again he introduces traditional material to provide the theological justification for the instructions in 3:1-2. The density of theological assertions, including an abundance of terms otherwise absent from these letters, and the lofty, formal tone of the passage set it apart from the surrounding material and suggest an origin in the baptismal liturgy of the church. The connection between exhortation and warrant is somewhat simpler here: God's gracious mercy toward sinners provides a model for Christians to follow in their dealings with outsiders, whether pagans or, presumably, the opposing teachers. The rich theological content of the passage surpasses, however, the author's immediate rhetorical needs and documents the author's Pauline heritage, both in the overall structure of the argument and in details of its wording.

Following a widespread pattern of early Christian preaching, the passage opens with a list of vices that define the degeneracy of the pre-Christian life (see also Rom 1:29-31; 1 Pet 4:2-3). The list is intended to be illustrative, not exhaustive, and probably derives in large part from traditional material. Nevertheless, it fits well into its context in this letter, reinforcing its largely stereotypical polemics and exhortations. The reminder of former disobedience (Gk. *apeitheis*) comes, for example, hard on the heels of an exhortation to obedience (Gk. *peitharchein*). Being led astray and ruled by passions is the way the author has described the current lives and impact of the opponents (2 Tim 3:2-6, 13; 4:3-4; cf. Titus 2:12). The final two items on the list are nearly synonymous: "hated" or "hateful" (Gk. *stygētoi;* NRSV: "despicable") and then, more explicitly, "hating one another." These words describe a complete absence of concern and affection for others and therefore an absence of community. Thus they contrast sharply both with the goal of the author's exhortations (2:4-5; 3:1-2) and with his description of God as filled with "goodness and loving kindness" (v. 4).

To highlight the contrast between believers' former and present lives was, of course, a basic application of vice lists in Christian writings (1 Cor 6:9-11; Eph 2:1-7; Col 3:5-8; 1 Pet 4:2-3), but the critical feature of *this* passage lies in its description of God's saving action. Once again the author refers to the first coming of Jesus as an epiphany (Gk. *epephanē*; NRSV: "appeared"), but here it is described as an epiphany of God's goodness and loving-kindness, not of God's grace. Goodness and loving-kindness are, of course, synonyms for "grace," but the two new terms have been carefully chosen with the intended function of this theological passage in mind.

"Grace" in the Pauline tradition is almost exclusively reserved to define God's act of saving mercy. On the other hand, goodness and loving-kindness (Gk. *chrēstotēs kai philanthrōpia*) were widely used by contemporary writers to describe the actions of humans (Plutarch *Comparison of Demosthenes and Cicero* 3; Isocrates *Evagoras* 43), and in hellenistic Judaism to describe both God and humans. In fact, in hellenistic Jewish writings, heavenly goodness and loving-kindness are presented as models for human actions (Philo *Special Laws* 2.141; *Letter of Aristeas* 208), and that is the intended application here. Believers are to be gentle and courteous in their actions toward one another and especially toward outsiders because this is how they experienced God's action in their own lives when they were themselves "outsiders." The author's use of terms associated with both human and divine acts to define God's nature enhances this moral application.

A second theological point is also important for the author's argument, the very Pauline point that God "saved us, not because of any works of righteousness that we had done" (cf. Rom 3:24, 28; 4:2-5; 11:6; Gal 2:16, 21; Eph 2:8-9). The author has a keen appreciation of the Pauline message of grace (1 Tim 1:13-14; 2 Tim 1:9). In a letter that mentions good works so frequently (2:7, 14; 3:1, 8, 14), a reminder of this message is important, especially the

message that grace was bestowed apart from "works of righteousness." The author assumes (again in good Pauline fashion) that
good works result from, and do not precede or evoke, God's grace.

In this passage the author (perhaps influenced by the traditional
material he uses) speaks of God's having "saved" us (and thus of
"God our Savior"), whereas Paul spoke of God's having *justified*
us, with salvation reserved for the future (v. 5, cf. Rom 3:24;
5:9-10). Nevertheless, the author retains the eschatological tension
of Paul's thought, for, though "saved," the believer possesses only
the *hope* of eternal life (v. 7; see also 1:2; Rom 5:1-5), not its full
reality—a point the pseudonymous author of Ephesians has nearly
missed (Eph 2:5-7).

A string of words, linked together too loosely to permit any
rigorous analysis of their logical connection, associates the act of
salvation with water (literally "washing," Gk. *loutron,* a reference
to baptism), rebirth, renewal, and the Holy Spirit. These associations are common in early Christian writings (John 3:3-8; Rom 6:4;
Eph 5:26; 1 Pet 1:3-5), but this author does not develop them, even
though they were traditionally associated with the moral life that
is his primary concern. This is, in fact, one of the very few places
where this author speaks of the Holy Spirit (cf. 1 Tim 4:1; 2 Tim
1:14), and here he only alludes to the rich Pauline teachings of the
role of the Spirit in the work of moral renewal (Rom 8:1-17; Gal
5:16-26) and its connection with the hope of eternal life (Rom 5:5;
8:15-17; 2 Cor 1:22; 5:1-5). The role of the Spirit is only one of
several ways that this author understands the transformed lives of
believers. Grace certainly has a role in the process (2:11), as does
sound apostolic teaching (1 Tim 4:6) and scripture (2 Tim 3:16).
And godliness itself, though a goal of this transformation, is also
an agent of it (1 Tim 4:7-8; 2 Tim 3:5).

The author closes the passage with the familiar endorsement,
"The saying is sure" (see comments on 1 Tim 1:15), which also
points to the traditional nature of the theological material. The final
verse repeats earlier exhortations to Titus to promulgate the instructions he has received (2:1, 15), but here the author uses a more
emphatic verb ("insist on," Gk. *diabebaiousthai*). A purpose clause
summarizes the goal of the exhortations in 2:1–3:8, but does so in

general terms of good works and profitability. The relationship between the exhortations and the church's witness is not repeated here (cf. 2:5, 10), but the author moves seamlessly into a final word about the opponents (3:9-11).

◊ ◊ ◊ ◊

"All people" (NRSV: "everyone"), according to this passage, are to be treated with gentle courtesy (3:2). With this phrase, which repeats the universal emphasis of 2:11, the author certainly includes all non-Christians. Though the point is not made explicit here, this charitable attitude can be expected to promote the gospel as much as the socially prescribed respect for order encouraged in 2:2-10 (see 2 Tim 2:24-26), for courteous actions of Christians directly mirror the gospel message of divine grace. The author thus reveals an understanding of the theological grounding of Christian behavior that is clearly rooted in Paul's perspective, but in fact surpasses it. In Romans, for example, Paul urges the Christians of the capital city to "welcome *one another* . . . just as Christ has welcomed you" (15:7; see also 15:2-3). That is, in imitation of Christ, believers are to provide a gracious welcome to other Christians with whom they disagree (see Rom 14:10), but Paul does not extend the application to outsiders. This author does.

According to the wording of the passage in Titus, though, this gentle attitude should also include other Christians, including rebellious opponents, for the phrase "all people" is all-inclusive. This message, however, stands in some tension with the way the author has actually dealt with the rebellious teachers. His description of them can hardly be described as courteous (1:10-16), and the instructions to muzzle and rebuke them sharply are far from gentle.

This self-contradiction suggests an astonishing lack of integration of word and deed. It may be that, in writing this, the author really had only non-Christians in mind and intended to continue here the encouragement of behavior that would promote the gospel in Greco-Roman society. One could conclude that where truth and the integrity of the community were at stake, harsher methods had his tacit approval. Yet in 2 Timothy it is explicitly stated that *opponents* are to be corrected with gentleness. The letters thus offer a mixed ethical message, much like that of Matthew's Gospel, which includes both the gentle words "love your enemies" (5:44) and the bitter invective of chapter 23. In Titus, one side of the message is supported by the message and experience of divine grace; the other by a pagan prophet (1:12).

Final Exhortations Concerning Opponents (3:9-11)

The argument flows so smoothly from 3:8 into these verses that they barely constitute a new section, even though the content changes significantly. Having urged the faithful to devote themselves to things that are profitable (Gk. *ōphelima*) and noble (Gk. *kala*), the author now urges Titus to avoid things that are unprofitable (Gk. *anōpheleis*) and worthless (Gk. *mataioi*). The former he defines as good works; the latter, not as evil works, but as the verbal disputes and debates characteristic of the opponents. This leads to a set of brief instructions on how to deal with these opponents should they persist in their actions. The verses contribute nothing new to the portrait of these opponents but, with 1:10-16, frame the exhortations to orderly obedience with warnings about the disruptive activities of the opponents.

◊ ◊ ◊ ◊

This is one of the many places in these letters where the author depicts the opposing teachers as engaging in vacuous verbal debates instead of profitable actions (1:10; 1 Tim 1:4; 6:4, 20; 2 Tim 2:23). Such charges were also common in philosophical circles as a way of belittling opponents (Philo *Preliminary Studies* 53; *Migration of Abraham* 171; Dio Chrysostom *Discourses* 32.10; 54.1) so they may shed little light on the actual situation here. The references to genealogies and the law repeat earlier comments linking the opponents to Judaism (1:14; 1 Tim 1:4, 7) but add nothing concrete about the nature of that connection. The important point—-from the author's perspective—is the contrast between the opponents' worthless discussions and the solid actions he himself advocates. Titus is literally urged to go out of his way to avoid (Gk. *periistasthai*) such discussions, but he and the rest of the faithful are to put before themselves as their goal (Gk. *proistasthai*) the good works outlined in this letter.

As in 1 and 2 Timothy, the author holds out some hope that the opponents may be dissuaded from their speculations (1 Tim 1:20; 2 Tim 2:25), for he advocates giving them several admonitions before taking stronger measures (see also Matt 18:15-17). Here, though, he seems less sanguine about the possibility of reform and focuses on what to do when they are not persuaded to change. The solution is simple: "Avoid them" (see also 1 Tim 4:7; 2 Tim 2:23). Avoidance seems a somewhat milder response than that described in 1 Tim 1:20, where certain persons were "turned over to Satan." The turning over to Satan, however, was intended to have a corrective, pedagogical effect (see also 1:13), whereas here the offender's status seems irremedial. Such a person is perverted (literally, turned inside out, entirely altered) and persists in sinning (the implication of the present tense Greek verb, *hamartanei*). Though it is the author who insists on the separation, he names the opponents as the ones who create "divisions," not only because their teachings have destabilized the community (1:11) but also because they have brought the separation upon themselves (NRSV: "self-condemned"). From the author's point of view, of course, this avoidance was a protective strategy to eliminate internal divisions and restore order; he would not have recognized it as divisive.

The adjective used in verse 10 to describe the opponents (Gk. *hairetikos*) derives from a verb that means "to choose." As defined here, however, the choice is one that affects the integrity of the community, and the word has the additional nuance of factious or divisive behavior (so NRSV: "anyone who causes divisions"; see also 1 Cor 11:19; Gal 5:20). Since the opponents were earlier identified as those who reject the truth (1:14), the Greek word almost carries the meaning of its English cognate, "heretic," but the emphasis in this passage is on the divisive results of their behavior, not their doctrinal error (cf. 2 Pet 2:1).

◊ ◊ ◊ ◊

With this closing reference to opponents, the author returns to the harsh tone of 1:10-16. The moderate behavior advocated in 3:2, insofar as it is relevant for dealing with opponents, seems to be exhausted by the two admonitions Titus is instructed to give. These admonitions probably correspond to the sharp rebukes mentioned in 1:13, but the focus has shifted from their intended goal of correction to their expected failure.

The author of this letter shares Paul's concern over divisive activities within the church (Rom 16:17-20; 1 Cor 1:10-13; Phil 2:1-4). He does not, however, reflect theologically or christologically on the problem (cf. 1 Cor 1:18-31; Phil 2:6-11). Instead he offers in this letter a number of concrete suggestions, including silencing opponents, correcting them, treating them gently, and, here, avoiding those who persist in their divisive behavior. As elsewhere in these letters, the author shows no interest in substantive debate. If the rebukes are not successful, contact with the opponents should be terminated. He emphasizes the social consequences of the opponents' activities (causing divisions) and responds with punishment in kind (exclusion). As if to underscore the social implications of this punishment, the final, personal instructions in the letter (3:12-14) illustrate what *inclusion* looks like.

TRAVEL ARRANGEMENTS AND GREETINGS (3:12-15)

The letter ends as many Pauline letters do—with travel plans, greetings, a concluding exhortation, and a benediction (see Rom 15:22–16:23; 1 Cor 16:5-24; Phlm 22-25). The realistic personal details in the passage seem to pose a challenge to the hypothesis of pseudonymous authorship (see also 2 Tim 4:9-22), yet they are not incompatible with it. The pseudonymous Cynic epistles, for example, though largely filled with exhortations, also contain references to travel plans ("Chaerophon . . . will probably also come to you . . . "), requests for hospitality ("Phyrnichus the Larissaean, a disciple of mine, . . . will not require much from you since he is a philosopher"), and family news ("Xanthippe and the children are doing well"). These personal details not only enhance the verisimilitude of the Cynic letters but also, in many cases, provide an anecdotal illustration of a philosophical ideal (Malherbe 1977a).

◊   ◊   ◊   ◊

Several individuals are mentioned here, two of whom are known from other New Testament writings. Tychicus is described elsewhere in the New Testament as one of Paul's traveling companions and coworkers, though he is not mentioned in the undisputed Pauline letters (Acts 20:4; Eph 6:21; Col 4:7; 2 Tim 4:12). He or Artemas, an otherwise unknown individual, is to replace Titus on Crete. The earlier description of Titus's assignment on the island made no reference to his imminent replacement and seemed, in fact, to presume an extended, if not permanent, stay (1:5, 13; 2:15). However, the request for Titus to do his best to join Paul (the same request is made of Timothy, see 2 Tim 4:9), together with the request that Titus send Zenas and Apollos "on their way," provide the immediate excuses for the letter, which otherwise is filled with exhortations of no obvious urgency.

There were a number of cities in the ancient world named Nicopolis ("Victory City"). It is likely that the author had in mind the Nicopolis on the western coast of Greece. It lay close to Paul's known travel circuit, though there is no other evidence that he ever visited that city. It was, however, customary to avoid sea travel in the winter, when seasonal storms made sailing particularly dangerous (Acts 27:12; 28:11; 2 Tim 4:21).

Zenas is also unknown apart from this reference, though Apollos figured prominently in the early Christian mission in Corinth (Acts 18:24–19:1; 1 Cor 3:5-15; 16:12). Here the two men are probably to be understood (within the letter's fiction) as the bearers of the letter, which also would function as a letter of introduction for them. The request to Titus and the Cretan church to "send [them] on their way" uses a Greek word *(propempein)* that had become almost a technical term in early Christianity for providing financial assistance for a trip (Malherbe 1977b, 68). Thus in Acts and the letters various church workers are "sent on their way," that is, they are given hospitality (food and lodging) and money to support them on the next stage of their journey (Acts 15:3; 21:5; Rom 15:24; 1 Cor 16:6, 11; 2 Cor 1:16; 3 John 6).

The exhortation to good works in verse 14 repeats the words of verse 8, but now in support of the concrete request of Christian hospitality. The issue, however, is not to meet *"urgent* needs"

213

(NRSV), which suggests a crisis, but to provide for the "necessary needs" (Gk. *tas anagkaias chreias*)—the necessities of life (Dibelius and Conzelmann 1972)—of the traveling Christian workers. To do so is to be "productive" or fruitful—a reference to the tangible results of an active faith that has expressed itself in generous deeds of service to others.

◊ ◊ ◊ ◊

If, as we have assumed, this letter is pseudonymous, the setting provided by these final verses is fictitious. Yet it is not therefore meaningless. Two important messages emerge from the personal requests and greetings. The first is the ethical message found throughout these letters: Christian faith must result in concrete acts of charity or "good works," here exemplified by the sharing of resources to meet the basic needs of traveling Christians. The second message is more subtle. The opponents have just been charged with divisive activities, quarreling, and dissension and have as a consequence been ejected from Christian fellowship. By way of contrast, the final verses of the letter paint a portrait of healthy Christian fellowship, which includes companionship, affection, and material support for a wide network of coworkers. This vigorous and supportive group bears visible fruit, while the squabbling of the opponents is "unprofitable and worthless" (v. 9). The author has used the traditional features of a letter's closure to send an object lesson on the social behavior that comports with the goodness and loving-kindness of God.

SELECT BIBLIOGRAPHY

WORKS CITED IN THE TEXT
(EXCLUDING COMMENTARIES)

Allan, John A. 1963. "The 'In Christ' Formula in the Pastoral Epistles." *NTS* 10:115-21.

Balch, David L. 1981. *"Let Wives Be Submissive . . . ": The Domestic Code in 1 Peter.* SBLMS 26. Chico, CA: Scholars Press.

Bassler, Jouette M. 1984. "The Widows' Tale: A Fresh Look at 1 Tim 5:3-16." *JBL* 103:23-41.

Bousset, Wilhelm. 1970. *Kyrios Christos,* 5th ed. New York: Abingdon.

Bultmann, Rudolf. 1955. *Theology of the New Testament,* vol. 2. New York: Scribner's.

Collins, John N. 1990. *Diakonia: Re-interpreting the Ancient Sources.* New York and Oxford: Oxford University Press.

Danker, Frederick W. 1982. *Benefactor: Epigraphic Study of a Graeco-Roman and New Testament Semantic Field.* St. Louis: Clayton.

Donelson, Lewis R. 1986. *Pseudepigraphy and Ethical Argument in the Pastoral Epistles.* Tübingen: Mohr-Siebeck.

Elliott, John H. 1981. *A Home for the Homeless: A Sociological Exegesis of 1 Peter, Its Situation and Strategy.* Philadelphia: Fortress.

Ellis, E. Earle. 1992. "Pseudonymity and Canonicity of New Testament Documents." In *Worship, Theology and Ministry in the Early Church: Essays in Honor of Ralph P. Martin,* edited by Michael J. Wilkins and Terence Paige, 212-24. JSNTSup 87. Sheffield, England: Sheffield Academic Press.

Fiore, Benjamin. 1986. *The Function of Personal Example in the Socratic and Pastoral Epistles.* AnBib 105. Rome: Biblical Institute Press.

Furnish, Victor Paul. 1984. *II Corinthians.* AB 32A. Garden City, NY: Doubleday.

Gamble, Harry Y. 1985. *The New Testament Canon: Its Making and Meaning.* Guides to Biblical Scholarship: New Testament Series. Philadelphia: Fortress.

Harris, Murray J. 1980. "Titus 2:13 and the Deity of Christ." In *Pauline Studies: Essays Presented to F. F. Bruce on His 70th Birthday,* edited by Donald A. Hagner and Murray J. Harris, 262-77. Grand Rapids, MI: Eerdmans.

Harrison, Percy N. 1921. *The Problem of the Pastoral Epistles.* London: Oxford University Press.

———. 1964. *Paulines and Pastorals.* London: Villiers.

Holmberg, Bengt. 1978. *Paul and Power: The Structure of Authority in the Primitive Church as Reflected in the Pauline Epistles.* Philadelphia: Fortress.

Johnson, Luke Timothy. 1978/79. "II Timothy and the Polemic Against False Teachers: A Re-examination." *JRelSt* 6/7:1-26.

Karris, Robert J. 1973. "The Background and Significance of the Polemic of the Pastoral Epistles." *JBL* 92:549-64.

Knight, George W., III. 1968. *The Faithful Sayings in the Pastoral Epistles.* Kampen, Netherlands: Kok.

Lefkowitz, Mary R., and Maureen B. Fant. 1982. *Women's Life in Greece and Rome.* London: Duckworth.

Lightman, Majorie, and William Zeisel. 1977. "*Univira*: An Example of Continuity and Change in Roman Society." *Church History* 46:19-32.

MacDonald, Dennis R. 1983. *The Legend and the Apostle: The Battle for Paul in Story and Canon.* Philadelphia: Westminster.

McDonald, Lee Martin. 1988. *The Formation of the Christian Biblical Canon.* Nashville: Abingdon.

McEleney, Neil J. 1974. "The Vice Lists of the Pastoral Epistles." *CBQ* 36:203-19.

Malherbe, Abraham J. 1977a. *The Cynic Epistles: A Study Edition.* SBLSBS 12. Missoula, MT: Scholars Press.

———. 1977b. *Social Aspects of Early Christianity.* Baton Rouge, LA: Louisiana State University Press.

———. 1980. "Medical Imagery in the Pastoral Epistles." In *Texts and Testaments: Critical Essays on the Bible and Early Christian Fathers,* edited by W. E. March, 19-35. San Antonio, TX: Trinity University Press. Reprinted in *Paul and the Popular Philosophers,* by A. J. Malherbe. Minneapolis: Fortress, 1989.

Malina, Bruce J. 1981. *The New Testament World: Insights from Cultural Anthropology.* Atlanta: John Knox.

Meade, David G. 1986. *Pseudonymity and Canon: An Investigation into the Relationship of Authorship and Authority in Jewish and Earliest Christian Tradition.* Grand Rapids, MI: Eerdmans.

Oberlinner, Lorenz. 1980. "Die 'Epiphaneia' des Heilswillens Gottes in Christus Jesus: Zur Grundstruktur der Christologie der Pastoralbriefe." *ZNW* 71:192-213.

Pfitzner, Victor C. 1967. *Paul and the Agon Motif: Traditional Athletic Imagery in the Pauline Literature.* NovTSup 16. Leiden, Netherlands: Brill.

Pomeroy, Sarah B. 1975. *Goddesses, Whores, Wives, and Slaves: Women in Classical Antiquity.* New York: Schocken.

Prior, Michael. 1989. *Paul the Letter-Writer and the Second Letter to Timothy.* JSNTSup 23. Sheffield, England: Sheffield Academic Press.

Skeat, T. C. 1979. " 'Especially the Parchments': A Note on 2 Timothy IV.13." *JTS* 30:173-77.

Stowers, Stanley K. 1986. *Letter Writing in Greco-Roman Antiquity.* Library of Early Christianity. Philadelphia: Westminster.

Treggiari, Susan M. 1991. *Roman Marriage: Iusti Coniuges from the Time of Cicero to the Time of Ulpian.* New York and Oxford: Oxford University Press.

von Lips, Hermann. 1979. *Glaube—Gemeinde—Amt: Zum Verständnis der Ordination in den Pastoralbriefen.* FRLANT 122. Göttingen: Vandenhoeck & Ruprecht.

Wendland, Paul. 1904. "Σωτήρ." *ZNW* 5:335-53.

Wolter, Michael. 1988. *Die Pastoralbriefe als Paulustradition.* FRLANT 146. Göttingen: Vandenhoeck & Ruprecht.

Young, Frances. 1994. *The Theology of the Pastoral Letters.* New Testament Theology. Cambridge: Cambridge University Press.

COMMENTARIES (BOTH CITED AND NOT CITED)

Barrett, Charles K. 1963. *The Pastoral Epistles.* The New Clarendon Bible. Oxford: Oxford University Press. — Concise volume consisting of insightful footnotes on the text of the New English Bible. Assumes pseudonymous letters containing authentic fragments.

Brox, Norbert. 1969. *Die Pastoralbriefe.* RNT 7.2. Regensburg, Germany: Pustet. — Argues vigorously for pseudonymity and places letters within the wider context of early Christian pseudepigraphy. Provides a full and scholarly commentary on the text with helpful excursuses on important topics. A significant scholarly resource.

Dibelius, Martin, and Hans Conzelmann. 1972. *The Pastoral Epistles*. Hermeneia. Philadelphia: Fortress. — Translation of the fourth edition of a respected German commentary (1966; 1st edition, 1955). Authors assume pseudonymity, provide a wealth of background material from Greco-Roman literature, and offer learned excursuses on important exegetical issues.

Fee, Gordon D. 1988. *1 and 2 Timothy, Titus*. New International Biblical Commentary, rev. ed. Peabody, MA: Hendrickson. — Intended for lay evangelical readers. Assumes Pauline authorship and a context of false teaching by some elders of the church. Highly readable and responsible exegesis.

Hanson, A. T. 1982. *The Pastoral Epistles*. New Century Bible Commentary. Grand Rapids, MI: Eerdmans. — Presents a running, balanced review of the opinions of other scholars. Views letters as a "miscellaneous collection" of materials by a pseudonymous author with no unifying theme or development of thought.

Hasler, Victor. 1978. *Die Briefe an Timotheus und Titus (Pastoralbriefe)*. Zürcher Bibelkommentare: Neues Testament 12. Zürich: Theologischer Verlag. — Brief but often original and provocative commentary. Assumes pseudonymity.

Holtz, Gottfried. 1965. *Die Pastoralbriefe*. THKNT 13. Berlin: Evangelische Verlagsanstalt. — Learned commentary on the Greek text, interspersed with useful excursuses. Assumes the letters were written by a secretary with Paul's authorization. Promotes a questionable hypothesis about the pervasive presence of eucharistic language in the text.

Houlden, James L. 1976. *The Pastoral Epistles: I and II Timothy, Titus*. Pelican New Testament Commentaries. Harmondsworth, England: Penguin. — Provides text of the letters, commentary on the content and context of each paragraph, and useful information on individual words and phrases. Assumes pseudonymous authorship.

Hultgren, Arland J. 1984. *I-II Timothy, Titus*. Augsburg Commentary on the New Testament. Minneapolis: Augsburg. — Brief, readable commentary reflecting sound exegetical judgments. Assumes pseudonymity.

Jeremias, Joachim. 1981. *Die Briefe an Timotheus und Titus*. NTD 9, 12th ed. Göttingen: Vandenhoeck & Ruprecht. — A very brief volume (67 pages of text and commentary) originally published in 1937. Assumes the letters were written by a secretary relying on oral instructions from Paul.

Kelly, John N. D. 1963. *A Commentary on the Pastoral Epistles: I Timothy, II Timothy, Titus.* Black's New Testament Commentaries. London: Black. — Argues strongly for Pauline authorship, either directly or through a secretary.

Knight, George W., III. 1992. *The Pastoral Epistles: A Commentary on the Greek Text.* NIGTC. Grand Rapids, MI: Eerdmans. — Learned and lengthy commentary on the Greek text. Provides a wealth of detail about vocabulary and grammar but offers less help in identifying the flow of the argument. After a careful review of the critical arguments opts for Pauline authorship.

Merkel, Helmut. 1991. *Die Pastoralbriefe.* NTD 9/1, 13th ed. Göttingen and Zürich: Vandenhoeck & Ruprecht. — Short commentary (112 pages of text and notes) replacing Jeremias's volume in the NTD series. Assumes pseudonymity.

Quinn, Jerome D. 1990. *The Letter to Titus; A New Translation with Notes and Commentary and An Introduction to Titus, I and II Timothy, The Pastoral Epistles.* AB 35. New York: Doubleday. — A helpful, scholarly commentary that is accessible to the general reader. Offers both detailed notes on the words of the Greek text (with English translations) and comments about the shape and context of the argument. Well written and carefully argued; the result of a lifetime of study of these letters. Assumes pseudonymity.

Roloff, Jürgen. 1988. *Der erste brief an Timotheus.* EKK 15. Zürich: Benziger Verlag; Neukirchen-Vluyn: Neukirchener Verlag. — Provides detailed analyses of the context and structure of each section of text and insightful commentary informed by theological acumen. Lengthy excursuses address significant interpretive issues. Clearly the best available commentary on 1 Timothy. Assumes pseudonymity.

Spicq, Ceslas. 1969. *Saint Paul: Les épîtres pastorales.* 4th ed. 2 vols. Ebib. Paris: Gabalda. — Provides an extensive introduction (311 pages) and an extraordinary wealth of background material and philological information about the Greek text. An essential scholarly resource. Assumes Pauline authorship.

Towner, Philip H. 1994. *1-2 Timothy and Titus.* The IVP New Testament Commentary Series. Downers Grove, IL, and Leicester, England: Inter-Varsity. — Engagingly written and intended for pastors. Assumes a direct connection with Paul, either as sole author or through his secretary.

INDEX

Acts, book of, 18-20, 23-24, 46, 89, 98, 128-29, 136, 164-65, 171, 177-78, 185, 213
Acts of Paul, 24, 30
age
    groups, exhortations to, 86, 91-92, 192-97
    of "real" widows, 92, 97
    of Timothy, 86, 154
Alexander, 46, 176-77, 179
apocalypticism, 20, 79, 82, 101, 105-6, 158-60, 169, 173
apostasy, 78-79, 110, 148
Aquila, 178-79
asceticism. *See* celibacy, opponents

benefaction, 105-20
bishop, 18, 30, 49, 61, 63-72, 74, 86, 90, 92, 99, 101, 109, 111, 140, 155, 185-87, 191, 193, 205
blasphemy, 43-44, 47, 49

canon, 18, 21, 100
celibacy. *See also* opponents (rejection of marriage), 26-27, 30, 61, 81-82, 93-94, 96-97, 105-6, 197
conscience, 20, 40-41, 46, 70, 80, 128, 189-90
creation, 25, 27, 60, 78, 80-82, 111, 114-15, 152, 168, 190
creeds and liturgies, fragments of, 24, 31, 33, 45, 49-50, 52-53, 101, 112-17, 122, 127, 131, 134, 138, 153, 178, 198, 200-202, 206
Crete, 18, 25, 177, 184-85, 190, 213

deacons, 18, 49, 63-66, 69-71, 83, 86, 90, 92, 99, 109, 111, 137, 194
deception. *See* opponents (as deceivers)

Demas, 175, 179
deposit (the preserved tradition), 20, 121-23, 133-34, 166
devil. *See* Satan
doctrine. *See also* teaching
    and behavior, 34, 41, 47-48, 56, 72, 77, 164, 193
    false, 30, 37-39, 81-82, 140, 149, 160, 170
doxology, 37, 45, 115-17, 181

elders, 18, 23, 30, 65-66, 82, 86-88, 90-91, 98-102, 104, 108, 130, 140, 185-88
emperor cult, 51, 116, 132, 200
Ephesus, 18, 20, 25, 37-38, 72, 136-37, 176-78
epiphany, 32-34, 53-55, 77, 115-16, 123, 131-33, 169, 172, 175, 179, 183-84, 199-202, 207
Erastus, 178-79
eschatology, 51, 111, 115, 119-20, 126, 130, 134, 137-38, 141-43, 145-46, 150, 163, 169, 172, 174, 177, 179, 199, 208

faith
    as belief, 48, 77-79, 134, 147, 150, 184, 201, 214
    as knowledge, 27, 155, 182
    as religion ("the faith"), 29, 44, 46, 79, 83, 112, 122, 163, 166-67, 171-72, 183, 189
    as virtue, 40, 45, 46, 61-62, 79, 86, 114, 154, 164, 193
    mystery of the, 70, 75
final judgment. *See also* eschatology, 32-34, 101-2, 137, 146, 169, 172, 174
fragments of Pauline letters, 21, 136, 174

genealogies, 39, 189, 210